T0381441

Endorsements

Anthea Tripp writes from personal experience with conviction, wit, and wisdom. Her openness, honesty, and witness of her faith lend a sense that the words are written personally for the reader. *My Soul Sings for You* is a pleasant and easy read.

Ann Miner, Author, *I Lift My Eyes, Bugs in the Baptismal,*
Buddy Finds A Home, Polly Possum's Wandering Path

We have been friends for 35 years and I never realized she had this writing talent! This is a great read, with poignancy, humor and faith throughout.

Don Watts, aka The Old Woodworker
Sugar Land, Texas

My *Soul Sings* for You

Spiritual Peace in the Life and Times of Now

ANTHEA GILLIAN TRIPP

WESTBOW
PRESS®
A DIVISION OF THOMAS NELSON
& ZONDERVAN

WestBow Press books may be ordered through booksellers or by contacting:

WestBow Press
A Division of Thomas Nelson & Zondervan
1663 Liberty Drive
Bloomington, IN 47403
www.westbowpress.com
1 (866) 928-1240

Because of the dynamic nature of the Internet, any web addresses or links contained in this book may have changed since publication and may no longer be valid. The views expressed in this work are solely those of the author and do not necessarily reflect the views of the publisher, and the publisher hereby disclaims any responsibility for them.

Photograph Credit to Mikhail Kalinin/Solent News for 'Smoke Signals' bird graphic used in design on the front cover

Scripture quotations marked KJV are taken from the King James Version.

Scripture quotations marked NLT are taken from the Holy Bible, New Living Translation, Copyright © 1996, 2004, 2015 by Tyndale House Foundation. Used by permission of Tyndale House Publishers, Inc., Carol Stream, Illinois 60188. All rights reserved.

Scripture quotations marked ESV taken from The Holy Bible, English Standard Version® (ESV®), Copyright © 2001 by Crossway, a publishing ministry of Good News Publishers. All rights reserved.

Scripture quotations marked NASB are taken from The New American Standard Bible®, Copyright © 1960, 1962, 1963, 1968, 1971, 1972, 1973, 1975, 1977, 1995 by The Lockman Foundation. Used by permission.

ISBN: 978-1-9736-7234-0 (sc)
ISBN: 978-1-9736-7235-7 (hc)
ISBN: 978-1-9736-7233-3 (e)

Library of Congress Control Number: 2019912681

Print information available on the last page.

WestBow Press rev. date: 9/18/2019

To the community of Sturminster Newton, which I consider my home away from home. Whenever we visited my elderly parents, who resided in Bridge Street for twenty-three years, this delightful township and its friendly inhabitants lovingly embraced my family and me.

In Sturminster, surrounded by lush green pastures and wooded copses, I savored the serenity of long walks in the countryside. Often while resting near the old mill, my soul sought refuge from the busyness of routine life. I inhaled peace as I cast the cares and pressures of a demanding world upon the still waters of the meandering River Stour.

I pondered the universe as it is in the life and times of the present. In the sacred silence of solitude, my spirit soared as I sensed the still, small voice of God whispering my name, calling me to express my thoughts and write them down in a book. Revived, my weary soul began to sing.

I am eternally grateful to the community of Sturminster Newton. A piece of my heart will remain there forever.

Sturminster Newton Mill viewed from the bridge

Contents

Acknowledgments

To my beloved mother and father. Thank you, Mum and Dad, for loving me and giving me life. I'm so grateful to God for choosing *you* to be my parents. You each have taught me so much about living life to the fullest. I love you both with all my heart. I rejoice in where you now reside. Oh, that the music of my soul would reach you in heaven.

I wish to express gratitude to my husband, Chuck. You are the love of my life. I am eternally thankful for your patience, encouragement, and enthusiasm for my writing and for never complaining about the hours I have spent tapping away on my computer in order to complete this book. You have always been and forever will be the wind beneath my wings and my greatest inspiration. You have my forever love.

To my three beautiful children, David, Stephen and Chandra, you make me proud. Thank you for your unconditional love and for cheering me on to write. You always bring joy and meaning to my life. I love you with all my heart, and I thank God for entrusting me with your souls. It is such an honor to be your mom. Raising you and loving you has been my most joyful and fulfilling journey, and I am a better person because of you three.

To Shelley, Leslie and Dany, thank you for marrying into our family. To Stacy, thanks for embracing our family as your own. You are all loved and cherished. I thank each of you for all you contribute to my life. As faithful followers of my blog, and avid advocates for my book, I am humbled and grateful for your support.

To all my grandchildren and great-grandchildren, I love you dearly. You light up my life and instill in me a hope for the future. Thank you for sharing your love, laughter, and enthusiasm for life. You bring out my very best self.

To all my dear friends, I honor your friendship. Thank you for loving me through all the ups and downs of life and business. I appreciate your unwavering loyalty and support. I value your enthusiastic encouragement. You've been influential in the completion of this book.

To Gary Morse of Gary Morse Ministries, I am grateful for you and the gift God bestowed on you. Thank you for being the catalyst who spoke truth to me. You inspired me with the confidence to take writing to the next level, to heed the Word of God, to express myself more passionately, and to bare my soul. Thank you for reading the introduction to my book and for granting permission to publish your response and words of encouragement, as quoted here.

"Let me just say how much it blesses me to hear how a word spoken in due season can help establish, position and enrich one's life. I pray that you will continue allowing your life to be aligned and pliable for His kingdom."

In His service, Gary Morse

Introduction

"You have a book in you!" exclaimed the prophet.

"You will write," he proclaimed. "No matter the time of day or night, heed the call and write. Don't worry about sleep. Write down your thoughts! There's a writer inside you. Express your emotions and describe your experiences. Write about family and everything you've learned from your life and times, the good and the bad. All of it. You've got a story to tell. You *must* tell it!"

This book is the result of an encounter with destiny that catapulted me into a whirlwind of action, compelling me to author *My Soul Sings for You*. Many years in the making, this book was merely a smoldering dream placed on the back burner of life until an invitation to a friendly gathering became a significant tipping point in my life.

In December 2014, I had cautiously agreed to join a group of friends for an evening of worship and praise that included a biblical message from a guest speaker referred to as "a prophet." I confess I'd never met or given much thought to modern-day prophets, and I had no idea what to expect, so I ventured there with hesitation but also with an open mind. After the main event, the prophet selected individuals randomly and proceeded to prophesy specifics related to them. Based on their reactions and responses, he was accurately zeroing in on what was happening in their lives and dispensing words of encouragement.

Meanwhile, I wanted to slide off my chair and fade into the background. Better yet, I would have welcomed the power to become invisible. I was not looking for any spotlight to shine on me that night, but I was hemmed in with no obvious way to escape the intimacy of the crowded room. Toward the end, Gary, the prophet from Gary Morse Ministries, looked directly at me for a few seconds quite intently before announcing enthusiastically and very confidently, *"You* are a writer!"

What? I wondered. *How in the world he could know that?* As he continued to speak to me, he encouraged me to do more of what I had been doing for several years. I had already changed the tone and increased the frequency of my blog posts, but I hadn't thought about my writing in quite the same way as he depicted. He suggested I should elevate my writing to a new level and a greater depth of expression. I sat there spellbound as this insightful gentleman, whom I'd never met before, proclaimed accurate details about my life at the time. Being somewhat of a skeptic and not knowing him, my first instinct was stoic apprehension. However, I quickly dismissed any distrust, silenced the questioning chatter in my head, and focused my attention on his words—words that rang of undeniable truth. The prophet was indeed correct. He was right on the mark with all he described of me *then* and all that has *since* transpired in the last few years! Though far from being an accomplished writer, I am nevertheless a writer of sorts, and five years previously to this gathering, after many weak starts and failed attempts at writing regularly in my blog, I had created *Anthea's Anthology,* for which I have currently written more than one hundred articles and short stories.

Simply stated, I *love* to write. Let's face it. Anyone who can scribble daily entries in a five-year diary from the age of fourteen to eighteen years has got to enjoy writing, or the person would have tired long before completing it. I still glance occasionally inside that tan-colored journal, which is filled with handwritten notes, and I am always intrigued by those entries from many years ago. They are reminders of events, activities, and people I've long since forgotten with the passing of the years. Every page from cover to cover is filled with my teenage scrawl, some entries in pencil, others in black, blue, red, or green ink. Mind you, the penmanship often leaves much to be desired, but a five-year account of my life and times in colorful words is hidden within a leather-bound diary bearing a brass lock to keep my deepest thoughts and actions private and away from parental prying.

My faithfulness to the diary morphed into a writing habit. As life progressed and I married, busied myself raising a family, traveled the world to wherever my husband's military career landed us, I would write long letters to family and friends and compose newsletter inserts for the annual Christmas cards.

After founding Get Super Healthy, our health and wellness business for more than thirty-eight years and counting, I wrote the monthly newsletters and a few amusing children's stories to entice youngsters to make healthy food choices! As the age of technology exploded, I graduated to electronic newsletters, built a business website, and authored all the content. I found my greatest passion and outlet for literary expression in *Anthea's Anthology*, my blog, where I freely pour out my emotions in words.

I always *knew* I would write a book *someday*. There was *no* doubt in my mind. I envisioned the book sitting on a shelf. I saw my name on the cover. It was a foregone conclusion that my book would get published *one day*. This book was in the future. I would start it when the Spirit moved me, when I had more time, when I had something valuable to contribute to others, when I stopped traveling, or when I achieved the pinnacle of success in my business. *If this, if that, and when all the stars align!* It had become a far-off, *someday* thing.

I wasn't sure what genre of book I would write, but I knew the content had to inspire my readers in a meaningful way, contribute to their lives, meet them where they lived, speak to their challenges, and breathe love into their hearts. I yearned to help restore souls that were crushed by the world. Whether I would accomplish this through fiction or non-fiction remained a mystery even to me for a long time. As I've shared, my dream was barely smoldering. I kindled it by writing in my blog until the timing was right. I had shoved my untitled book on the back burner of life, awaiting a spark of inspiration to fan the flickering flames into a roaring furnace of passionate writing.

I am grateful to the prophet. He was the catalyst. His words ignited the confidence and assurance I needed to plan the purpose of my book seriously. He inspired me to believe in myself and in my ability to convey a meaningful message. When I voiced concern that writing a book might distract from my calling to impact others through the health and wellness industry, he posed a thoughtful question.

"What if you could reach more people with a greater impact through your writing?" he asked. It was food for thought—a new way for me to view my writing. A different perspective is always beneficial.

After my encounter with him, I wrote more frequently and more passionately, and I began to bare my soul unabashedly as I wrote on a variety of timely topics about life and family. My followers responded positively and asked for more. Many thanked me for putting into words what they felt and wanted to express but hadn't or couldn't. I soon saw a pattern emerging in my blog posts—the foundation for this book. I wrote timely entries about life in today's world, which I refer to as *the life and times of now!*

I also discovered something about myself. I was in a holding pattern of faulty thinking. It was a huge aha moment.

You see, for many years I had not allowed my light to shine as brightly as I knew it could. The chatter in my head repeatedly told me I had little to contribute. There were more successful, more experienced, and more articulate writers. There were published authors who could express a message better than I could, so I unwittingly dimmed my light and silenced my voice, and worse still, I toned down the intensity of my soul's song. I listened to everyone else sing their songs, and I praised their literary accomplishments. I bought and recommended their books.

Meanwhile, I accepted the lies I told myself. I began to believe them. I wasn't good enough. I wasn't deserving. As I discounted my worth, confidence in my ability was shaken. I underestimated the intrinsic value of my own life's song. As soon as I recognized this negative pattern, I resolved to change my tune. There would be no more blowing out my candle. The fire in me was ready to burn bright, and since I was the one holding the match, I must strike it.

The time had come to shine my light—brighter and stronger.

I would sing my God-given song from the depths of my being like the little bird on the front cover, the bird singing his heart out. What you now hold in your hands is music from my soul. I sing an anthem to my Creator and you, my reader. I hope my stories will touch you in ways that help you navigate your way through similar experiences and circumstances in your life and relationships.

This book addresses the life and times of now—the beautiful but often overwhelming life in which we find ourselves. We are always racing for time, wishing for more of it, and wondering why there is never enough to accomplish all we want. With that in mind, I have organized my short stories under chapter headings so that you can pick up the book when you have small blocks of time and read a topic that speaks to you in the moment. There is no distinct beginning or ending to the book, so you can start anywhere, but I encourage you to begin at the front and read every page in order to receive the full impact and blessing intended.

In today's crazy world of busyness, it's easy to fall into the trap of always going, doing, and pursuing. I've been in that mode, always moving, never taking time out to renew or to just be. We submerge ourselves in goals and activities to advance our careers, to elevate our status, or to secure bigger salaries to support our families. We sacrifice our physical well-being and sanity to provide our children with every single experience available, enrolling them in multiple and continuous planned activities that leave little time for spontaneous play, and in doing so, we further overload our burdened work and home schedules, which steals more and more of our time, energy, and will.

Many of us are slaves to the persistent and continuous demands of our personal and business emails, incoming texts, and instant messages, all demanding immediate attention twenty-four hours a day, seven days a week. We strap ourselves to our electronic devices either by choice or by necessity. It's easy to lose ourselves in the virtual world of social media, resulting in the dulling of our senses in a state of foggy oblivion and missing the vibrant beauty of the reality surrounding us at any given moment.

We feel we're missing out on the simple joys of life.

As if all these things aren't enough, at some point in life, we will inevitably face business or family challenges ... or both at the same time. That's the worst! Then there are relationship issues that unexpectedly demand attention and drain us emotionally. Situations surface that we've never faced before and are unsure how to handle. They come to us in the form of wayward children, divorces, elderly parents, unpleasant bosses or coworkers, or a variety of challenging circumstances that burden us with physical, emotional, and mental stress.

We dream of a simpler life, a quieter existence devoid of the hustle and bustle, yet we are trapped in the merry-go-round of an overscheduled life that offers little or no room to be still long enough to apply a solution, even if we had one ready to implement.

We can find ourselves with no white space left in our heads or anywhere in sight. We know we're missing out in life but have no time or inclination to seek what's lacking.

Sometimes we catch whispers from the depths of our souls imploring us to seek rest and restoration, and although we may acknowledge their pleas, we seem helpless to devote the time and attention to feed their hunger. While juggling and tending to all the other priorities in life, we neglect the very essence of our beings. We disregard our spiritual selves, and so our underwhelmed souls continue to thirst, unrequited.

As you read, I pray that your spiritual side will be awakened or at least affirmed and that your emotions are stirred by real-life stories from my journey through many years and experiences in life. I hope these stories instill in you a desire to nourish your soul intentionally. Maybe something I share will ignite a fire in your being. I hope so.

Within these pages are valuable lessons about family and life in all its glory, gift-wrapped for you in true short stories. These writings are refreshingly raw and real, and I hope they will touch your heart and evoke a full range of emotions that resonate with you. You'll laugh at the humor in situations, you'll shed tears of sorrow at life's losses, and you'll rejoice in its triumphs. Maybe you'll identify with and be blessed by the words I write.

I hope that your spirit will soar, that your heart will rejoice, and that your soul will sing. If by some chance, the world has crushed your soul, I pray my words of God's hope and restoration will encourage you, bless you, and lead you to joy. And until you give voice to *your* song, may I assure you that my soul sings for you.

All glory be to God.

CHAPTER 1
Legacy of Love

Life is good. Love is better!
—Donald Lee Allen

A Forever Kind of Love

Of all the emotions known to humanity, surely love must be the single most powerful one. In this first chapter, love is the center of each story in the collection.

As a confirmed romantic, forever and a day is the nature of the relationship I had envisioned as a teenage girl. Oh, to find the kind of love to last for eternity and beyond. To fall in love passionately and live happily ever after! While I was realistic enough to understand that love and marriage are risky and not all couples stay together (usually because of unforeseen circumstances), a lasting, passionate relationship was what I hoped for and prayed for as a young woman.

In my teens I often wondered what the man of my dreams would look like, where and how I would meet him when the time came. How many children would we have, and where we would live? Would he be as intense and passionate as me? Would we share the same values? Of course, all these questions and fantasies were like castles in the sky because they were way off in my future. I pictured them coming after I finished college, after I had been teaching for a while, and when I'd met enough different men so that I would recognize Mr. Right when he appeared!

Life is lovely in the way it twists and turns. I've learned always to expect the unexpected and to smile at my Creator's sense of humor. Little did I know that God had different plans for me! He presented me with my life partner while I was still in my teens. That was definitely not in *my* plan! I hadn't bargained on a blind double date. I thought I was meeting up with an old school friend to go to a movie. A rendezvous with a man I didn't know was the furthest thing from my mind at the time. I wasn't ready for the love of my life yet. Not in any way, shape, or form. It was way too soon. After all, I had things to accomplish, places to go, and life to experience. I needed to grow up and live a lot more, travel, and gain more maturity.

But there he was, standing in front of me, a handsome American GI and not at all what this proper English girl would have initially viewed as her lifelong partner, but as it turns out, he was everything I had ever dreamed of in a man.

At first, I didn't think much about him at all, and a serious relationship was not in his plans for sure! *What kind of a name is Chuck anyway?* I thought as I studied his face. *Now Charles—that I can understand.* My friend had sprung the blind double date on me, and I was in a state of such surprise that I reluctantly trailed along. However, after the movie my blind date and I quickly went our separate ways, quite happy to have shaken the other one off with no further thoughts.

One should never underestimate destiny playing its hand or God executing His plan. You can call it fate, coincidence, or whatever you wish to label it, but a few weeks later, a chance encounter at a busy bus stop in downtown Oxford brought us unexpectedly face-to-face for a second time.

Deep in the thought of getting home after a long day at school, my eyes focused far into the distance beyond the line of traffic, searching for any sign of the familiar red double-decker bus that would carry me home in time for dinner. I was paying little attention to those in the queue in front and behind me and was oblivious to all the workers and shoppers hurrying by. In my peripheral vision, I barely caught a glimpse of a faint shadow passing. I sensed a draft of air waft my hair as something brushed my overcoat, but in the city that's nothing unusual as people scurry hither and thither at quitting time, so it didn't occur to me to turn and see who had nudged my arm. I kept my gaze on the horizon, intently searching for a glimpse of the bus.

Suddenly, I was nudged again as the passerby backtracked and looked intently into my face. It was a few seconds before I remembered who this dark-haired, handsome man was. Yes, the one standing in my space. He had passed me by initially by a few strides, but he came back for a closer look at me. Perhaps because our first encounter had been at night and now it was in broad daylight, he wasn't sure who I was. He could have kept right on walking, but he didn't. Something prompted him to stop, and before I realized what was happening, I heard him say "I know you!" Then I realized who he was. We reconnected quite by chance. Or did we?

My longed-for bus was rapidly approaching, and just as the burgeoning queue hustled me on board, he asked to see me again. He invited me for a do-over, a follow-up date after the first uncomfortable blind date. While my head was saying no, my wayward and far-too-forward mouth betrayed me and said yes!

A touch of his hand on that subsequent date reached in and stole my heart. There was a third date, a fourth, and a passionate kiss, and the rest is history! With love, when you know, you know. We both knew very quickly that we were soul mates and wanted to spend the rest of our lives together. I would have followed this man to the ends of the earth, and for nineteen of his twenty years in the US Air Force, I pretty much did just that. I loved every minute of our time and travels in military life!

I am talking about Chuck, my amazing husband of fifty-five years. He's my best friend, my biggest cheerleader, my rock, the wonderful father to our three children, the grandfather to five grandchildren, and at the time of writing this, a great-grandfather to three adorable little boys and a beautiful little girl!

I often wonder where all those years have gone. We've shared an incredible journey in life. So much give-and-take on both sides, so much learned from each other and with each other, victories celebrated and yes, some tears over defeats and disappointments. But it all keeps us on our toes, right? For us, marriage is a lifelong commitment, a decision to love one another in sickness and in health until death do us part—whatever amount of time God grants us.

When people discover we've been married for more than fifty years and are still together and even more surprisingly, still in love, they often ask us, "What's your secret?"

The secret is there is *no* secret! It's all about love! Loving unconditionally, accepting each other, and learning to live together is a big part of it. Maintaining a willingness to be understanding first and then seeking to be understood is a practice we learned over time. It's important to know that giving is not always a fifty-fifty split with each partner. The proportions vary. Sometimes one gives eighty-twenty, and at other times the percentage is reversed and is twenty-eighty. There are many different combinations. But one thing is sure. Having a generous heart is a crucial component.

A marital relationship is one of life's most significant challenges and deepest joys. It's a love that grows stronger each year, and that continues to be our vision of married life. We've never measured our marital success by worldly goods, for we believe that it is love alone that cements a marriage. That doesn't mean we don't like our *stuff*. We certainly do appreciate fine things, but we don't use material markers to measure our happiness. The real way to measure a marriage is in the depth and breadth of the loving relationship.

It's a togetherness that endures through all kinds of weather. It's not just present when life is easy, the sun is shining, and everyone's having fun, but it's also present in how a couple stands up to the pressure tests when the skies turn dark and the fierce storms of life hit, knocking you to your knees. Challenges of financial stress, disagreements, forced separations because of work, and unexpected tragedies will test a marriage like nothing else. We've suffered through our share of tumultuous times, and there's no doubt that the storms rocked our boat; however, they didn't sink us. We stayed the course, and our marriage stayed afloat. What carried us through and enabled us to weather each storm was the power of love for and commitment to each other. An unwavering determination to grow closer and stronger despite the hardships was beneficial too.

But humanity was not the creator of love. God is love, and *He* teaches it to us. We love because He first loved us. The measure of true love is given freely and joyfully accepted just as God's love for us is provided to us freely and unconditionally.

It's not coincidental that Corinthians 13:4–7 is one of the most chosen readings at weddings. The verses lay out the power of love and contain the recipe for a foundation upon which to build a lasting union. Love never fails. I am always amazed at the power of love. Even though loving someone can be heartbreaking at times, it's essential to know that during the greatest challenges, love often grows deeper, and two people create a stronger union. I am so grateful that Chuck and I found each other, that we work on ourselves and our relationship, and that we persist at overcoming the inevitable darts and arrows that life deals us. I'm happy that our love grows and flourishes as we continue to walk this winding path of life together, continually learning. We're so grateful for our family and friends, and most of all, we're thankful for our God, for His infinite love and faithfulness to us and our marriage. He's always been the center of our lives, even though there have been many times when the humdrum of daily routine or the upheaval of an emotional situation sent us reeling off track and captured our time and attention, sadly causing us to take our eyes off Him.

While *our* eyes were turned away from Him, *His* gaze remained fixed continuously on us. He is indeed a faithful God, and He is infinite love!

Be completely humble and gentle;
be patient, bearing with one another in love.
—Ephesians 4:2 (NIV)

Dancing the Skeleton
Out of the Closet

The saying goes that every family hides a skeleton in the closet, and I'm the first to admit that our family is no exception to that idiom. I know of at least two—and probably more—bony structures skulking in the musty darkness of an upstairs wardrobe or hiding behind mothball-scented clothes in an ancient closet. There are surely secrets in our family history that enshroud discreditable or embarrassing facts that some would rather not acknowledge. They have painful or demeaning secrets about themselves or involving others whom they choose to protect. It's private information that might prompt a raised eyebrow or a judgmental, tongue-clicking *tisk tisk*!

George Bernard Shaw, the Irish playwright, was once quoted as saying, "If you can't get rid of the family skeleton, you'd best teach it to dance!" I assure you I'm not one to reveal *any* confidences entrusted to me by others, but I have no qualms about divulging my own. However, there is one exception. If it were to cause others pain, shame, or embarrassment, I would leave the dead skeleton to lie and rot to dust for eternity.

The time has arrived for me to waltz out the skeleton that's been locked away in our family closet for more than fifty years.

But really, the waltz is far too proper and elegant a dance for my skeleton. The provocative moves in the more passionate, smoldering Argentinian tango are a more fitting coming-out dance to accompany the reveal. Keep that thought and vision in mind as we proceed.

Dancing this skeleton out of my closet is a long-awaited and joyful celebration for me. Although many who know me will be surprised, some even shocked, this story is not so much about unveiling a deep dark secret as it is about speaking the truth, setting the record straight, and keeping a promise. We all have made mistakes in life, said and done things we wish we hadn't, or caused pain to others by our thoughtless, selfish actions. We are only human after all, and while those various transgressions result in regret, there are some things I believe are sacred, namely telling the truth and honoring a promise.

I'll start with *the promise*. In 1963, my parents implored me to keep a secret. It was *my* secret, but by telling them, I also made it theirs. My mother, whom I admired more than any other woman in my life, had taught me since I was young that if I had a secret or was asked to keep someone else's circumstances in my confidence, I should never betray that trust. And if I was ever tempted to blurt it out, I should immediately run to the nearest deserted field, sit down in the center, and whisper what was on my mind to the tall grasses and wildflowers. In that way, my mother advised, I'd never feel regret at revealing a secret to the wrong person, who might be tempted to share the juicy little tidbit and cause others pain and suffering. My mum was indeed a wise woman. But let's get back to the promise.

I can vividly recall sitting with my parents in the living room the night after I'd painfully confessed the secret I'd struggled with for several weeks. Their initial anger at my tearful admission the day before had subsided and was replaced by something much worse. Their faces mirrored devastation and the emotional strain of disbelief, sadness, disappointment, and fear. As for me, I sat in silence, my guts tangled in a knot, my head hung in shame and utterly humiliated. I was a formerly happy, confident young woman of eighteen, and now I was reduced to an inconsolable pile of disgrace and submission. I was brokenhearted, and so were they. To make amends for the shame, pain, and suffering I'd inflicted on them, I would have agreed to *almost* anything.

I needed redemption.

I conceded to keep our secret safe with only a very few trusted and necessary exceptions. My parents demanded a solemn promise from me that night. I must never reveal my circumstances to anyone during their lifetime. Out of love and respect for my parents and to redeem myself, I kept that promise until about two years ago. Some of my friends will know that to be accurate and can confirm I never breathed a word to them. After my mother died and when it appeared my ninety-five-year-old dad no longer cared if I kept the secret, I cracked open the closet door and permitted a few trusted friends to peek in at the skeleton. After concealing the messy facts for many years, the guilt and self-condemnation made it imperative that I speak out and correct the record. Truth and solemn promises are both sacred to me, but these had been in conflict for me for far too long. At last, the chains enslaving me to the promise have fallen away. I have been set free.

So now I must dance out my secret skeleton into the light of day to reveal the truth.

After spending three years in East Africa, much of the time at a girl's boarding school in Nairobi, Kenya, my father's teaching assignment in Uganda ended, and we returned to England. I was barely seventeen years old, and I was enrolled in a school in Oxford to complete my A levels, specifically English literature and foreign languages, before attending Salisbury University to follow in my father's footsteps and enter the teaching profession. That plan was not meant to be. Two weeks after arriving back in Oxford, I reacquainted myself with a friend I'd known since we were five years old, and that changed the course of my life forever.

As you now know from reading the previous chapter, I met the love of my life through that old school friend, so let's pick up the story from there. After several months of dating and having fallen madly in love, I approached my parents with the idea of becoming engaged to be married. That went over like a lead balloon. Their only child wanted to marry an American serviceman and leave England for the United States at such a young age. To them, that would never happen! Not only did they refuse to entertain the idea of a marriage in the future—I don't blame them at all—but they forbade me to ever see him again. Plus my dad told Chuck never to contact me. I was heartbroken.

Remember that you should never reckon with the power of love!

We refused to be apart and began to meet in secret. I found excuses to go out for this or that, and yes, I'm ashamed to confess that I lied numerous times about my whereabouts. Luckily for me, I had a certain amount of freedom because of my academic schedule along with practices and matches on the school tennis team, so I could maneuver around and squeeze in clandestine meetings with Chuck, who worked different shifts at the US Air Force base. I was happy to turn eighteen in January 1963 but not sure why. It didn't mean much in those days, except one could legally consume alcohol, which was not a huge motivator in my life. It was merely a milestone number for me. However, to marry without parental consent in the early 1960s England, you had to be twenty-one years old. What? Three more years to wait to marry the love of my life seemed like an eternity. The yearning to be together was magnetic and overpowering.

Not long after my birthday, I awakened one morning feeling very nauseous; however, the feeling passed after I ate breakfast, and so off to classes I went. A couple of days later, the same feeling occurred, but this time I vomited clear liquid. My stomach took longer to settle after that. Riding the bus to school was a real challenge. I had to hold back the urge to vomit. Queasiness continued intermittently for a few weeks. A couple of times my mother asked me what was wrong. Surely, she must have suspected my dilemma. I couldn't ignore it anymore, and reluctantly, I scheduled a doctor's appointment. My suspicions were confirmed. Positive.

I was pregnant. I was unmarried. I was only eighteen. I was ashamed because in those days an unwed pregnancy was considered shameful and the pregnant woman was viewed as brazen. I was still at school in the last year of my A levels. I was terrified, and I felt alone. But I was loved by an amazing honorable man who loved me so deeply that he would have given his life for me. Thank God for that because there was so much more for us to face.

How in the world can I break the news to my parents? I thought. I prayed and asked God's forgiveness for my sinful indiscretions, for disobedience and lies to my parents and for the pain I was about to inflict on my dear mum and dad. Have you ever had to divulge a painful secret to people you love, knowing they will be devastated, heartbroken and disappointed in you? If so, you will understand the depth of my torment. It was brutal. I lost weight. I stressed and stressed and went over in my mind what I would say and the time

I would choose to reveal the secret, and I imagined their reaction and how I would deal with whatever their responses might be. I admit that it was one of the most difficult times in my life. I had to dig deep within my being to extract the strength, courage, and humility to do what was necessary. There was no hiding this secret. My condition would soon become evident, and the secret within would begin to blossom outwardly as the beautiful little life inside me advanced toward the second trimester.

I mustered all that was in me and confessed to my parents. No, it didn't happen the way I'd planned. I had envisioned I'd be calm, brave, and in control of my emotions, at least outwardly, and that I would choose an appropriate time. Instead I fell apart unexpectedly. One day in early March, overcome with emotion, I burst into tears, and crumpling into a heap like a rag doll, I blurted it out, incapable of containing myself one more moment.

I'm pregnant.

I was unprepared for their reactions, although I should have realized that when people are shocked by devastating news, their responses are emotionally charged and unpredictable. They can say almost anything—hurtful things, things they may mean and feel justified saying in the heat of the moment, cruel comments they later regret, retaliatory words, reactive and angry accusations. The blast I received contained them all, and I knew I deserved the assault, so in fear and trepidation, I passively let my parents' rant play out. Inside I was dying. It was a living nightmare. I wanted it over and done with, but it was out of my hands. The rant continued for a very long time.

My father reacted with white-faced anger, and the names he used to describe my behavior cut me to the core. In all fairness I had lied, been disobedient, and done the unthinkable, so what could I say in defense of my behavior? Nothing. Overwhelming emotion muted me, so it was impossible to explain that my condition was a result of passionate love between two young people who desperately wanted to be together for life. A couple of times I opened my mouth to speak, but my voice would not oblige, so I took the barrage of anger and humiliation in silence and emotional numbness as my dad ranted, raved, and loudly threatened me and the father with a list of reprisals for what seemed like an eternity. What can I say? I was his only child, and I might as well have stabbed him in the heart. I deserved it, didn't I? I was raised to be accountable for my actions, so I knew I had no choice but to suffer the consequences.

Everyone responds differently to stressful situations such as I'm describing. We're all unique individuals, so we should expect differing reactions. I had optimistically hoped one of my parents, even though shocked and devastated, might show a smidgeon of compassion, wrap their arms around their terrified daughter, and while not condoning the behavior, reassure me that I was loved no matter what and that we'd get through this together. I soon realized my hopes were too high.

My mother didn't react with anger exactly. It was disdain. I don't know which was worse, anger or contempt. But the worst came the next day when my father, the headmaster at a local primary school, called in sick and stayed at home. That's when I fully understood the extent of the harm I had caused. My dad could overcome anything. He was one strong individual. He was small in physical stature, but there was no limit to his inner strength. He exceeded his limit that day. It was the only time I ever saw Dad cry. I caught a glimpse of my mother standing over him, comforting him as he slumped in his chair. His head in his hands, he sobbed like a baby. I was so ashamed of the suffering and devastation I'd imposed on two of the people I most loved in the whole world.

My dad had plenty of time that day to devise a plan of action for my future. He didn't consult me or take my feelings into consideration about the arrangement. That was Dad, a take-charge kind of a guy, and I know he just figured I was undeserving of any input. Later that evening is when I solemnly promised my parents to keep the secret. I'm sorry to say that after I had promised, my parents sprang two options on me. You can guess what they might be. Both were so foreign to my sensibility, especially since my father was adopted and had dedicated much of his life in the search of his biological parents. (But that's a story for a different book.) I was horrified and terrified at the suggestions. My dad couldn't be serious. I only know that when backed into a corner and emotionally distraught, desperate people can resort to severe measures that they otherwise would never contemplate and certainly would never carry out. And my dad was desperate for all of this to go away. I defiantly refused to consider any option except keeping my baby, so to avoid family disgrace and to shield my dad from embarrassment in the community, I was banished.

I agreed to go to Scotland in late August to stay with a loving aunt until such times as I delivered my precious baby in October. Meanwhile, it was suggested I wear the strongest girdle available to conceal my bloated abdomen, and I would complete the school year and receive my credentials. I was to stay and play on the school tennis team, and I was ordered to breathe not a word to anyone. Remember that my father was a school headmaster and a firm disciplinarian. Somehow I managed to make it through the school year and passed my A-level examinations.

I continued to beg my dad to give his permission for me to marry Chuck, but he would entertain no notion of a marriage, civil or otherwise. It would not happen. He would not consent, and he certainly would not give his blessing. His response was to arrange a meeting during which he unleashed on my courageous lover a repertoire of the most uncomplimentary naval terms he could muster. He secured an appointment with the USAF base commander, and to appease my dad and maintain a good relationship with the local civilian community, he agreed to look into transferring Chuck to another base in the future. Dad's determination to prevent a marriage at all costs seemed somewhat ironic to me. A different father might have chosen the shotgun wedding, insisting on marriage to make his daughter honorable and his grandchild legitimate. It's especially interesting behavior because Dad himself was illegitimate, born to an unwed mother and given up for adoption. But not *my* dad! He would save his daughter at any cost from what he considered a significant mistake. He was willing to do anything and everything in his power to prevent a marriage. And in the short term, he succeeded.

It's only fair to add here that while I yearned for forgiveness from my dad and longed for his unconditional love and acceptance, I always knew deep down that I was loved, even though he never spoke the words. I knew he sincerely felt he was doing the right thing for my future by separating me from the love of my life and my child's father. He just chose measures that seemed so extreme to me. Meanwhile, my mother had softened and forgiven me, and she even tried to influence my father to give consent for me to marry. All her attempts failed. Dad refused to consider marriage as an option.

So life continued in an awkward and very strained fashion. By the grace of God, I finished school. Chuck and I communicated via letters and infrequent telephone calls from a public phone booth, and the longer we were apart, the more determined we were to be together. Our love grew deeper, and our resolve stronger. Then in August I was taken off to Scotland, accompanied by both parents with two prearranged stops along the way. One I knew about, and the other was a total shock. First, we stopped at the home of a family friend and a doctor, who examined me and confirmed all was well with the pregnancy. The next stop in the Midlands was an appointment with an adoption agency. I had no foreknowledge of this and was sideswiped. It was one last-ditch effort to persuade me that I'd be doing the right thing in giving up my baby so that he could have a better life and provide joy to a childless couple.

At first, I was confused as to where I was and who the woman in front of me represented. She seemed very matter-of-fact as she sat behind her desk with the three of us facing her. She leaned over a stack of official-looking papers on her desk, a pen poised in her hand. I was in a foggy nightmare. I wanted to escape, to wake up and not be there. *I might be pregnant, but I'm no dummy,* I thought to myself. As I soon realized what was happening, I became quiet and defiant. I listened to the adoption agency representative state all the reasons an unwed mother should give up her child.

As she spoke, I was silently listing all the reasons it would benefit my child to stay with his natural mother, who already loved him and wanted him. So I respectfully and calmly *refused* to sign any paperwork. I was adamant. There would be *no* adoption of *my* baby. I would never give him up. I would not put my child through the heartbreak my dad had experienced when he discovered at age twenty-six that he was adopted and subsequently spent his entire life searching for answers.

I vowed to break that generational cycle. I would do whatever it took to keep my child.

In Scotland, I felt loved and accepted by my aunt and uncle and maternal grandmother. It was just what I needed—time to think, time to attend medical appointments and classes to learn about birthing a child and the responsibilities of motherhood. I shared lots of lighthearted laughs with my supportive relatives. Chuck and I communicated regularly, and three weeks before our son's birth, he arrived and stayed at a nearby bed-and-breakfast. He put an engagement ring on my finger, and we resolved that we would somehow find a way to be together. We never gave up hope that my dad would concede, that he would consent to our marriage.

October arrived, and on the seventeenth day, our son was born. Chuck was in the hospital waiting for the news, and he was the first visitor to see and hold our boy. What a joy! Then came my mother the next day. She immediately fell in love with her grandson. My mother brought reassurance that she would continue to try to persuade my dad to accept the idea of marriage. A few days later, Chuck had to go back to work. My mother returned to Dad, and I moved to the home of another aunt and uncle who had a three-year-old little girl. Thank God for loving relatives.

Between October and February, many things changed. My father conceded and did an about-face when Chuck's commanding officer confirmed Chuck was ordered to move to a different base in England! Then my dad insisted on a white wedding in the church to keep up appearances. What a switch! I was happy to oblige, but once again, I was sworn to secrecy and reminded of my promise. So I walked down the aisle in white, the guests unaware of the backstory—that is, all except for a few relatives, my bridesmaid, and Chuck's best man. A small reception followed. We spent one night together in a hotel in Stratford-upon-Avon, and the next day my parents met us and brought baby David with them. He'd not attended our ceremony. For several days before the wedding, he'd been cloistered in my parents' house, cared for by one of my amazing maternal aunts who'd been coerced by Dad to pass him off as her own. Chuck was granted a transfer a few weeks before, so our little family officially began life together in a new town.

The secret was safe, the promise kept.

In retrospect, the entire 1963 year was character-forming for me. It was a time of forced personal growth and maturity. It changed the trajectory of my life and *who* I would become as a woman, a wife, and a mother. It transformed me into the daughter I was destined to be in all the remaining years of my parents' lives. I learned to give them unconditional love freely and generously with no expectation of anything in return. And hard as it was, I kept my promise. I did not reveal the secret. I learned to tap into the Holy Spirit within me and allow His love to prevail over my weaker, worldly attempt at love. The circumstances surrounding all the pain and suffering shaped me into who I am today. I know who I am … and whose I am. I thank God for His faithfulness and for loving me. I am grateful for His forgiveness for my transgressions. As I experienced God's presence in my life and understood He had a plan for me, my faith in Him grew stronger.

What challenged me that year changed me. What knocked me to my knees also bolstered my faith. What could have broken me strengthened me. Gratitude reigned over resentment. Patience, belief, and hope conquered doubt, fear, and despair.

In life's struggles God favored me with a wonderful loving husband, a beautiful family, and a life I love. After we were married, my mother quickly fell in love with Chuck, and during a four-year period, my father slowly warmed up to him. Over time he grew to love my husband and thought of him as the son he'd never had.

Love is powerful.

So now that the skeleton has danced brazenly out of my closet after all these years, I rejoice that at long last the record is straight, the truth is out, and I have honored my solemn promise. If I could choose to change anything at all, I'd have openly exposed the truth of my predicament from the beginning and never had reason to hide my circumstances and conceal a skeleton in the closet. But then this story would not exist, and there would be no overriding messages. After reading this story, I hope you sense the theme of love I've woven into the pages.

We all want to be loved and accepted, don't we? Unconditional love is the ultimate gift we can give to our parents, our children, and those around us. Love is powerful. It heals. It changes hearts. It lifts. It keeps no record of wrongs. It always protects, always trusts, and always preserves. Love rejoices in the truth. It hopes. Love never fails.

From Whence You Came...
Thither You Go!

I've always subscribed to the belief that who you are today—at least in part—is a result of how and where you grew up, who influenced you most, and what you made of yourself in the meantime. I am most intrigued by the *why* part. I love to glance back at the early years and correlate the ways some people are and how their pasts helped form who they are today. The connection is usually unmistakable, and if you dig deep enough, I'm sure you will find it quite fascinating and as enlightening as I do, for glancing back lends understanding to who we are as people. While I don't suggest you live in the past or get stuck there, I would encourage you to venture back long enough to reconnect with some memories. Acknowledging your roots and early beginnings does have merit.

Have you ever heard of Keddie? A few years ago, Chuck and I visited this small railroad settlement in Northern California near the Feather River Canyon. Named after Arthur Keddie, who surveyed the railroad that cut through the Sierra Nevada Mountains in the early 1900s, this small community is situated alongside the former Western Pacific Line, the route traveled by America's most beautiful passenger train, the California Zephyr. Nearby is a unique and dramatic split in the railway tracks in the shape of the letter Y, and it dominates the terrain and overlooks the Spanish Creek tributary of the magnificent Feather River Canyon hundreds of feet below. The driving of a golden spike at the center of the trestle, known today as the famous Keddie Wye, marked the completion of the Western Pacific Railroad in 1909, and even today, one hundred years later, the Feather River Route still provides a vital transportation link as part of the transcontinental freight rail network.

My husband, Chuck, has always loved the mountains. Given the choice of a day trip to the beach or the mountains, he will predictably choose the latter every time and without hesitation. Once you hear where he spent his childhood years, you understand the *why* I alluded to at the start of this story. It stems back to the roots, from whence he came.

There are no words to adequately describe the awe-inspiring beauty of the surroundings where Chuck grew up during the mid-1940s to the late '50s. It doesn't come alive or hold as much significance until you stand amongst the cluster of log cabins at Keddie and realize that this was one of the most pristine places for a youngster to grow up. It was also a time when the world seemed to possess more innocence.

The sun dancing through the majestic sugar pines leads your eyes to the green treetops and then on to the thickly forested mountains above and the bright blue sky in contrast beyond. You hear water gushing, and your attention turns to the Feather River as it meanders through the canyon behind the log cabins. You can't help but imagine the laughter from children of a bygone day rafting down the white waters in rubber tire tubes while friends cling to the old swinging bridge high above the river, cheering and jeering them on.

You look skyward and take a deep breath of pure mountain air, invigorating you and heightening all your senses. As you slowly wander along the narrow trails amongst the cabins, you catch the scent of pines, and your feet crunch on the thick carpet of pine needles and cones. You're so tempted to gather some of these beauties, and you wish you could; however, you know you must leave them behind where they belong with the beauty of the moment.

For more than twelve years, Chuck lived with his parents and siblings in one of the authentic log cabins nestled in the small settlement of Keddie, where his father worked for the Western Pacific Railroad. It was a booming little place in those days with a restaurant, a general store, and other amenities to support families who resided there; however, it's now a mere skeleton of its former self, and sadly the buildings are mostly uninhabited and in desperate need of repair. Save for a few cabins that showed signs of inhabitants, an eerie silence reigned in this tiny place, which now resembled a ghost town, so we quickened our pace and soon found the cabin where Chuck had spent his formative years.

It's so easy to see how life influenced him during that period. Growing up in those days in that environment accounts for so much of who he is. Chuck is comfortable in his skin. He knows who he is, and there's no pretense about him. He is independent and self-sufficient with a strong sense of commitment and personal responsibility. He is a devoted husband and father who is loyal and dependable, the type of man who gets the job done, and he doesn't fuss or whine as he's doing it. He is passionate about the mountains and has great respect for nature with a deeply rooted love for the wild outdoors. He holds a special admiration for wolves. Oh, by the way, he's fiercely protective of the second amendment.

As I said, you can trace much back to those early years … from whence he came. His father's job with the railroad meant he worked long hours away from home, and Chuck, being the eldest boy in the family, volunteered for many of the household chores and responsibilities, amongst which was collecting logs and chopping wood. He viewed the woodcutting as *his* job, so he took great pride in doing it well and in storing the provisions that resulted. It was his joyful offering of love to the family unit. As a teenager, he spent hours and hours in the woods, exploring every nook and cranny, mostly alone. It was just him and his friend, the trusty 0.22-caliber rifle. You can understand the independence, self-sufficiency, and respect for nature that he developed from those early experiences as he roamed the canyons and woods.

I knew Chuck was a godly man, but for a while I couldn't fully understand why he wasn't keen to attend church—that is, until one day in the early years of our marriage when he shared a compelling experience that had impacted his young life. Here we go again, back to days of yesteryear to make sense of today. There's always a little clarity hidden somewhere in the roots of the past!

This story lends clarity to Chuck's reluctance to attend church when he and I first met. It dated to when he was a boy of about twelve years old. He invited a close friend to accompany him to their little community church, which had been instrumental in his walk with God, including attendance at several summer church camps. Neither family were churchgoers, but the two boys were keen to attend. So one Sunday, they set out on their bikes, and as they were racing downhill toward the bridge that crossed Spanish Creek, Chuck hit a car and flew over the top, landing many feet away on the edge of the nearby bridge. He awoke in the hospital, diagnosed with a concussion, and for a few days, he was unable to move his legs.

If you think about that incident for a moment, it's easy to understand what could happen in the mind of a young boy who was excitedly racing to church to worship his God when he was suddenly stopped in his tracks and almost killed in the process. What conclusions might a child draw? Did he think he wasn't supposed to go to church? Did he start to believe that bad things happened if you decided to seek God? A sensitive, young boy might be reluctant to repeat that experience. In this case, the apprehension stuck with Chuck for years.

But God plants His seed of love in our hearts, and these continually beckon to us. Sooner or later we will seek Him until we find Him. As Chuck and I stood in that very same spot together, I imagined how he must have felt while he recalled the incident and his accompanying feelings, which ranged from childish excitement on the way to church to shock about the sudden crash to the fear of waking up in a hospital bed, confused and wondering why God had allowed it all to happen. It was therapeutic to relive those moments as an adult with a mature perspective on life and God.

The saying goes that you can never go home, but I don't buy into that. Not only *can* you go back, but perhaps you should make it a *point* to go home if for no other reason than to connect with your roots and remember from whence you came. It's sometimes helpful to view the past through the lens of the present. It's always fulfilling to understand the why, what, where, and when of who you are, isn't it? If you've never taken the time to dive into your past, to examine your roots, and to get a sense of who you are in relation to where you came from, I encourage you to do it soon. It's enlightening and fulfilling. And it might provide the wings upon which you soar into the future.

> The greatest gifts you can give your children are the
> roots of responsibility and the wings of independence.
> —Denis Waitley

You Will Always Be My Babies

My Dearest David, Stephen, and Chandra,

The longer I live, the more I believe in miracles, especially the miracle of life. What a fantastic Creator is our God to bless us with you three children. With each pregnancy, the moment I felt that first flutter of movement deep within me, assuring me you were alive and kicking, I was awestruck by the wonder and magnificence of human life. How miraculous that two tiny cells can collide, multiply, form precious human flesh, and thirty-nine weeks later, produce a beautiful baby. A union of love delivers more love. A precious child is entrusted to our care, and we must nurture and raise him or her to the best of our ability.

I have loved every moment of this journey with each of you. I will love you through eternity.

I never cease to be amazed that you've all grown up to be *normal, happy, healthy, and productive* adults with a capacity for love and deep regard for others. You have self-esteem, confidence, and belief in yourselves and your Creator. I fell short at motherhood along the way too many times to count, and I'm the first to admit it was by the grace of God you turned out so well. When I screwed up, He showed up. In many ways I grew up with you. We learned together. If I could go back in time, I'd change the way I handled some things. I wouldn't be so intense, so demanding of perfection, or so protective. I'd correct less and overlook more. I can truthfully admit that raising children was one of the most challenging experiences I've ever faced, but it was also one of the most enjoyable and rewarding!

My dear children, although you are mature adults with children of your own, you three will always be my babies. I bore you, raised you, held you, kissed your hurts away, dreamed of your future, and marveled as your personalities developed. A mother's love runs deep for her babies. It is infinite and unconditional.

I adore all our beautiful grandchildren, and they light up my life. I'm so grateful for each one; however, the truth is your children are your babies, and *you* are mine. I love my five grandkids no less than I love you and the unique bond with them is every bit as special as yours and mine but just in a different way. You will always be my babies no matter your age or circumstances. When you hurt, I hurt. When you suffer, I feel that pain. When I see you happy, my heart sings with an indescribable joy. Your welfare has always been paramount to me, and thus, it will ever be. Once a mom, always a mom. All three of you have children of your own, so you will understand firsthand the depth of a parent's love.

What an honor it is to be entrusted with living souls to nurture, guide, and love forever. Children are blessings.

Since my mother passed, I have acquired a new status. I'm now the tribal *matriarch*! I must confess that being the matriarch of the family is indeed unnerving. Not only does the title and position cause me to tremble in my boots, but when I think of whose shoes I fill and those who bore the important role of family matriarch in generations past, I'm somewhat intimidated.

It's also empowering to know that an exclusive title of honor is reserved for the eldest mother in the family, not because of any special deed or claim to fame and not because she's qualified or deserving but because she simply inherits it by default. The title is bestowed on her for merely being the senior mother in the clan! A new name brands me— matriarch. Whoop! The distinguished description alone instills confidence and infuses me with a renewed sense of purpose and a meaningful standing within the family hierarchy. Now I get a title to lend credence to my current roles of mom, grandma, and great-grandma. Amazing!

You should know that my mother once admonished me in a moment of frustration, and although I can't remember what precipitated the comment, the words hit me hard. The comment cut me down to size. "If you're half the mother your grandma was, you'll be doing well!" Mum knew how to put things into perspective. She had a concise and disarmingly authentic way with words, always delivered at the perfect time to put everyone and everything in its proper place. Despite the sting of the hastily spoken zinger, she spoke the truth, and I knew it. I could not argue.

In the realm of motherhood, my maternal grandmother excelled. She was like the mother superior. She passed that excellence on to my mother, who, as the eldest daughter in the family, happily assumed the honor and carried the banner forward. She conscientiously and lovingly shared family news, offering encouragement, comfort, advice, and wisdom as she nurtured her eight siblings and their families near and far in much the same way as a shepherd tends his flock.

My mother and grandmother were daunting matriarchs. They have set the standard high for those who follow. Both were highly domesticated women, amazing homemakers, and cooks. Everything was baked from scratch, and clothes were hand-sewn. My grandmother darned socks while my mother even ironed my dad's underwear. Where in heaven's name did they find the time and inclination? I must confess I haven't touched an iron in months! Ouch! Oh, they didn't have the distraction of social media for one thing!

My grandmother raised nine children successfully. My mother had one child only—me. My mother also worked full-time, and she did all the shopping and the housework. Plus she still managed to entertain friends, often on the same day she mowed the lawns and trimmed the hedges. She skillfully provided guests with sumptuous meals on a shoestring budget. Goodness me!

As I think about these two special women today, I marvel at them, and I am full of admiration and love for them. Yes, I'm in awe of what they did each day for their families. They accomplished so much in their lifetimes, but what is most meaningful and what I desire to emulate as a new matriarch myself is not related to what they did or how they did it but rather *who* they were and *how* they lived their lives.

Each in their unique way, they were influential and independent thinkers and women who were ahead of their time. They were kind, loving, loyal, and fiercely protective of their family to a fault. God help anyone who messed with their offspring. I may have *that* one down. They exuded authenticity, epitomized motherhood, and adhered to strong family values. They were selfless to a fault too. They bore hardship and challenges with fortitude. No, they weren't perfect, but they each sported a happy, bright smile, maintained their sense of humor no matter what life dealt them, and placed their faith in God.

I asked your dad the other day what he thought a matriarch was! He responded, "A mother boss!"

That's so funny, but it's not the kind of matriarch I envision myself to be. I wish to embrace the role of honor with grace, dignity, and truth. I aspire to be a matriarch willing to accept a certain amount of authority that comes with age to speak with wisdom from firsthand experience. I want to be one who gently and kindly influences others positively to instill values by example and to lovingly speak the truth even though some might prefer I remain silent. I promise to strengthen the family unit, and no matter the challenge, I'll be the first to cry, "Circle the wagons!"

The more I think about the term matriarch, the more I warm up to it. I think it implies a mother's genuine concern for all generations in the family tree, not just for my three children but for the grandchildren and their children.

And it even implies care for other people's children. Maybe with God's help and the right attitude, I can live up to and do justice to the powerful matriarchal legacy inherited from my mother and grandmother, leaving a meaningful impact on the lives of multiple generations.

Thank you for your love and the blessing you are to both Dad and me.

All my love forever,

Mom

Here's a message to all parents reading this: As a great-grandmother, I've gained some wisdom and insight on raising children. Mostly by trial and error and learning from mistakes that often make me cringe now. Aging brings about some distinct benefits though. Over time I've improved like good wine and mellowed like an aged cheddar cheese. I've heard people say that we should have grandchildren before we raise our children. Of course, that's impossible, but I get what they mean. Mellow is helpful, but the best advice to new parents entrusted with the precious souls of children is to always lead with love.

We parents bring children into the world with no idea on how best to rear, teach, guide, and discipline them so that they will be strong yet sensitive and assert themselves but also learn to conform to certain behaviors. They must learn to be kind to others but not be doormats. They must learn to be respectful and respected. They must learn to love others and be lovable! There are so many more things of importance in child-rearing. The list goes on.

Even if there were a complete manual for parents, there are always exceptions to every rule. Children are all individuals with their own set of unique genes and temperaments. In theory, everything sounds good. Most advice reads well in a book. In practice, it's so different as any parent knows. In real life those little sleeping angels can turn into raging, defiant, screaming, and kicking apparitions in the blink of an eye, people we might be tempted to disown.

Isn't your child like that? And if your child isn't, I have no words for you.

Children will test our patience and our endurance and cause us to have random thoughts about tearing out handfuls of our hair, grabbing *them* by the hair, or screaming back at them at the top of our lungs in sheer defense, frustration, or retaliation!

Does any parent ever do that?

I confess I screamed like an alley cat at least once or twice! No, wait. That happened far too many times. I often apologized to all my children for being too quick to lose patience or raise my voice and hand in anger at their behavior when they were growing up. Sometimes they might have driven me to it; however, often it was my knee-jerk reaction, and the response was undeserved. Whether the former or the latter, I regret losing it sometimes. Just be aware that children will push boundaries we set for their good, and they will *demand* limits not set by acting out in an unattractive manner. Often they will run amuck until you set a boundary. By the time you do establish one, you may feel so insane that you draw an unrealistic, harsh line in the sand, and you dish out an overzealous discipline.

It seems children live to challenge rules, suggestions, and authority, especially their parents' rules. The grandparents, of course, can do no wrong. It's one of the joys of being a grandparent. It often seems that a child's objective in life is to test their will against you, the parent. Do they do it? You bet they do!

Our kids tested us, and they did it every day. If our little darlings did it, maybe yours are doing the same. It's the nature of the little beast. I have seen two-year-old children twirl their parents—both at once, mind you—around their tiny little fingers. I have been the one twirled, and I've been the twirler, so I'm permitted to talk about this! When you're in the moment, you're in the heat of battle. Depending on whether you're the child or parent, you're trying to win, or you're attempting to survive. If you're an innocent bystander looking on, you may think, *Wait a minute. Who's the parent here? Get a grip, and act like it. Take charge, and assert your parental authority!*

That's easier said than done! Am I right, parents?

But there is *good* news! Most children turn out fine despite the occasional traumatic episode or mishandled situation by an ill-advised parent. We all know most parents love their children dearly and see them as blessings, contributing joy, purpose, and meaning to life. Children teach us a whole new perspective on unconditional love that far outweighs the day-to-day challenges of child-rearing. We parents experience the most amazing personal growth. We learn the greatest restraint ever, and it's all free training! Your child is the trainer that causes you to aspire to new heights of patience and maturity! It might also be called self-preservation!

I love this saying, but I don't know where it originated. "Grandchildren are God's reward for not killing your kids!" I for one am *so* grateful for God's grace and His mercy on me for my inept parental skills in the past. We are better parents and better people today because of our child-rearing experiences. We learned so much from raising our children. You might say they taught us a lot, including an increased sense of humor, more patience, greater understanding, and endless love.

Chuck and I have three amazing children who delight us and make us proud parents and grandparents. As a great-grandma with five grandchildren and four great-grandchildren, I feel so blessed, and I love them with all my heart.

If there is one bit of wisdom out there for parents to learn, implement, and practice daily, it is to model the way to live. You must set the example and adhere to the Golden Rule and heed what's laid out in the following guidance:

Children Learn What They Live

If children live with criticism, they learn to condemn.
If children live with hostility, they learn to fight.
If children live with ridicule, they learn to be shy.
If children live with shame, they learn to feel guilty.
If children live with encouragement, they learn confidence.
If children live with tolerance, they learn to be patient.
If children live with praise, they learn to appreciate.
If children live with acceptance, they learn to love.
—excerpt from a poem by Dorothy Law Nolte

May God Bless all children and parents in the world!

And he took the children in his arms, placed
his hands on them and blessed them.
—Mark 10:16 (NIV)

The Drawer Upstairs

It's been years since I gave any thought to the drawer—the one on the shadowy landing at the top of the stairs, the top one in the antique, dark oak chest of drawers that seemed so high to me as a child. I could barely stick my nose over the top drawer to catch a glimpse of the contents inside.

It's not surprising I'd given no thought to it. It's been more than sixty years since I visited my grandparents' house and a good sixty-five years since I last peeked inside the drawer. An incredible amount of time has passed since then, and I doubt the beautifully crafted chest of drawers is even in existence today, let alone the treasures concealed within.

Perhaps what's more mysterious to me is why those memories suddenly came flooding back to me. Why now? Random thoughts of the drawer have monopolized my mind for the last few weeks, and try as I might, I have no rational way to explain their persistent presence. Even when I banish the thoughts, they bounce right back a few minutes later! It's all very puzzling!

At times like these, I'm compelled to write. For me it's not about writing to an audience or following. It's about getting thoughts out of my head and onto paper to unclutter my mind, making room for more ideas, different views. I think of it as pouring out feelings in words. Adamant expressions that hold on tenaciously until the written words release them.

Let's return to the drawer.

It was dark and shadowy in the landing area on the second floor in my grandparents' house. The ceiling light was dingy, and it gently swung when it was switched on; however, it was intriguing as well as a little scary to a young girl. The floor creaked eerily and moving shadows formed on the walls in sync with the swaying light. Parked against one wall in this small hallway leading to two bedrooms was an old oak chest of drawers with ornate brass handles at each end of the stack of five drawers. I've no idea what was hidden away in the lower drawers. The only one that mattered to me was the top drawer—my grandfather's drawer.

Grandad would occasionally take me by the hand and guide me upstairs to the top drawer on the landing. At the age of six or seven, I could barely see the contents as I peeked over the top on tiptoe. I loved that drawer. I felt so privileged that my grandfather entrusted me to hold treasures in my little hands that were very meaningful to him, mostly significant because of the poignant memories or emotions those items stirred within him.

How I wish I could remember everything in the drawer. Alas, I do not!

What I do recall vividly is the musty, moldy smell that escaped whenever he opened the paper-lined drawer to reveal the various treasures. I would never have dared to touch anything without invitation, so Grandad would select something, describe it, tell a short story, and hand me the object. Goodness, these old treasures captured my attention and imagination every time! I was enthralled. Sadly, I cannot remember the accompanying stories. It was too long ago.

I do know there were old coins of foreign denominations that he'd brought back after serving in the British Army in World War I—coins from France, I assume, since he was deployed in the trenches there. I believe there were a few old wristwatches and one pocket watch and chain he promised to give me eventually. There were his WWI medals and ribbons and an assortment of other trinkets like small pen knives, padlocks, keys, and other odds and ends.

I was seventeen when he died at seventy-seven years old. I never received the pocket watch, and I don't know what happened to it; however, I do have the WWI medals and a few coins. Perhaps most importantly, I have one or two more treasures from my grandfather.

I have unforgettable and wonderful memories of trainspotting with him and my dad. We'd go off on the weekend just for an afternoon to a busy train station and spot the old steam engines. Each had a unique number on the engine, and when we spotted the train as it passed by on the track or at the station, we'd enter the engine number into the little book of trainspotting.

And when I had measles and was confined to bed, itching all over, he'd ride his bicycle several miles up and down hills to our house to visit me. Now that's love! He would sing hymns to me and read me stories, and when I asked, he'd tickle my feet. It was something that distracted my attention from the unpleasant childhood illness and calmed down the itchiness of the fiery red rash. He was there every day I was laid up in bed, and he helped me get through the childhood illness.

The most treasured item was his Easter gift to me in 1952—my first Bible. The inside front cover bears the following inscription: "To Anthea, Easter 1952. And thine age shall be clearer than the noonday. Thou shalt shine forth, thou shalt be as the morning. Grandad."

Of all those prominent in my life as a little girl, I have to say without a doubt that it was my grandfather who led me to the Lord, influenced my faith, and exemplified the life of a godly man. He was a gentle caring man of extreme faith and conviction. I'm so grateful to my grandfather for his love and for taking the time to teach me, spend time with me, and hum hymns to me. I thank him from the bottom of my little girl's heart and this grown woman's soul. I will always love him, and I'll never forget him.

My hope for every child is that they have special souls in their lives to pour kindness, love, and faith into their hearts, impacting them in the same way that my grandfather did for me.

And thine age shall be clearer than the noonday; thou
shalt shine forth, thou shalt be as the morning.
—Job 11:17 (KJV)

Grandchildren Complete
the Circle of Love

I was up before the crack of dawn today. It was just me with God and my random thoughts. It's always annoying when I wake up so early when it's the weekend. Don't most people get to sleep in longer? Isn't that the expected Saturday treat, especially for the oldies among us? You know, those folks who used to be known as moms and dads but who through no fault of their own, are now permanently branded as grandparents simply because their children chose to have offspring of their own. Funny when you think of it that way, isn't it? Mind you, I'm not complaining. I love being a grandparent, but the *older* part that accompanies it, I don't so much enjoy.

With any luck, your turn to be a grandparent will come as it did for Chuck and me and as it did for our son David, who is also a grandpa. I would laugh louder except the joke would be on me because if he's a grandfather, what does that make me? A *great*-grandparent. I console myself with the thought that if grand is good, great is better. But it's still *older*. There's no getting around that hurdle.

Anyway, the other day I was in the supermarket, and I heard a mom admonishing her child who was pitching a royal tantrum. "I brought you into this world, and I can take you out!" she snapped, clearly on her last nerve. The kid appeared to be in no danger. In fact, he wasn't at all fazed by the threat, and I'll reserve judgment on her comment; however, I immediately thought at the time, *No, silly, don't take him out. You'll never be a grandma. You'll be eliminating a whole lot of joy in your future!*

If you're a parent yourself, you identify with this mom and the challenges of rearing children. It's not a piece of cake at times. Parenting is a new learning experience every day, but as a grandparent, you discover a whole new world of fun and joy every day with no responsibility attached! You haven't experienced life in all its glory until you understand what it's like to be a *grandparent.* I wish that for you. It's magical.

> Grandparents are the footsteps to future generations.
> Grandchildren are the dots that connect the
> lines from generation to generation
> —Lois Wyse

Things change overnight when you upgrade from parent to grandparent. How many times have you been that parent who complains to your kids that money doesn't grow on trees? When the grandkids arrive, you spend it as if it does. Whatever they want, it's no problem!

You know how your kids, especially the young adult variety, think you know nothing? Your perfect grandkids think you walk on water! It might be because grandparents listen carefully to what their grandchildren say. But it goes beyond hearing the words. Grandparents have gained wisdom by practicing on *their* children. Generally, grandparents are less rushed and preoccupied, so they have time to give their undivided attention to the words, facial expressions, and body language of their grandkids. They can read between the lines and pick up on things left unsaid. It's a sixth sense that grandparents have.

Do your kids take you for granted? Are they mildly bored to see you? Your grandkids see you and run full speed at you to give you a knock-you-down bear hug! Do your kids get impatient and roll their eyes at you because they've heard your stories before? The grandkids beg for more! Do your kids interrupt you in the middle of a sentence, anticipating what you're going to say even before you say it? Not your *grandkids*. They pay full attention and hang on your every word.

Do your kids dismiss your wisdom and advice with a shrug? Get this! Your grandkids seek it out and thank you for taking the time to provide them with your guidance. Is getting your kids to help you like pulling teeth? Your grandkids will do anything you ask without any grumbling, and they'll thank you for allowing them to help! Do your kids think you've forgotten how to parent? Your grandkids love you because you *don't* parent them.

After all, you're the grandparent, remember? *You're* all fun and warm fuzzies.

I can't help but chuckle as I write this because life is wonderful in so many crazy, unexpected, and beautiful ways. Even within generational disparity, there is order and continuity, and for each generation, there's a little payback too. What goes around comes around. Best of all, we gain a deeper understanding and enlightenment as each generation walks the path of their parents and grandparents before them. It's the cycle of life.

It's the circle of love.

Among the joy, love, and satisfaction of raising a family, there are inevitable challenges, frustrations, and struggles. At times, exasperation and desperation show up, but there are wonderful rewards derived from raising children so that they become productive, purposeful, loving adults who contribute to society. One of the best bonuses is the arrival of grandchildren. There's no greater joy or blessing than that of your children, but the next is your children's children. Thank You, God, for Your treasured gifts of love.

> Grandchildren are the crowning glory of the
> aged; parents are the pride of their children.
> —Proverbs 17:6 (NLT)

It's Not Happiness If the Joy Doesn't Last

A few years back, I realized I'd progressed beyond turning into my mother and may have morphed directly into my *grandmother*. I know that sounds a bit weird, but bear with me.

Since I adored both my grandmothers, I'm honored with the association to be like them. I learned so much about courage, loyalty, love, and the meaningful things in life from my grandmas. Despite the eye-rolling and sighing from this teenager who thought she knew better, and apart from often dismissing their words of wisdom as corny or redundant, much of what they said permeated my being. Over the years their words echoed in my head at times when I most needed some internal wisdom, courage, and strength. I thank God for their love for me and the persistence and patience they granted me as their wise words often fell on deaf ears.

Today the world is all about immediate gratification and instant everything! Thinking we can have it all right now and pay for it later is pervasive in the present times. And oh, how we do pay at times! My grandmothers did not believe in instant gratification, and they certainly never practiced it. Their belief systems supported the idea that if something was worth having, it was worth waiting for, saving for, or not having at all.

Proverbs were the rule of the day from my grandmas. I often heard many different ones, and although I pooh-poohed much of what they were saying as being old-fashioned or fuddy-duddy quotes, their words stuck with me and permeated my mind and soul. As I grew in maturity and life experiences, I became more thankful for the sayings they had recited. I was even more grateful that I have grasped the meanings of those proverbial messages, and when the grandmotherly lessons replayed in my head, I implemented them into my life for the most part.

Proverbs are simple little sayings with deep wisdom and value. They're laced with a good dose of common sense and wrapped up in short but catchy phrases such as the following:

- A stitch in time saves nine.
- A penny saved is a penny earned.
- All good things come to those who wait.
- A fool and his money are soon parted.
- A soft answer turns away wrath.
- Don't teach your grandma to suck eggs.

Instant gratification means feeling happy in the moment, but unfortunately, that quick rush of happiness often doesn't endure. As the shine from our impulsive action tarnishes, our temporary happiness wanes. Remorse sets in, and we find our hasty decisions have stolen the very joy we sought. I'm the first to admit that in the past I've ascribed to and experienced firsthand the delight of instant gratification, which I've soon regretted, but then I've also known lasting joy. I know which I prefer. How about you?

Sacrificing a little today to have something better tomorrow has produced *more* joy in my life.

One of the greatest joys for Chuck and me as a young married couple was choosing to save a monthly sum of money for four years and paying cash for a car instead of driving a new car that would have financially strapped us. Anticipating the purchase and feeling a sense of accomplishment as the savings accrued was surpassed only by the exhilaration of a cash deal and owning the car from day one with no required payments. That was ongoing joy! That trumped driving it off the lot and being indebted to monthly payments for the foreseeable future.

When we decided to switch careers and start our in-home business, we knew that there was only so much time in the day. We couldn't give up our current jobs, so we had to carve out additional time for a while to make our business a success. We understood it would take time and effort to establish. We knew we'd have to sacrifice some things in the beginning to produce something of higher value in the future. We were willing to do that. It was our choice.

To quote my grandmas, "Anything worth having is worth waiting for and working for." Sometimes one must forego a little pleasure today and endure some temporary pain to secure a better tomorrow. Sacrificing some things *today* isn't easy, but the payoff and lasting joy are *so* worth it.

Speaking of pain, that reminds me of one more message I frequently heard, "That which doesn't kill us makes us stronger!" I wonder if that's the truth or only partly true. We'll examine that idea later in the book.

Dearest grandmas, you are my heroines! I love you dearly and thank you for all the proverbs that have enriched my life and guided me in the right direction, saving me from myself and the temptations of instant gratification on many occasions.

My dear readers, what proverbial sayings have influenced you in significant ways?

> One generation shall commend your works
> to another; they tell of your mighty acts.
> —Psalm 145:4 (NIV)

The Power of Handwritten Notes

They lay there on my bedroom chair, unceremoniously wrapped up in plastic bags of various dimensions and origins, carefully packed and then unpacked from my suitcase. I'd lovingly albeit randomly placed them there on my return from England after my mother died. There they remained, piled up in the same spot. They hadn't moved for several weeks!

A cursory glance would reveal a heap that resembled a cluttered mess of meaningless stuff, but on a more in-depth examination, one might catch a glimpse of an old jewelry box, a photograph, a lace handkerchief, a book of poetry, or a seemingly insignificant piece of tattered paper peeking out from behind its humble, crumpled container. Then there was a copy of Mum's remembrance ceremony revealing her beautiful, smiling face. She was always smiling and looking up at me as the picture lay on the chair seat.

Within those bags lay some of the little things I rescued from her belongings. I found them hiding in a coat pocket, her wallet, a handbag, a cardboard box, a travel bag, or drawers in a bedside table—poignant remnants from my mother's life. These were unique treasures she valued dearly. Meaningful memories were embodied in each item, memories that ignited love deep within.

Every day I looked at the pile on the chair as I walked past. The presence of the items weighed heavily on my mind, but each time I glanced at the assortment, I quickly banished the thoughts that rose to the surface from the depth of my emotions. Why could I not bring myself to sift through her belongings? Was I *that* busy, or was I subconsciously putting it off? The truth was that I wasn't ready to venture down memory lane and risk the inevitable ebb and flow of grief that accompanies the loss of a loved one. I needed more time, more readiness, and more acceptance.

The day finally arrived when the ever-present reminder awaiting my attention got the better of me. I finally decided to tackle the pile, unable to bear the jumbled mess on my chair. I knew the assortment was for my eyes only and the touch of my hands alone. Nobody else could do it for me. I sat on the bedroom floor and unfastened each bag. I sorted the contents one container at a time into various categories—old photos with old photos, recent ones with recent; jewelry with jewelry; books with booklets, letters with letters, and a separate stack for cards, papers, and random memorabilia. As I handled each item and placed it in its appropriate pile, I realized this was no muddled mess of memorabilia. Instead there was a distinct sense of order, a consistency in message, and a common theme connecting all these treasures, even though I'd gathered each item from its unique hiding place and they were all scattered about in different locations in my mother's house.

Oh, joy! What unexpected gifts I received, all wrapped up in words of beautiful expression, much like the threads of sentiment woven into a beautiful living tapestry of love. You see, I discovered so much more than the mere face value of these items, which I'd intended to preserve in my mother's memory. I was enthralled and blessed by handwritten notes and heartfelt expressions of love. Some were from long ago, and others were more recent. There were inscriptions on the back of photographs, postcards, inside greeting cards, and within beautiful letters, some dating back years.

Some letters spanned dozens of years, characterizing family members or chronicling events in their lives. I read declarations of thanks, words of gratitude for loved ones, encouragement to go on, and professions of everlasting love, all preserved on scraps of paper. I found letters from my grandma, some from *my* children and grandchildren. Others were from Mum's extensive family of siblings, revealing their thoughts and feelings voiced in affectionate words, each written in distinctive handwriting. One letter was from Mum's younger sisters who were with my grandmother as she lay dying. One of the aunts was describing to my mother how *their* mother was staring intently at something at the end of her bed and how she, my grandmother, asked the attending nurse to wipe her eyes so that she could see *her* mother more clearly. What a blessing.

These meaningful writings are priceless treasures I'll cherish and pass to the next generations. As I relished every beautifully written word, love and admiration flooded over me. I savored each message and explored every thought as I surrendered to the emotions flowing from the writer, but I also experienced emotions that the recipient of the letter, my mother, would undoubtedly have felt as she read the sentimental words meant for her.

What a beautiful legacy of love we leave behind when we preserve the thoughts and feelings of others expressed in their written words. It's powerful! We can see life as it was through their eyes, visit places they've been, attend events they've enjoyed, and experience emotions that moved them. We come to know them and understand them, learn who they were and what they stood for, even though *they* are long since gone.

Handwritten expressions have a far-reaching power. We can even relive our own life again and again through words as we journal about our own experiences and recount lessons we've learned. How fascinating it is to revisit memories we or others have recorded in writing. Oh, the power that lies within journaling.

How delighted I was to find two small Bibles in their original and worn boxes, and underneath, or inside each Bible, I uncovered extra special photos and love notes from each family member. The near and dear ones, the ones deemed worthy of protecting, were wrapped in God's holy Word.

I found a tattered note from my grandmother wishing my mother a happy twenty-ninth birthday. Grandma expressed sincere devotion to my mother, who treasured the words and probably read them time and again, even years after her beloved mother was gone. Then I came along sixty-six years later and discovered the little note among other treasures, and I am blessed in multiple ways— once by Grandma's beautiful sentiments, second by the loving way Mum honored the letter, and third through the opportunity to bless *my* children and grandchildren with this heart-warming story.

> Every moment and every event of every man's
> life on earth plants something in his soul.
> —Thomas Merton

My mother cherished simple things in life, many sentimental little gifts. Something from each grandchild was folded up under her Bible. What joy those gifts of love must have provided her so that she would honor and protect them in such a way. Can you imagine the emotion that overwhelmed me in the discovery?

And now the blessing has been passed on. The next time our family gathered, those gifts were returned full circle to their original owners, now grown men and a woman with their own families, and they now understand how greatly their grandma cherished those little gifts—gifts they took time to write many years ago.

It's the circle of love! It's a powerful thing.

Considering all the high-tech convenience in the present times, I suspect the art of writing notes in longhand is quickly disappearing. It's so easy to shoot out an email, comment on Facebook, schedule an automated birthday card, call on a cell phone, or Skype in person. I, too, am guilty of choosing these methods of communication. But when all is said and done, I must confess there's nothing quite so meaningful than inking a blank page with personal words and expressions of love that kindle a fire in the heart of a dear one and inscribing a sentiment that has the potential to live on in the hearts of others. These pages are special, worthy of tucking away in or under the Bible, housed next to God for safekeeping. These are endearing handwritten expressions to read again and again and to revisit at will, and we must safeguard them as a lasting remembrance to touch the next generation. They're so impactful and far-reaching.

I'm wondering what you think as you read this story. Do you handwrite letters and love notes in cards? Do you keep a journal where you share your innermost thoughts and feelings? Here's something to ponder. You may never know where your written manuscripts may eventually end up, the impact they have, or who may be blessed by what you write!

> Oh, that my words were recorded,
> that they were written on a scroll.
> —Job 19:23 (NIV)

CHAPTER 2
Laughter Ignites Joy

Primroses laugh betwixt the snow, and ignite the woods with joy

Lighten Up and Laugh

Laughter is the best medicine they say, so here's something to consider. If you decide to take life less seriously and you learn to have a good laugh at yourself, you will never cease to be amused! I'm personally a great example of a woman who is amused at herself. Almost every day I can find some silliness in something I say or do that gives me a reason to laugh.

Take this situation not long ago. I had plenty of laughs all because of my silly antics! First off, I decided to forgo the sandwich I lusted after for lunch to keep a promise (to myself and others) to eat a boatload of greens at each and every meal for twenty-one days!

So what's funny about that? You'll soon see.

Everyone who knows me realizes I'm conscientious about eating clean and living green. Our business is about getting *super* healthy for goodness sake, so that explains a lot. Some would say I live, eat, breathe, and promote healthy living 99.5 percent of the time, so healthy food has routinely been in my daily life for almost forty years! I love protein smoothies, but that green brew in front of me on the verge of fermenting was not the usual tasty, green yumminess I had whipped up in the past!

What in the world happened to it? I daresay it was nutritious for me, but the slick green slime resembled pond scum, and I half-expected a frog-like creature to emerge. After drinking half of it, I confirmed that it did indeed taste like pulverized earthy and moldy moss mixed with river water and frog parts!

"Down the hatch, Anthea!" I encouraged myself as I winced at the appearance. "You're a wimp and a phony if you don't finish to the last drop." I chugged it down. I emptied the glass. Almost immediately my stomach churned, and I felt a strong urge to gag it all back up. While I was thinking about suppressing that reflex action, a loud growling from my stomach startled me, and I felt a five-second explosive cleanse about to hit me and the porcelain throne!

As I remember this episode, I laugh out loud at the silliness and humor of the things I do and say. After *that* disaster I vowed I'd return to my old faithful green smoothie recipe that tastes wonderfully delicious and is healthy too. I'm still grateful for the experience though. It's good to be adventurous and try new things, and it provided me with the opportunity to laugh at myself. A good laugh is always appreciated and welcomed.

Do you know that a hearty belly laugh can save your sanity *and* extend your life? Yes, it can ... for a few more minutes. I am serious, my friend. You can laugh at me if you like, but it's healthy for you. You must take advantage of every opportunity to enjoy laughter because every minute you're able to extend your life is valuable and counts. It all adds up!

Did you realize laughter is that powerful? It's true. Studies show that laughter is *good* medicine and helps in a few ways! It turns out that laughter positively affects human health in three ways— physically, mentally, and emotionally.

According to Robert Frost, "If we couldn't laugh, we would all go insane!" It's good to laugh. No, wait. It's imperative to laugh, and you *must* lighten up and laugh at yourself. Laugh often before others do! You can lead the way by laughing *first*, which lets others know it's okay for them to enjoy a chuckle, not at your expense but as a gift from *you*.

It's a double blessing for you—*your* amusement and the laughter of those who laugh with you rather than at you. Are you ready for more humor?

We have a garbage can in the kitchen with a motion detector. The lid flies open in response to anything that moves. Chuck loves it. I dislike it intensely! It's so much easier and quicker for me to lob the trash into an open can than stand in front of the motion detector, wafting things at its sensor, waiting for the lid to respond. I feel like a nutjob standing there, waving at a garbage can. I find it very frustrating, and I often wonder how many minutes I waste there in a year. If I were to add up all the five-second increments of time I wait for the lid to fly open, what would the count be? I have endured this annoyance out of love for my man. I'll do anything for my honey. If it wasn't for him, I'd have trashed the bin long ago!

One day in the recent past, I was busy and somewhat preoccupied— at least that's my excuse—as I gathered dirty clothes for washing. Armed with a bundle of smelly gym clothes, I positioned myself squarely in front of the clothes hamper in the bedroom and stood there for a moment or two. I was waiting for the lid to flop open!

Yes, I seriously did that. I woke up after a few seconds and manually lifted the lid, but not before I almost died laughing at the stupidity of it all. I was so thankful no one was watching me at the time, but here I am now sharing my craziness with the world. I'd say my action was due to conditioning at best and insanity at worst. It's more likely it was neither. I was probably distracted, or my brain was overloaded, a common affliction for many of us in the life and times of now. In the world of today, we are overwhelmed. Too much is going on. There are too many things to do, and there's so much to remember. It's no wonder we have memory lapses and outages in our wiring.

Such is life. Stay calm, and laugh on. It's healthy for you. What funny things have you done or said that cause you to crack a smile or collapse into a pile of giggles?

> She is clothed with strength and dignity,
> and she laughs without fear of the future.
> —Proverbs 31:25 (NLT)

Spandex Stretches My Patience

When my good friend and I lived in the same town, we would have a ladies' day out now and then. It was usually a shop-until-you-drop kind of day. I'm talking *all* day! We'd drive ninety minutes to a huge shopping mall, arrive when it opened, and leave when the doors hit us in the rear as they closed. Then we'd stop for dinner and get home in time for bed. Our men thought we were nuts. They were probably right, but those were the good old days. It wasn't that we always spent too much money or came home with more than we could carry. It was just the delight of the shopping experience itself. When you find a great bargain and some cute clothes that fit, it can be quite rewarding, but it can also be a terrific stress reliever. The best part is the camaraderie and enjoyable experience. It's an event you want to repeat.

Looking for just the right outfit and finding it can bring lots of pleasure, but something has changed all that for me! Spandex has infiltrated the stores. It has crept into the shops like a thief in the night, and worst of all, it's disguised in the prettiest cotton pants hanging innocently on a perfectly normal-looking hanger. *The nerve of it*, I thought. *It's in everything and everywhere and pretty much in every brand.* Lately, it has become the bane of my shopping experience. I am out to get spandex. And I don't mean *get* as in buy. It's more like I want to kill it with a vengeance.

Do you know what spandex is? It's a polyurethane fiber known for its exceptional elasticity. It is stronger and more durable than rubber. It does have some redeeming features. It's soft and light, and it stretches, so it's appropriate for the proper occasion. I *love* it in undergarments, swimsuits, workout clothes, leggings, and other sportswear where elasticity is appreciated. But in my opinion, it needs to know its proper place. Spandex should not be woven into natural fibers!

My annoyance is not with the fabric itself. Alone or combined with other stretchy fibers, it's fantastic! My complaint is that spandex hasn't just stayed with rayon, viscose, polyester, and other synthetic fabrics that are *intended* to stretch but has invaded natural materials, including cotton and linen, giving them an unnatural elasticity that they typically don't have. Now *that* drives me to distraction and recently has deprived me of some shopping fun.

It took a while for me to catch on to the spandex ruse. But the game is up. I now know that it isn't only in certain types of clothes where I might want expansion for comfort. It has slithered into street clothes that I assumed were cotton and held their shape. Spandex is sneaky that way! It's a tease and a trickster, and before I knew what was happening, it was an intruder in my home. It was all over my closet. I've been the victim of a veritable home invasion by spandex. It's maddening that it resides in my cotton clothes, especially in my jeans and dress pants.

A couple of years ago, this *really* got to me. I bought a pair of cute pants that were a perfect fit when I tried them on in the store. Ah, it's so good to find pants that fit correctly. They even looked great after I washed them and put them on the first time. A couple of hours later after sitting for a while, they felt a little looser. *I must be losing weight*, I thought to myself. *I could have sworn these pants were tighter this morning*. Anyway, I went about my business and later caught a glimpse of myself in a mirror. Horrified, I did a double take.

What in the world? I turned and looked back over my shoulder, aghast as my worst suspicions confirmed what I'd feared. What I saw is not the kind of eye-catching perky look that every woman hopes to see but a drooping derriere of the most unattractive kind. The seat of my capris had bagged out, and I had joined the ranks of the baggy-pants brigade. Hey, let's face it. At my age I want all the lift I can get. I want toned, not saggy! My trainer and I spend serious workout time on my gluts to compensate for Mother Nature and the relentless pull of gravity, so I don't need a synthetic fiber sabotaging the results of my killer workout with its irritating stretch component.

I consoled myself with the idea that I must indeed be losing weight and that I could always get a smaller pair of pants. I continued with my day. By evening, I just knew I'd lost ten pounds by some miracle. My pants were so loose they practically fell right off when I unzipped them. An awful thought occurred! *Maybe I have a serious illness. No, Anthea, banish the thought! Your clean eating finally caught up with you, and you lost ten pounds of bloat all in one day.* At last, my efforts to lose a few unwanted pounds had paid off! I congratulated myself. The power of positive thought had prevailed again.

I climbed on to the scale eagerly. Disbelief hit me as I stared at the numbers. That can't be right. I got back on, only for it to mock me again. It showed the same weight. "Liar, liar, pants on fire," I accused. "Are you stuck on the same number? You are wrong! My pants just fell off me a moment ago." I regained my composure and calmly stepped off the scale, and holding my breath, I gingerly got back on one toe at a time. The number had changed. It was *up* a pound! Now that's just plain wrong. No way! Frustrated with the numbers on the scale, I decided to teach it a lesson. I slid it under the bathroom counter so it was out of sight. I delivered a well-deserved time-out.

"Spandex, you are a rabble-rouser of the worst kind," I muttered.

It took several times of wearing the spandex/cotton blend pants before I realized that almost all my newer ones were doing the same thing. They would fit in the store and after washing, but if I wore them longer than thirty minutes, they would bag out in all the wrong places. If I rewashed them, they'd fit, and if I wore them for more than thirty minutes, they'd stretch. It was the same sequence over and over like a broken record. The stretchy fiber manages to overpower the cotton fibers that usually keep their shape. I don't know about you, but I like my clothes to fit when I put them on *and* when I take them off. Now I have a closet full of cute pants that I dislike.

So I decided to go shopping for 100 percent cotton pants that hold their shape. The hunt was on! I mean this was serious business. I was on a flare-your-nostrils, find-it-at-all-cost, don't-care-what-price mission to secure pants that fit and had zero spandex. At this point, *cute* was not mandated. I'd gladly accept a little bit of *ugly* if only the garment would fit and not contain *any* trace of stretchy synthetic fibers.

I went from low-end to high-end stores and back again with very little success, but I learned a lot! First, I learned that spandex is not in an item of clothing based on one's size. It's in the larger sizes, and it's also in the size a toothpick would wear. Second, I learned what to do to make the hunt easier. You head straight for a rack of pants, disregarding the size, color, style, and cost. Your sole goal is to reach the nearest label disclosing the fabric content. You can always pick the right size and color once you establish that the material used in the collection meets your criteria.

You start with the label, which is not always visible. Sometimes it's concealed in an inside seam, and you must unsnap one side of the garment from its hanger to reach in and find the tag that displays the fabric content. You're looking for the precious label that states the item is 100 percent cotton. Good luck. There is an overabundance of various blends with cotton and the stretchy fibers. You can find cotton pants all right; however, the beast is ever-present, and the fabric contains anywhere from 1 percent on up. If it has only 1 percent, it's passable if you're desperate. Two percent is very questionable, but 3 percent and higher will hurl you into the baggy-pants brigade faster than your head can spin over your shoulder to glance at the unpleasant sagging behind.

I apologize for yet another pun, but what's the bottom line? A hundred percent cotton pants are scarce. Grab them when you see them, pay whatever the asking price, and when you do find them, never leave them alone in your cart. Don't tell anyone where you found them, or your supply will vanish.

I've decided that in present times, we're stuck with spandex blends. It's commonly woven in with all nature of fibers. It's not going away. I can't influence the fabric manufacturing industry, so I must change either my attitude or my strategy. I *do not like* stretchy synthetic material in my cotton clothes, so I must be more strategic.

My recent foray for a skort (skirt with built-in shorts) slammed it home this week as I searched for 100 percent cotton skorts that were hard to find. I finally found some cute skorts in one of my favorite stores, and I grabbed a couple to try on. They were obviously cotton. Then I remembered to check the label, and I noticed it said 3 percent spandex woven in with the natural fibers. How sneaky. That changed things up a bit. I needed a different strategy. So I carried three pairs into the dressing room—the size I am and two sizes smaller. I won't be fooled into buying my real size if it contains spandex. *That's* something to keep in mind, my friends.

Oh yes, you sneaky synthetic fabric. I am on to you. I will play your game, I thought to myself in the dressing room. *I will squeeze into a size smaller. Then when you stretch, you'll be the perfect fit.*

The dressing room became my mini gym for squats and knee bends. My new strategy is the squat-and-stretch test. You try on the garment, and then you get into a wide-legged stance with your feet pointing out and do as many sumo squats as you can in thirty seconds. The idea is to see how much the material will stretch. There's an advantage to this test too. The more squats, the more muscle toning in the right places. I put on a skort, and it was just a perfect fit; however, I knew better now. The fit would never last. Whoosh! Off it came! On went the next garment, but this one was one size smaller. Hmmm, it felt pretty good, a little neat maybe but okay. It was time for more squats and knee bends to determine if it would stretch.

At this point I was beginning to feel a bit obsessive. You probably think I am too. The thought of hidden cameras crossed my mind, and I started to chuckle at how ridiculous I might appear. Always remember that laughter is beneficial, especially when you're the butt of your *own* joke. I proceeded to do the squat test. Ten to fifteen squats later, I assessed the situation! Indeed, they stretched out just like I thought they would. I rejected that size. They were already too loose in thirty seconds. Whoosh! Off came the skort, and I squeezed into the smallest size. Whoa! A wee bit tight, but maybe that means they'd be just right after wearing for a while. A few more squats to make sure the material expanded and loosened up to my squat-and-stretch test. That size passed. Perfect. It was time to buy!

A new skort was in the bag. I bought the one that was a wee bit tight to start, but I knew after a few minutes, it'd fit just right. The next day I wore the skort all day. As guessed, it loosened up, and by nighttime I felt like I'd lost inches; however, I knew better. I hadn't lost weight or inches. It was just time for a wash to tighten the fabric. And so the ridiculous cycle resumes.

Spandex has changed my shopping experience! The only tag that used to matter was the price tag. Now I've morphed into an obsessive-compulsive label-reading maniac, avoiding spandex at all costs, and the store clerks think I'm neurotic. Spandex may have infiltrated my space and stretched my patience, but one way or another, the fun will return to my shopping excursions … along with a few squats and a few laughs.

My dear friends, is it just me, or do you feel the same way about the invasion of synthetic fibers into natural cotton fabrics?

The most wasted of all days is one without laughter.
—E. E. Cummings

How Was Your Flight Today?

Over the years we've traveled millions of miles on flights, first at the government's expense when Chuck's military assignments turned us into globe-trotters. Then there was the travel we did for our personal pleasure. But we also flew to many vacation spots as part of the incentive for luxury travel that we earned from our business success. Perhaps what I most recall and enjoyed in recent years are the forty-eight round-trip trans-Atlantic flights to the United Kingdom. We visited my parents at least every six months for twenty-three years.

On one occasion I was flying solo on a British Air flight. It was emergency travel home to England to be with my ninety-five-year-old mother who was very unwell and bedridden, and I sensed it was her time to meet her maker. I didn't know what lay ahead. I only knew I needed to get there fast. The wrenching in my gut divulged an urgency to be with her. Over the years I've learned to pay attention to those specific gut instincts as I recognize the Holy Spirit prodding me.

It was with a heavy heart that I settled into my appointed seat. I was content to be alone with my thoughts. I was hoping to rest and enjoy some solitude, to prepare myself for what I'd face at my journey's end. How would I find my mother's condition and my father's state of mind? What would it be like in an unfamiliar bed-and-breakfast where I'd be staying since the spare room at my folk's house was occupied by the live-in caregiver? I was not inclined to socialize with my fellow travelers. I wasn't up to chitchatting or exchanging pleasantries of any kind, even though I'm usually quick to smile and befriend people. I merely wanted to be left alone with my thoughts. Had I been able to snap my fingers and become invisible, I'd have chosen to do so.

You're probably wondering by now why this story made it into the chapter about laughter since the reason for travel and the mood I've described is rather sobering and not at all funny. Despite my demeanor and the severity of the circumstances, I usually can see the humor in situations, and I do believe that laughter is good for us, so if you bear with me, you'll understand that even in the worst of times, one can find some comic relief. Maybe it's also good to *look* for a little humor to lighten the intensity. In this case, the humor came to me in ways I couldn't have foreseen. Life can be fascinating.

So how was my flight across the Atlantic that night? I replied politely to the British customs official's inquiry, "Um, fine. Thanks. Not too bad. Well, it could have been worse."

Miraculously, I saw the humor hidden in the situational comedy on that flight. The comedy of errors saved me from losing my mind, flipping out, or embarrassing myself with a stream of uncharacteristic profanity. Maybe it even helped me avoid physical injury.

What about that woman across the aisle from me? The one who reached rudely in front of me to take a spot in the overhead above *my* seat? Yes, that one. The one with the giant case she could barely lift. It could have been a whole lot worse had she not taken time to wash her underarms before leaving home. As it was, I held my breath longer than I thought I could in view of her unshaven armpit, which was just an inch or so away from my nose. The temptation for me to nudge her with my elbow was overwhelming. The thought played out in my mind. I smiled to myself at the vision of me elbowing her chubby midsection, but I resisted the temptation to execute the blow. After all, we were still at the gate. They could forcibly remove me from the plane, and that wouldn't have been good.

Yes, things could have been worse.

The parents of the sick, runny-nosed, screaming child in the row ahead of me could've slapped me instead of glaring at me like I was a bug when I calmly and lovingly suggested a way they might lower their kid's fiery temperature of 102 degrees at thirty-nine thousand feet. After two hours of their child's constant screaming, his feet kicking everything in sight, including the seat in front of him, the parents were visibly panicking. They were flapping and frantically wringing their hands. This behavior had two flight attendants dancing like circus monkeys as they scurried up and down the aisles, trying to figure out how to help the unruly child and calm the distraught parents. It was chaotic.

Well, wouldn't you have made a kind and helpful suggestion? Perhaps something as simple as a cold, wet washcloth on their child's forehead could help lower that raging fever. Did they not understand that with all my experience with kids and grandkids, I *might* have some valuable input? It's just possible I know a wee bit about soothing a two-year-old with a miserable fever. I know they thought about taking a whack at me because they were as out-of-control as the child. My first clue was when the mother lurched toward me in her anguish but caught herself in time. And I escaped with another killer look.

Oh well! Get on with it then! I thought. But the truth was that I wanted the noise to stop as did all the passengers. The idea of a little peace after two hours of uncontrolled, nonstop shrieking will cause people to resort to extreme measures. I thought about a few ways but restrained myself from implementing them. Arriving in the United Kingdom with a black eye would not be good. Yes, it could have been worse.

Eventually, the sick child wore himself and his parents out, but then the teenager with a permanent scowl on his sulky face who was seated at the end of the adjacent row went into high gear. With his long skinny legs, he reminded me of a daddy long-legs spider. He fidgeted in his seat and appeared to be hyperactive with attention deficit disorder. While everyone else jumped at the chance to get some sleep, he began to tap his feet incessantly in tempo with his nimble thumbs, which were clicking away at lightning speed on the controller buttons for his video game. I tried to look on the bright side to avoid more agitation. I thanked God for small mercies. At least his identical twin was not in the empty seat next to me.

Yes, it could have been way worse.

The individual somewhere nearby with the uncontrollable rectal sphincter could have launched smelly burps in between the horrendous stink bombs exploding from his other end every few minutes. I couldn't sleep even with my face covered with my scarf, which now doubled as a mask. Now it was getting humorous. *What a flight*, I thought. *What next?*

It was terrible, but it could have been so much worse. A wheel could have fallen off the plane as we landed, or we could have plunged into the Atlantic or ended up as an ornament on the

Westminster Abbey spire instead of the skillfully smooth and safe landing the pilots dealt us.

In the end, arriving safely at the destination is all that matters! I remember thinking how very grateful I was for so many blessings and a few unexpected chuckles. Happily, I had both feet on the ground, and after a good night's sleep in my peaceful bed-and-breakfast, I'd be energized and psyched to face whatever life would throw at me the next day.

> A well-developed sense of humor is the pole that adds
> balance to your steps as you walk the tightrope of life.
> —William Arthur Ward

Skip the Senior Shuffle

Tim Conway is one of my all-time favorite comedians. He's well-known for playing the role of an elderly gent with a shuffling gait. This "older than dirt" character played by Conway was slow to think, slow to move, slow to react, and even slower to speak. He was painfully slow in fact.

The live audiences would laugh hysterically at the antics of this somewhat senile but lovable individual so skillfully portrayed by Mr. Conway. It is said the actor would often ad-lib his lines, which both confused and amused his costars, causing them to burst into uncontrollable fits of laughter. The show was humor at its finest, taking a real-life situation and conveying the humorous side of human nature and circumstances. As we've mentioned already, laughter is the best medicine. Well, isn't it?

The senior shuffle is a walking gait where the feet never lift off the ground but slide forward one foot at a time and an inch at a time. As you might imagine, *shufflers* travel nowhere fast. Elderly people often walk with this gait. It arrives when they grow physically weak with little or no muscle strength in their legs and are too infirm to lift even one foot off the ground. To do so might risk losing balance, ending in a terrible fall. If you've never seen anyone with the senior shuffle, I suggest you Google Tim Conway and senior shuffle. You can also find it on YouTube. Then watch a few minutes of this hilarious acting.

In situation comedy the portrayal of the senior shuffle is humorous, but it is not so funny for those who must live the role in real life! Aging is an inevitable and natural part of life, but the signs and symptoms seem to escalate once one turns fifty or so! As many people exclaim, "Old age is not for wimps," and it's definitely not for the fainthearted. It seems there's a new challenge every day. I had a reality check several years ago when I ended up with three herniated discs, which I'll tell you about in a minute.

Like most of us older folk, I want to look, feel, and be as young as possible for as long as life blesses me. How about you? In my opinion, optimum health means being mentally and physically fit with the absence of disease. I am totally into preventative measures, and since I'm way too cowardly even to entertain the idea of plastic surgery, I ascribe to natural antiaging alternatives. That translates into a monthly chiropractic tune-up, deep tissue massage, aerobic exercise three days a week, strength conditioning twice a week, and slathering an all-natural, high-quality antiaging skin care system on my face morning and night. I round that off with a healthy diet, sensible supplementation (which includes a cellular antiaging tonic), mental stimulation to retard the memory issues, daily spiritual nourishment, lots of quality time with loved ones, and multiple doses of laughter.

What more can one do to retard premature aging? Not much. The rest is in God's hands.

You don't have to be eighty or ninety to be afflicted by it! It descended on me like a ton of bricks and as fast as a bolt of lightning a while back when I got overly enthusiastic about maintaining bone density. On one doctor's flippant recommendations, I took to a regimen of jumping rope daily. It was called skipping in *my* day, and that's what I should have done. I should have *skipped* it altogether.

"You need only jump for three minutes a day, and it will do you a world of good!" said the physician.

On the third day of jumping up and down and ignoring the jarring impact, each time my feet collided with the ceramic tile in our entryway, my innards were about to tumble out. It was then that my bulging L-4 disc collapsed onto my L5 and that the L5 crunched on top of the SI disc. The result was intolerable pain from three herniated discs that laid me up for several weeks. The first fortnight I moved with the dreaded senior shuffle, but it beat crawling on the floor, which was my mode of mobility for day one and two. It was no picnic. The pain was unbearable. But good came from it!

I admit it took digging deep, but I was determined to prevent my physical condition from affecting my emotional and mental composure. Physical pain plus depression is a downhill slide. That's not what I wanted. But it's easier said than done when pain is involved. I struggled for a couple of days, but with regular ice packs, gentle stretching, pain cream, and several doses of alfalfa tablets daily, the pain subsided sufficiently to be tolerable. For those who aren't aware, alfalfa contains natural anti-inflammatory properties. So what if my toilet deposits turned green and I mooed like a cow a few times? Swallowing some concentrated alfalfa compressed into tablets is a small price to pay for a little pain relief. The vision of me mooing like a cow, plopping green pancakes, or stomping my foot repeatedly at the ground produced some much-appreciated laughs at my plight! Laughter lightens up many sobering situations.

As an entrepreneur, I teach my team that attitude is everything, and since my business partners were privy to my behavior, I knew I had to practice what I'd been preaching. I needed an attitude adjustment. How does one adjust one's attitude? You *choose it.* You intentionally try your hardest to make the best of a bad situation. You step up, show up, and increase positive affirmations. You practice mind over matter. You visualize yourself as you want to be, and you do what it takes to make it real. You monitor what you're saying to yourself in your head. You eliminate negative input from any sources. After a while, you'll believe what you're saying. Then you'll soon see results manifested from the adjustments.

It's amazing what you can do from a prone position. You can conduct business on the phone with a headset and laptop. That's what I did on and off all day long. I ran our business from the bed, talking from a reclined position, all thanks to modern technology. Interacting with people was fun, and entertaining helped to pass the time as I caught up with friends and clients. Meanwhile, my beloved hubby waited on me hand and foot in between building a massive deck in our garage for extra storage. Yes, it's incredible what we can do when unfortunate events challenge us.

I had plenty of time to think while I was confined. I resolved to take my daily exercise more seriously. I decided to retain a personal trainer once I recovered. I would accept the advice of my orthopedic surgeon who said, "No impact sports, including running and jumping. Instead you can swim! Continue to see your chiropractor, and follow the regimen he advises. Buy a pair of good walking shoes, and wear them out. Walking is the best exercise for you."

Lastly, I vowed never to accept the senior shuffle as being inevitable at *any* age unless it's due to serious injury. It is preventable, so I decided I would always strive to skip the senior shuffle. But I would no longer physically jump rope.

How do you avoid the shuffle? Well, that's up to you to decide what you're willing to do to stay as young, strong, and healthy as possible. But one thing is for sure. All research and clinical studies agree that you can retain muscle strength as you age if you take the necessary actions. Getting older doesn't mean you have to get weaker. It's never too late to begin, and you're never too old to start.

Staying active is good, but it's better to intentionally schedule aerobic and strengthening exercises. Please take advice from the voice of experience. Challenge those muscles, get into the gym, do the resistance exercises, and build some muscle density. Maybe hire a personal trainer if you need to learn some techniques, but get going. Do it regularly for the rest of your life. Promise yourself you will start it today. You'll be very thankful as time goes by, and you'll grow stronger and healthier.

I'm grateful that my injury resulted in a *positive* outcome. There are so many lessons to learn in life that make us healthier, happier, and more joyful! When you build muscle mass and strengthen your core, your back and legs will be stronger than ever, and your chances of bypassing that old-age gait are much higher.

Will you join me? Let's skip the senior shuffle!

> Nobody grows old merely by living a number of years.
> We grow old by deserting our ideals. Years may wrinkle
> the skin, but to give up enthusiasm wrinkles the soul.
> —Samuel Ullman

CHAPTER 3
Animal Anecdotes

Furry friends add fun to family life.

Furry Frenzy

Have you noticed that we learn to snuggle with furry things from an early age? Long before we bounce into this world, kicking up our chubby little legs and gasping for our first breath, preparations for our arrival are in full swing. Adoring parents and relatives are all so eager to welcome the precious new life, and they lovingly place a wide variety of soft, cuddly critters wherever the baby will be. The cradles, cribs, dressers, and prams are all adorned with plush stuffed animals ranging from big to small and covering all the colors of the rainbow. The baby's space is full of love … and furry things.

Teddy bears, puppies, mice, rabbits, ponies, elephants, and virtually any other animal you can name are all baby-proofed, sanitized, fluffed up, and lined up like an informal greeting party, patiently waiting to welcome a baby into the family. Do you remember your favorite stuffed animal as an infant? Mine was a small furry bear that was light beige in color with brown eyes that twinkled. He smiled with his eyes! His name was Worcester, and while I cannot remember why that name stuck, I know for sure he was a dearly loved bear. He was stroked and kissed so much during my childhood that the poor fellow's fur wore off in large patches, exposing his bare skin. Sadly, one eye fell out and was lost.

This chubby little girl often smothered him with her motherly bear hugs. It was not uncommon for her to wake up from a deep sleep to discover the annoying lumpiness beneath her back was none other than a crushed Worcester. It was a very squashed and indignant teddy who had miraculously escaped suffocation. The fact is that I almost cuddled him to death over the years, but not quite. Luckily, he lived to tell the tale, and my goodness, what a tale he could tell. Thankfully, he is still with us, ancient and weary and not so furry anymore. But he's loved. He always has been. However, with age he's also earned a great deal of respect and reverence. This small furry bear is a cherished part of the family nowadays, and he proudly observes life from behind the safety of his glass front door, his dignity restored.

I often wonder what he thinks of his sedate life today. Do you think he misses hugs and kisses from that exuberant little girl? I like to think he's simply content to be still, to sit and watch life on the sidelines. I'd hate to think he was pining for his crazy, younger days. Having lived a long and full life, giving and receiving love, I feel he's very happy where he is. After all, home is a good place to be.

As we reach toddler age, we become fascinated by furry things that *move*. Of course, we still love our favorite stuffed toys, but as we grow more aware of our surroundings, we are attracted to the kind of fur that purrs. We become enthralled by those little creatures with soft, silky, floppy ears and tiny pink tongues that flick in and out and smother us with wet kisses. We discover kittens and puppies, the playful variety, and before long we're imploring our parents to give us one of our very own. We want living pets to stroke and cuddle, to love on, to play with and provide us with comfort in the darkness of night. We want special furry friends who love and understand us, ones who must endure our toddlers' hands and all nature of unrestrained fascination, which is often manifested in tail-grabbing, fur-pulling, ear-tweaking, and other bodily assaults, all delivered in the name of love. Poor fur babies!

That's how it all begins. A four-legged bundle of joy invades the household, one who loves unconditionally and truly believes he or she is one of the humans in the family. Oh, how we love our family pets and rightly so, for they bring us another dimension of joy and playfulness. They fill up our lives with love, entertainment, companionship, and welcome comfort in life.

They enrich our lives for the length of their lives. But alas, all too soon, the time arrives for them to cross the rainbow bridge, and tears fall unrestrained as we mourn their loss and prepare their resting places complete with headstones and graveside farewell ceremonies. Although we never *replace* the one departed, as time passes and sadness fades, our hearts prepare to embrace and lavish love on new pets … and then another … and another.

A veritable parade of pets march through our lives!

As a child, I had several pets, but none with fur. My pets were not the kind to hug! Who wants to embrace a cold, wet, smelly fish or a squirmy newt? They're fun to catch and fascinating to watch, but there's nothing cuddly about them. While the neighborhood kids had dogs and cats, I had fish. We caught these scaly creatures when Dad and I cast our fishing lines into the river and hooked a likely candidate. They were reeled in and added to the bright orange carp residing in our garden pond. Of course, I did *like* the fish, and I cherish the memories of summer fishing trips where Dad and I bonded on the riverbanks, while Mum sat peacefully under a shady tree, reading until we worked up sufficient appetite to dive into the delicious picnic she'd assembled.

My dad banned certain animals in our household. I was not allowed to have a dog, cat, or even a mouse or hamster. Dad would not agree to it, and no explanation accompanied the rule. But in addition to the pond fish, I did have Joey. This green budgerigar parakeet could repeat a few human words, and he was learning to say more until he spied the love of his life flying around in our back garden. He tweeted to her, which caught her attention. Then he whistled his little heart out with a beautiful love song. She heard. Fairly soon, she flew onto the living room windowsill, and when we gently opened the window, she flew inside, circled the room once, and landed on top of Joey's cage. We opened his door. She hopped in. That was that—no more elocution lessons for our talking Joey. He ignored all our attempts to engage him in conversation. He only had eyes for his mate.

Joey showed little interest in us at all until we arrived with food or opened his cage door so he and his love could fly around the living room, flapping their wings and depositing droppings on the pelmets above the curtains, which evoked a lot of tongue-clicking disapproval from my poor mother, who had to clean the messes. Occasionally Joey would flutter onto a willing shoulder or alight on an outstretched hand. He might briefly nuzzle into the crook of a neck or peck at an ear before flying a few more laps around the living room, chasing his lady.

Eventually, Joey and his love graduated to an aviary on the back patio, but not long after moving into their new home, a loud crash in the middle of the night got all of us up in a hurry. Maybe a cat jumped on their living quarters and tipped it over. We'll never know, but what I do recall vividly is the open door to an empty aviary. The birds had flown the coop and were never seen again, and a little girl was brokenhearted for days, wondering what became of them. The empty aviary remained in place on the back patio with the door open for weeks until my parents dismantled it. I remained ever hopeful that my two feathered friends would return home. They never did.

Then there was my first pet, Timothy, who carried his house around on his back. He was a beautiful tortoise. You'll hear about him later, but after the birds, there were no more pets for me until I had a family of my own.

Life with Chuck and our three children produced a variety of pets, all of which had four legs and sported fur coats of sorts. Well, doesn't every family need and deserve a pet or two? Perhaps the continuous stream of furry ones we owned compensated for the lack of cats, dogs, and rodents in my childhood. Or maybe it had more to do with my husband and kids, who had this uncanny knack for picking up strays that stole their hearts, rendering them powerless to reject any lost, orphaned creatures. The most likely answer is that our pets came into the family because we all love animals, especially dogs. Yes, we do have our favorites.

I think about our procession of pets as the furry frenzy. Mind you, in some cases, the nature of the animal was such that the term furry *fury* might have been more fitting. We had at least two such animals! The thing is that you never know what you're in for when you take in a stray! Suffice it to say, our pets were dearly loved and treated as members of the family. Well, almost all of them. Over the years the entire menagerie brought us love, companionship, joy, laughter, protection, and frustration on certain occasions. One species grossed us out but taught us a lot about nature.

Yes, we humans can learn much about life from the animal kingdom. I dedicate this chapter to all God's creatures, the wild ones and the domesticated ones. How beautiful are the beasts of the earth, sky, and sea? They are beyond wondrous, and I thank our Creator for His gift of so many varieties, especially pets. In this chapter you'll hear more about some of our family pets and their antics as well as a few wild animals.

> Until one has loved an animal, a part of
> one's soul remains unawakened.
> —Anatole France

Timothy Tortoise

May I ask you a question? If you're a parent and you plan to delight your child with a pet, what are the first two animals that come to mind? You're probably picturing a fluffy puppy or a furry kitten, aren't you? Of course, there are other favorite creatures, but dogs and cats do seem to top the list of pet choices for most families.

Here I will point out that I said *most* families! Just not ours.

Dogs and cats were not allowed in our home. Not ever. It didn't matter whether they belonged to a friend, neighbor, or relative. I understood the whole "no dogs" rule because Dad had his very own reasons for not allowing Mum and me to have a dog. It wasn't that he disliked them. On the contrary, my father loved all members of the animal kingdom. Well, most animals. Cats were not among his favorites, even though *he* had one as a child. According to Dad, cats are sneaky, self-centered, cruel animals who kill for sport and derive instinctive pleasure from torturing their helpless prey by toying with them rather than making a clean kill for survival reasons. My dad would go to great lengths to chase off any cat found trespassing in our garden or caught in the act of stalking a poor defenseless bird or small rodent. Dad had his favorites! He adored birds.

Let me be clear. Dad wasn't against dogs just because they are dogs. He thought they were beautiful animals and much more pleasant than cats. It was their tongues my dad couldn't tolerate. To be more accurate, it was the slimy wet licks he abhorred. He would back up into a wall to avoid a dog licking his hand, and ironically enough, any time we encountered a dog, the animal immediately always targeted him.

While studying microbiology, Dad had viewed slide samples of canine saliva under a microscope and learned from advanced science classes that humans can contract deadly diseases from *certain* bacteria found in dog saliva. So convinced was Dad of the potential effects posed by dog saliva that I saw him leap in the air and move his hand out of the way like lightning to avoid an overzealous tongue-licking, saliva-dripping puppy dog that aimed its tongue at any patch of exposed skin, be it his hands, arms, or legs. I'm not disputing the validity of this claim. Nor am I judging my dad for being alarmed at the potential threat. I'm just saying that was his justification for steering clear of dogs. And he protected his family from any such risk by refusing to own a dog.

Honestly, I can't remember if I specifically asked for a dog or not, but most kids go nuts over puppies and kittens. All my friends had them, so I'm assuming I would have expressed the desire for one at some point. The good news is I don't seem to have been permanently scarred from missing out as a youngster, although I made up for what was lacking in childhood by embracing an abundance of dogs and cats as an adult.

Anyway, I had Timothy. "Good Old Timothy" as I called him.

Timothy was my pet tortoise, and I loved him dearly. He was my very first real pet, and I was responsible for his care. And I did so very conscientiously. We fed him the best tender pieces of lettuce and other greens available. When my folks were growing vegetables at the bottom of the garden, he would crawl into the furrows and help himself to some of the tender new shoots. Surprisingly, my avid gardener parents were okay with that. After all, tortoises don't eat many vegetables, just little nibbles here and there, so nobody complained.

Timothy was mostly allowed to roam our back garden unrestricted with no cages or chicken wire to fence him in. He was king of the back garden, and he loved his safe hiding places. He would occasionally disappear as he discovered a new secluded spot to retreat inside his shell and snooze. I knew most of his secret haunts, so between you and me, they weren't really hiding places, but Timothy didn't know any different. Perception is everything. He thought he was safely hidden, and that's all that mattered.

Sadly, Timothy only lasted one summer with us. I want to tell you he had a long, happy life like Worcester, the teddy bear, but it wasn't meant to be. All I remember is winter came, and it was his time to hibernate. He was placed in a large box with straw and a container of water and then put in the shed out back. My pleas to keep him in my bedroom were rejected, and so off to the shed he went. Next thing I remember was a tearful mother telling me Timothy never woke up from hibernation. Of course, we officiated a tortoise funeral for him in the back garden, but that was the end of Timothy. There were no more tortoise pets for me.

As time passed, I recovered from the loss, and then one day, lo and behold, a new pet arrived—a feathered friend. Joey, the budgerigar, joined our family, and you've already heard his sad tale.

Thankfully, children bounce back with surprising resilience, so it wasn't long before my friends and I occupied our free time in the great outdoors, exploring the surrounding countryside, fascinated by the wonders of nature and all its little critters. We collected frogs' spawn and marveled at the amazing transformation of tadpoles into amphibians. We darted nimbly over stepping-stones as we chased newts in nearby streams. As I mentioned earlier, my dad and I also caught fish in the river at Port Meadow to stock the two garden ponds.

In retrospect, it was a charming time of life for a child growing up in the early 1950s in postwar England. We neighborhood kids were a ragtag bunch of boys and girls, but we enjoyed so much fun together as we played hide-and-go-seek, climbed the gnarly willow trees, rescued baby birds, mimicked mooing cows across the field, and marveled at ants carving their maze of passages in dirt-filled mason jars. We scoured the woods and fields for wildflowers and picked posies for our mothers. We chased fluttering butterflies with our homemade nets. We learned respect for the beauty of nature, and we fell in love with all God's creatures, great and small.

Ah, yes, life was good.

Horsing around with Socksie

It's been a while since I thought of Socksie, and it's been many years since she was part of my life. Isn't it fascinating how the mind works? One thought led to another, and there she was. She suddenly popped into my mind's eye as vividly as if it were today!

As a little girl growing up in the 1950s, life was fun, or at least it was for me. I know my parents must have struggled monetarily after surviving WWII and the aftermath that resulted in rationing of certain foods, difficulty finding housing and work, and a multitude of other challenges, but I was oblivious to all that. I was a happy, adventurous child living in a newly built housing development where it was the norm for neighborhood kids to play outside until well after dark, feeling free and running wild to explore the wonders of the small world in which we grew up. It was rural, and it was safe. It was a simpler life.

It was a beautiful time.

Our street backed up to a sizeable farm of undulating green fields. The view from my bedroom window was heavenly! My eyes feasted on the back garden which was the envy of the neighbors. It was small but beautiful and lovingly manicured by my parents. Our property had something else that made it unique. Besides

Timothy the tortoise, who nibbled at the young lettuce growing in the vegetable patch, it sported not one but two fish ponds that my folks had constructed, and in them were goldfish that we'd purchased and chub that we hooked in a succession of fishing trips to the Thames River in Port Meadow, Oxford.

I loved all that, but what intrigued me more was what lay beyond the garden and beyond the twisted, gnarly willow trees whose low branches leaned lazily over the small stream that gurgled alongside the bottom of our back garden. I could easily climb through the fence at the bottom of our garden, and I did so often, usually accompanied by a friend. Using a few strategically placed stepping-stones, I was across the stream, through the jagged hole in the prickly hedge, and into the vast wonders of a sloping green field that seemed endless to a youngster of elementary school age.

This field was Socksie's domain.

Socksie was another one of my four-legged friends, and she was no ordinary pony! You see, Socksie was a beautiful retired white cart horse with gigantic furry hooves. She was an enormous animal and somewhat intimidating to a small child; however, she was majestic, and she reigned supreme in her field. She owned it, and she knew it. She would toss her head to show off her flowing mane, and swish her tail, flaunting her superiority at the lowly cows who had to share a field in the neighboring meadow. Socksie roamed freely in her pasture surrounded by tall, thorny hedges on all sides, and if we sneaked into her domain, which my friend and I often did, we glimpsed yellow cowslips growing in clumps everywhere. The tallest and most beautiful wildflowers emerged from her horse droppings, which we called *dung*. I'd say that Socksie lived the good life in her well-deserved retirement. It was clear by her demeanor that she had led a full and hardworking life as a farm horse.

It was exciting and titillating to sneak into Socksie's field and dodge the dung heaps. If we crawled through one of several small holes in the hedge, we could play undisturbed at the bottom of her field, and if she was up at the top end of the hill, she was unaware of our presence. It was fun to gather blackberries from the hedges at certain times of the year or catch tadpoles in the babbling brook at other times. We were unnoticed by the grazing Socksie, but we always kept a watchful eye out for her because in all honesty, she scared us just a little.

No, wait! She scared us a lot.

Socksie towered over little girls of eight or nine years old, and from our side of the strong metal gate, we'd peak at her, timidly pat her neck, and marvel at the size of her hooves, which were as big as our heads! As we played in the field at a distance, she wasn't so scary, but up close we were in awe of this mighty steed. But she was a gentle soul really and welcomed the stale crusts of bread or fallen apples we brought to her as treats. That was no problem for us so long as the barrier of hedge or gate separated us.

I'm not sure what made us brave enough to advance to that next step to venture into her territory and hand-feed her treats inside the field. I think we just grew familiar over time as the friendship developed. It was a gradual process, getting to know one another, trusting one another, and respecting one another. It was kind of the same with human friends, but this was a relationship of two friends and a horse.

How or why things changed, I don't remember. But I *do* regret it. Maybe we were ten by this time and a little bored. Perhaps we were seeking a new thrill, but we grew braver and bolder. Soon we were horsing around with Socksie. We would confidently enter the field and fearlessly approach her, bearing gifts, usually a basket of stale bread crusts. As we approached, she'd see us and walk toward us to greet her friends. As soon as she reached our proximity, we chickened out, dropped the bread, and took off running like scared rabbits with our empty basket, leaving her to forage for the treats in the thick grass.

We repeated these antics over and over for several months. It became our game. We knew the boundaries, and so did Socksie. Or so we thought. As we became more and more mischievous and enjoyed the thrill, we allowed her to get closer and closer before we dropped the bread and bolted for the hole in the hedge. But the game changed one day when we naughty girls took advantage of our horse friend and began to tease this gentle soul by crying out, "Socksie, Socksie, here's your bread. Catch us if you can!" We'd run and drop the goods time after time, and she'd always stop to eat the gifts we threw down as we watched safely from afar.

The game ended the day she didn't stop.

The same scenario played out that day just like it had on other days. As she trotted closer, we dumped the bread, took off running, and stopped to watch her eat her treats. Not that day! She cantered past the crusts of bread and picked up her speed into a full-on gallop.

Heavens above! I could hear those thundering hooves pounding the ground, gaining on us, I caught a fleeting glimpse of flared nostrils, her mane flowing wildly and her tail straight out behind her. To top it off, she was neighing furiously at us, shaking her head, and with lips curled back, she exposed her enormous yellow teeth. I heard what seemed like bloodcurdling screams coming from this enraged creature.

They were not from her mouth though! The screams were the frantic, high-frequency screeches of two terrified girls running for the hole in the hedge.

What would become of us? I envisioned the worst—those teeth embedding themselves in my behind, losing a buttock and being deformed for life, or a hoof to my head, squashing it like one of the rotting cabbages Socksie loved to devour! "Run like the wind," I screamed to my friend, who was a faster runner and well ahead of me.

What, Anthea? Are you crazy? I thought. *You are the one who needs to run for your life!* It was every man for himself—every child in this case. My friend was already bolting as though a pack of hungry wolves were hot on her trail! I was struggling to catch up, bringing up the rear, easy prey for a justifiably enraged horse.

The hole in the hedge was visible. My friend was through, and I was almost there. I felt Socksie's hot breath from her angry snorts, and I heard my heart pounding louder than her hooves. As I plunged through the tiny hole in the hedge, ignoring the scratches, rips, and tears from the thorny brambles, I caught a forceful nose nudge from this incensed animal. The headbutt added a great deal of velocity to my exit. I flew through the hedge like a shot from a catapult! Socksie had evicted us from her realm. Triumphantly, she sauntered back up the hill to reclaim her peaceful existence.

Whew! We had escaped injury and learned a valuable lesson in life from a horse.

Do not tease animals. Always treat them with kindness and respect! In the same manner, don't taunt people. Never laugh at someone else's expense. Don't take advantage of others. Never betray the trust of a friend for any reason—not for entertainment, relief from boredom, self-gain, instant gratification, or any other purpose. Never take friendship for granted, for it is a precious treasure!

Cherish it.

> The only way to have a friend is to be one.
> —Ralph Waldo Emerson

Help! There's an Elephant on My Plate!

Elephants are some of my favorite animals. When I was little, I marveled at them in the zoo. I was fascinated by their acrobatic antics when the circus came to town, and at times I rode on their backs, squealing in delight as I hung on for dear life. But never have I revered them more than when I experienced them up close and personal in East Africa in the late 1950s.

It was a time when all the magnificent wild animals of Africa roamed free and untamed in their natural habitats. They were plentiful, and they were majestic. To a spellbound teenager observing them from her parents' small four-door sedan, armed with only a camera to shoot pictures of their beauty, they appeared gigantic, powerful, awe-inspiring, and sometimes terrifying. They *always* commanded the right of way, which was willingly given, preferably from a safe distance. I'm privileged to have experienced so many species in the wild, sometimes too close for comfort and in overwhelming numbers.

Of course, I've never had a *real* elephant on my plate. I have never tasted elephant meat, and I don't feel inclined to do so; however, I've figuratively eaten many in my time! In this adventure we call life, there is always a proverbial elephant lurking in the background, waiting for consumption, and the only way to tackle it is one bite at a time. We all know there's no swallowing an elephant whole. It's not possible, and it's not smart to think we can.

To me, the legendary elephant is any challenge in your life perceived as significant, daunting, and overwhelming. Maybe your elephant is weight loss or tackling that postgraduate course or paying off the debt that's run rampant. For some it could be writing a book or painting a picture or starting a business or running a marathon or any number of things. What's the elephant lurking in the shadows and standing in the way of *your* life?

Thanks to our society of instant gratification, no matter what it is we desire to have, be, or do, we not only want it, but we want it *now*. We've been conditioned to expect nothing less. Whatever happened to the idea that anything worth having is worth waiting for and working toward and that the journey along the road to success is supposed to be enjoyed, viewed as a learning opportunity and appreciated as an experience of great value.

I am disturbed by a lack of will in ever-increasing numbers of people I encounter in the life and times of now. More and more, I see an unwillingness to take on that elephant bite by bite. There's a pervasive attitude in society today that if the elephant is too massive to swallow in one gulp—and we know it is—there is no appetite for it at all. It seems that the *desire to try* vanishes, sometimes never to return. Many give up before they start, and in doing so, they reject the opportunity to tackle and overcome challenges that would serve to make them stronger. Goodness alone knows that in this world we all need patience, determination, and tenacity to survive.

Too many folks deny themselves the thrill of the hunt, the joy of success, and ultimately, the satisfaction of accomplishment because success isn't instant or doesn't come as fast as they thought it should. In this way, dreams die, and hope fades.

Let us recapture those dreams and reclaim our hope. Take on that elephant! Remember running a marathon begins with one small step, so take it! Then take another step forward followed by another, and over time victory will be yours. An artist creates his painting one brush stroke at a time. Fifty pounds of fat didn't accumulate in a day, and it won't come off overnight. Fifty pounds is lost one pound at a time. Think about it. If you lose a pound a week, in a year you'll have lost fifty-two pounds. Patience and perseverance are required. The most amazing of books started with a single blank page and a creative idea. A person wrote one word on the page followed by another and another until finally a great book was authored. What about your credit card debt? Make one payment here and one payment there. That's what we call "eating the elephant one bite at a time!"

What is *your* elephant? You know, the one you're refusing to eat that's lurking in the back of your mind driving you nuts! Think about it. Take that first bite, and don't let the sun go down on another day without starting. Get on with it. Take a stab at that elephant on your plate. Take pleasure in your dining experience. Savor each bite. When you complete your objective, revel in the fullness and satisfaction of accomplishment!

Bit by bit, one bite at a time, you will consume the elephant. It's so worth making a start!

Alligators Eat People

This morning while I was thinking about my time in East Africa (in the late 1950s), I remembered the inebriated golfer near Lake Victoria who accepted a *dare* to stick a postage stamp on the rump of a hippopotamus. He succeeded in placing the stamp on the hippo's gigantic rear. He won the bet, but at what cost?

I don't recall what the prize was precisely, but it wasn't much. Maybe the friends of the golfer offered to pay for his drinks at the nineteenth hole, or perhaps it was a small monetary wager, I don't recall, but I do wonder if winning the bet was worth the hospital time and a bazillion stitches. In my opinion, he was fortunate to live to tell the tale!

By now you might be wondering about my ability to focus on a topic. You're probably thinking, *Wasn't this woman's storyline something about an alligator? Why is she talking about hippos? What is the connection between hippos and alligators?*

They have a common attribute—massive bone-crunching teeth and jaws.

They have huge, razor-sharp, killer teeth that slash and tear flesh; enormous ugly teeth attached to jaws that can crush bones and lop off human limbs as if they were snapping a twig! These animals pack a deadly bite, and just about everyone knows it. So how did I arrive at this juncture? My thoughts about Africa led me to stories of biting creatures, which then morphed from a hippo to an alligator. I hope that makes sense.

A successful entrepreneur friend of ours is known for sharing doses of practical and concise information. He shares simple advice that speaks to me, not only in a business sense but on a personal level. I believe one can benefit from applying his wisdom to life in general. "Stay out of the swamps. Alligators live there. Alligators eat people."

It's a simple fact and absolute truth! Please don't overlook the wisdom in simplicity. If you don't want to set yourself up for pain, don't go where you know the potential for pain exists. If you don't want to be eaten by alligators, do not venture into the swamps, at least not willingly, and if you have no other choice, be very sure of the consequences of doing so. Go armed.

For example, if you're allergic to peanuts, you might not want to seek employment in a peanut factory. I'm just saying that's an example of an alligator! If you're obese and need to lose weight and you know your weakness is fried food, stay out of fast-food restaurants. That's your alligator. If you're in a destructive relationship that you know isn't good for you, get out of the swamp. That's your alligator!

Your alligator could be almost anything disguised in the form of a person, a food, a thing, an obsession, an addiction, a job, or a bad habit. How do I know?

I've been down to the swamps myself. I've seen the alligators. I stay away!

Sometimes the alligators are not visible. They sneak around and hide in still waters. They wallow in muddy shores or conceal themselves in the shadows under the roots of trees. You cannot always see them; however, you know that they live in the swamps and that their teeth, while not visible, are sharp. Their jaws are like steel traps, and their bite will dismember or kill. An unseen peril is no less deadly, so be aware, and know what lurks in the murky shadows.

Thank goodness we are free to make choices in life. Let's choose wisely. If you don't want to feel pain, don't set yourself up to receive it. It's bad enough that others can set you up with an unsuspecting sideswipe, so don't willingly go into the jaws of a man-eater and invite pain and failure into your life!

Instead, change yourself, and change what you *do*! Why would someone keep doing the same thing and expect a different result? Change your thoughts and your actions, and you will change your life. It's within your power to do so. Work on it. Just do it!

Let's circle back to the hippopotamus story. If you don't want to get ripped to shreds by a hippo, don't attempt to stick a postage stamp on its rear. Hippos don't like that, and they have big mouths, strong jaws, and sharp teeth. And alligators do too. Alligators live in the swamps. Alligators eat people. Stay out of the swamps. I leave you with a question only you can answer.

What is *your* alligator, and do you know where it hides?

Crocodiles are easy. They try to kill and
eat you. People are harder!
Sometimes they pretend to be your friend first.
—Steve Irwin

Robin, Where Are You?

Have you ever hummed a catchy tune or sung a song to yourself silently, perhaps one that randomly popped into your head and lingered on and on as if stuck in a loop on continuous play? No matter how diligently you try to purge your mind of the music, it keeps on playing unceasingly and altogether involuntarily like a broken record. Even if you love the melody, you will find it irritating after a while, and it can drive you crazy in some cases! Then suddenly, peace reigns in your head, and you realize the refrain vanished as unexpectedly as it appeared. The human mind is impressive.

The week leading up to Christmas 2016, something similar happened to me, but instead of repeated music, a vivid vision flashed before my mind's eye. It arrived unexpectedly and took up residence. I wasn't troubled by the repetitiveness of the image itself, which occurred several times daily throughout the week, although I was curious as to why it was happening. No, it ran deeper. What stood out was the poignant nature of the scene itself. It grabbed me and evoked strong emotion.

It struck a chord in my heart and touched my soul.

"Robin, Robin!" The stooped elderly gentleman called out from the front doorstep of his house, his breath penetrating the cold air in misty wisps. "Where are you, Robin?" he queried, peering across the frosty lawn in search of his feathered friend, all the while gesturing with his hand to reveal crumbs of bread that might tempt the little red-breasted bird to appear. Persistently, this kindly bearded soul whistled ever so softly and hopefully to the robin.

"I'm here, Robin! Robin, Robin, where are you?" he said.

The robin didn't come. His friend was nowhere in sight. Slowly, reluctantly, and noticeably disappointed, my dad stepped back into the warmth of his house and closed the door on the frosty night air. It was Christmas Eve. He was alone.

I felt sad.

This scene appeared in my mind several times a day that week. I didn't tell anyone. I kept it to myself because it was troubling, and I chose not to intensify my already heightened emotion by repeating the story. It also puzzled me. As a deep thinker, I like to know the reasons behind unusual occurrences, and this was out of the ordinary for me to obsess over a picture that popped into my head. I wondered why this was happening. Why had I conjured up this vivid scenario with my dad and the robin? Why did my mind reveal that picture? Was there a significance? Answers weren't forthcoming, so I attempted to erase the image of my lonely dad calling for a robin that didn't come by busying myself with holiday preparations. It was easier said than done.

I wondered why it was haunting me.

Do you ever ask yourself these kinds of questions and demand an answer? Do you take time in the busyness of the day to ponder the meanings of occurrences such as these?

Christmas is the most joyful, beautiful celebration of the year for many of us. It's a time for family, for love, for giving, and for rejoicing over the birth of our Savior. We must also remember that for some it's a time where loneliness and sadness prevail, and a few may even feel a sense of hopelessness.

I thought about my friend with no Christmas decorations caring for her husband after a stroke, another friend who had suffered a terrible fall and had fractured her patella, and a client who had confessed that she had no reason to keep on living. Even amidst the beautiful carols, the bright lights, and the reason for the season, Christmas can be a challenging time for those who are sick, suffering, or alone.

It was Christmas Eve, and all was calm in our house. All was bright from the twinkling tree lights reflecting in the glass coffee table. I was the only one still up. My eyes darted around the quiet living room. Presents under the tree patiently awaited morning discovery. The fragrance of winter berries lingered from the freshly extinguished candle. Cookies and milk lay on a plate nearby, anticipating Santa's arrival, lovingly arranged on a special plate by our grandson.

I savored those few moments of silence alone with my thoughts.

My mind wandered back to the morning and my daily call with Dad. He and I had not mentioned the robin since my visit to him in September. I hadn't shared my recurring vision of him calling out for the Robin who didn't come. I had convinced myself to no longer question why the vivid scenario wouldn't leave me. I assumed it was one of those inexplicable occurrences.

During the call to my dad that morning, I commented on his being alone on Christmas Eve and expressed how I wished we were together. Imagine how astounded I was when from out of the blue, he commented, "When I opened the front door to check the mail, the robin was waiting there, so I went back in and brought him some bread crumbs, which he happily gobbled up!"

My dad sounded so thrilled to welcome home his friend the robin. My heart filled with joy, and my soul began to sing! Who would have thought? The Christmas Eve Robin! These simple joys of life can make such a difference. But this isn't the end of the story.

I decided to do a little research on the meaning of the robin, and it turns out that in ancient folklore the appearance of a robin is significant. The robin symbolizes joy and spiritual renewal. The robin is a welcome visitor to the garden in winter, and if someone you love recently passed, it can convey the message that they're watching over you. The appearance of a robin can symbolize that you are deeply loved.

There's also a legend from long ago about the birth of Christ! The story goes that the robin got its red breast by tending to the fire in the manger. As the blaze began to burn out, a tiny brown bird appeared singing and flapping its wings. The draft of wind created by its wings made the embers glow brightly, reigniting the fire. Some of the hot sparks landed on the bird's breast, making it glow bright red. Mary declared that the bird and its descendants would forever wear a red breast as a sign of its kind heart.

These stories seem like mere folklore and legend to some, but to my dad and me, the return of the robin was so much more meaningful. Recently having lost my mother, and my dad his beloved wife, the robin was a symbolic reminder and reassurance that Mum loved us. I like to believe she was watching over my dad. This little bird brought joy into a lonely heart that evening and comfort to a loving daughter. In that brief encounter, Robin appeared with love in his tiny heart to convey a heaven-sent message from a beautiful soul in heaven to two souls here on earth. Oh, how we are loved.

Thank you, Robin!

> Hope is the thing with feathers
> That perches in the soul
> And sings the tune without the words
> And never stops at all.
> —Emily Dickinson

CHAPTER 4

High Days and Holidays

Seize every opportunity to unplug.

One More Birthday

How do you feel about your birthday? I wonder if you're excited to make it an extraordinary day, a day to rejoice and celebrate life or if you're someone who never gives it much thought, so it usually passes by quietly with no fanfare, no cake, and no celebration. To you, it might be just another day like any other. But perhaps you revere the day you were born, and you literally can't wait to celebrate it. You might even see your birth as a gift of life worthy of its annual celebration. I hope you celebrate your birthday every year no matter your age, for your life truly is a gift.

As for me, I love birthdays, mine and other people's too. The first thought in my head when I wake up on my birthday morning— even before I open my eyes—is always this: *It's my birthday today!* And I immediately feel thankful to be alive. I awaken and know where I am. I remember what day of the week it is, and I realize it's the anniversary of the day I was born. It's gratifying indeed. Mental acuity is never to be taken for granted, so that alone is worth celebrating.

It's going to be a fabulous day, I think to myself. *I'm alive. Today is the first day of the rest of my life.*

Of course, my birthday has dawned faithfully every year so far. I'm still here, so I'm living proof of that. I'm also thankful to see it arrive. I suppose I could view it as any other day or any other birthday since most don't signify any specific number or milestone. Let's say that the number representing the years I've lived on earth isn't that significant. It's only a number, and it doesn't define me. I like to view each birthday not as being older but as becoming wiser, more comfortable in my skin, bolder, more mellow, happier, and more thankful with each passing year. I place a stronger emphasis on being healthy, maintaining a sound mind, and staying young at heart. Quality of life is priceless, and having it gives one great cause to celebrate every day, not only on birthdays.

I sometimes wonder if I'll hit that triple-digit birthday. I hope so. To reach the distinguished title of centenarian will be amazing! Since I'm the conductor of my orchestra in this theater of life, I'll set the tone and choose the music for my special day each year. It will not be just another birthday. It's the anniversary of the day I received the most precious gift ever—life itself to design and craft as I so choose.

That's reason to rejoice. What a valuable gift it is, and yet in the humdrum of our daily living and all the noise that dulls our senses, it's easy to take for granted and pass it off as just another day or just one more birthday. Weird, random thoughts can influence behavior and attitude, so we must eradicate that which we do not wish to take on. I confess there have been times in the past when inferences such as those tried to invade my mind, but I quickly banished them. There's no such thinking allowed on my birthday.

On January 11, the day a sharp smack on the bottom startled me into the world, I took my first breath all those years ago. No doubt the slap was well-deserved for showing up as a girl when my parents expected a boy. Shortly after I was born, Dad said to Mum, "She looks just like Winnie Churchill!" Nice! Thanks a lot, Dad.

Was I chubby with a double chin? All right, so I was short, fat, and bald? Not that I remember hearing my dad's words, but there are tales told that remain unrefuted. When I bounced into the world, they (my parents) scrambled to find a suitable name for a girl. My beautiful parents just *knew* their newborn would be a boy, so no girl names were even in the running. My mother was reading a book during the last week of pregnancy, and the heroine took her fancy, so I received *her* name—Anthea.

No matter how I came by my name, I appreciate and enjoy it. It's a keeper. It's different, and I am partial to being unique. Why or how Gillian came to be my middle name is unknown.

Most birthdays I've done nothing significant. I haven't jumped from a plane or climbed Mount Everest. However, I do remember three birthdays quite vividly. My seventeenth was on board a ship bound for the United Kingdom as we returned from a three-year term in Africa. The memorable part was chewing tobacco. The sea vessel was small compared with cruise ships of today, so it was easy to socialize and make friends with the passengers and crew. A few of the teenagers bonded, and we hung out with a couple of the younger ship's officers. It was with this group of young men and women on my birthday evening that a game of dare erupted.

I was dared to chew tobacco. A crew member produced a plug, and I began to chew it vigorously. It was quite disgusting. I immediately regretted it, but as I was brought up as a young lady, I chose not to spit it out. Instead I swallowed it. It wasn't long before I felt violently ill and spent the evening hugging the toilet. I tried to pass it off as motion sickness, but since the sea was calm and I was worried about the health implications of swallowing tobacco, I confessed to my mother, who received the news more sympathetically than I had anticipated. The consequences of the dare were retribution enough. She and my dad had a good laugh over that one. I was so happy to oblige.

My fiftieth was a surprise party organized by Chuck and our daughter Chandra. I was lured away on some pretense, and when I returned, all manner of transformation had taken place in our home. Enlarged photographs showing me at every stage of life were hanging on all the walls, each bearing humorous captions. Friends came from far and wide, so there were lots of delightful human surprises. It was a memorable evening in many ways. My seventieth birthday celebration at our daughter's house was not quite so raucous an affair. The party was a little more sedate but every bit as enjoyable and unforgettable. It was filled with surprises such as the unexpected arrival of family and friends.

On birthdays I usually do change my routine a bit. It's a day I welcome long chats with friends near and far, and I savor special dinners with family. This year we had birthday cake *first*, and then we ate the main course. Another year I ate a significantly different breakfast from usual. I dug myself out of the regular rut of drinking my healthy protein shake, and instead I fired up the toaster, threw a chunk of whole wheat bread into it, let it sit until it got cold, and then plastered it with a hefty load of butter and coated it with a smear of homemade orange marmalade. You see, you must let the toast go cold so the butter doesn't melt. If it melts and disappears into the toast, the bread goes soggy. If you truly understand what's happening here, you'll get that it's all about having some toast and marmalade with your slab of butter. It's not a run-of-the-mill piece of toast and marmalade. It's a special treat!

I loved every bite too. I had no shame whatsoever. I don't have even an ounce of guilt attached to what I choose to eat on my birthdays. All options are on the table. The rule book goes out of the window for the day. "Happy butter to me! Happy butter to me!" I could sing. I enjoyed every bite. Dear friend, are you having a chuckle at the toast story? Look, it's true that as more birthdays come and go, we find some of the simplest of things can make us the happiest. If you're not there yet, your time will come. We must put fun and silliness into life now and then.

The fact is that on most birthdays I intentionally set out to enjoy the day. To live in the moment and focus more on *being* and less on *doing*—unless, of course, writing is considered doing something. Since I love to write, I find it a joy to sit and pour out random ramblings. As thoughts drop out of my head onto the paper, I'm often taken by surprise by what I read and the thoughts that surface from deep within. I find myself in places I never intentionally sought to go.

According to playwright Alan Bennett, when you're a writer, "You don't put yourself into what you write. You find yourself there."

Birthdays are more than milestone markers. Birthdays are the anniversary of the day we were brought into this world. I thank God for the privilege of life. As Marcus Aurelius stated, "When you arise in the morning, think of what a precious privilege it is to be alive, to breathe, to think, to enjoy, to love."

And to that list, I would add the ability to wonder at the meaning of life. Let's appreciate the freedom to choose how we spend each day of our journey as we travel through *this* life on our way to the next. I hope you're always grateful to celebrate the gift of a birthday.

God gave us the gift of life;
it is up to us to give ourselves the gift of living well.
—Voltaire

Every Vote Counts, and Each Soul Matters

How do you feel about elections?

For many years I had to sit on the sidelines, unable to participate in any election, as I was not yet a citizen of the United States. Neither had I voted in the United Kingdom, my country of birth, because I left before voting age. I was nineteen years old when I moved to the United States, and at that time in Great Britain, the voting age was twenty-one. You might say I fell between the cracks of eligibility.

So when I finally was naturalized as a citizen of the United States, I literally couldn't wait for the next election to come around so that I could have a voice. I was thrilled the first time I cast my ballot.

I love to vote. I consider Election Day one of the high days. It always feels so good to exercise my privilege to cast a ballot for candidates of my choice, and I especially enjoy being able to do it early to avoid the craziness of the official day. I'm so grateful for the freedom to vote my conscience with no fear of coercion, no mandate to choose a designated candidate, and no worry of reprisal for my selection.

Does it seem to you that the tone of elections has intensified and that the rhetoric becomes more hateful with each passing year? Have you noticed that the campaigning starts earlier and earlier and dominates the news long before the actual day to vote? Despite all the desperate attempts from candidates to garner votes along with never-ending chatter from mass media and political spin artists, we thankfully reside in a country where we, the people, still elect our governing body by casting a ballot. I thank God for that freedom. Around election time I always think about those souls who shed precious blood in past times to secure the right for each of us to vote our consciences.

> The ballot is stronger than the bullet.
> —Abraham Lincoln

The current times are full of intrigue. It's an exciting period in which to live. I wonder what the next election will bring and if the candidates will be loud and contentious. I've known a few elections in my time, but in recent ones the intensity of personal attacks, accusations, alleged lies, and corruption have reached an all-time high. I am not a fan of hate and personal attacks at any time, so I pray we become people who remain passionate to our political beliefs but refrain from vicious personal attacks against the opposing contenders and supporters.

No matter which side of the aisle you favor, I hope you desire civility, truth, and decorum from the candidates and their voters. I will be praying fervently for the direction of this great country. I hope you will too.

Here's the thing. We don't know what future national elections will bring, but when the kafuffle of the primaries calms down, we know we will probably end up with two presidential candidates with drastically opposing views on issues that face the nation.

Possibly their political platforms may be distinct opposites. If elected, one will take us down one path, and the other will go in a completely different direction. Nowadays the norm seems to be a vast political divide in views and policies between left and right. There's very little middle ground. There aren't many grey areas to diffuse and confuse the selection process.

It makes for an easier choice.

Well, it's easier if you have a clear vision of what you want this nation to be in your grandchildren's and great-grandchildren's generations, and you know what will secure that picture. It's easier if you refuse to listen to the opinions and agendas of all the spin artists (and others). It's easier if you choose to hear the candidates themselves and thoughtfully assess where each one plans to take this nation in the future. It's easier if you listen carefully to the words they speak and if you do your research and discern truth from exaggeration or untruth. It's easier if you set aside the minutia, spin, and noise and decipher which political platform and which candidates are your best choices and then decide if you believe they will carry out their promises.

Once again, I urge you to pray for discernment. Elections determine the course of our nation's history for years to come. By voting, we have an opportunity to have a valuable voice in creating history and determining the destiny of future generations. In my opinion, no election warrants folding your arms and sitting on the sidelines because you don't like either candidate. A no vote for one is probably a vote for the other. While I respect everyone's choice, I'm not a fan of throwaway votes to candidates who have so little support that they cannot possibly win.

And yes, we will hear all the media banter and the crazy polling numbers leading up to every election, and *no*, I don't believe they're always accurate. Neither should you. Polls can be skewed and misleading. So don't be discouraged by thinking the polls decide any election. Instead, get out, and *vote*. Be empowered. Do it! Then wait for the results *after* the election. Don't leave it to chance or to someone else's vote.

Every vote counts.

So let's follow each election process carefully. Be passionate about the outcome. If you're a believer, pray. Listen and think long and hard. Search your soul and determine your selection.

Cast your vote.

As a believer myself, I've experienced the power of prayer many times in my life, so why would I not pray for discernment and then listen intently for answers from God? I know many in both parties are praying people. That's a good thing. Our country needs all the prayer it can get. Thankfully, God loves every single soul because to Him *each* soul matters and *every* soul is precious in His sight.

> What, then, shall we say in response to these things?
> If God is for us, who can be against us?
> —Romans 8:31(NIV)

God is on the side of every single human soul. But the enemy is not! The devil is a liar, and he's the master of deception. He's also against God. He blinds people to the truth, creating havoc, confusion, and doubt. Don't be misled. Pray for our country, pray for the candidates, pray for each other, and pray for wisdom and discernment in your voting decision.

I suspect some voters will pray for God to be on the side of *their* candidate. Will you indulge me for a moment? There might be something more important than trying to sway God to choose the candidate *you* want. Instead, what if we asked ourselves *this* question: "Am *I* on the side of God?" Ponder that for a while. Knowing the nature of God, how does that influence your vote?

Blessed is the nation whose God is the LORD,
the people he chose for his inheritance.
—Psalm 33:12 (NIV)

Happy Pancake Tuesday!

This day doesn't fall into the category of a holiday, but I see it as another one of those high days. It's truly a day to celebrate and one that justifies enjoying some pancakes. If ever there was a day to eat pancakes, it's *this* day! Why? Because it's official Pancake Day!

It always falls on a Tuesday in February or March immediately preceding Ash Wednesday! In case you've never heard of it before, it's also known as Shrove Tuesday. It's always the day before the first day of Lent, a Christian observance that begins on Ash Wednesday. The date changes each year depending on the timing of Easter.

Many people voluntarily give up something during Lent, which goes from Ash Wednesday until Easter Sunday. Lent is forty days associated with fasting and avoiding rich, fatty foods. Many people all over the world choose to refrain from unhealthy foods, including sugary sweet and the fattening variety, and other overindulgences that are usually bad for their health.

Shrove Tuesday, known as Fat Tuesday in France, permits an exorbitant feast on the day and throws the health aspect out the window for twenty-four hours, giving people permission to eat up all the sugary, floury, creamy, sweet things so that they can clear these out of their pantries and refrigerators to be well-prepared for the fasting of Lent beginning the next day.

So what does all that have to do with pancakes?

It all seemingly started because pancakes are an easy way to use up sugar, flour, eggs, cream, and other rich, fatty, sweet edibles. Who knows how long ago it all began? Some say Shrove Tuesday was more of a pagan ritual before it was associated with Lent.

Be that as it may, watch out for Pancake Tuesday when it comes around each year.

My mother *always* provided us with pancakes on Shrove Tuesday when I was growing up in England, where people celebrate it more commonly than those of us in the United States. I managed to carry the tradition forward while the kids were at home, but somewhere along the way after they all grew up and left home and the busyness of life consumed me, I forgot about Shrove Tuesday and the pancakes.

My mother's pancakes were thinner crepes, and they were delicious. They were large and paper thin. We squeezed the juice from fresh oranges on them, sprinkled sugar all over them, rolled them up, and devoured them. I could never eat just one.

I've decided to reinstate the tradition of Pancake Tuesday in our household. I hope you'll consider joining us. To celebrate I'm sharing one of my favorite recipes for buttermilk pancakes. You'll see it on the next page. No, they're not out of a box. They're my own creation made from scratch, perfected from years of trial and error. They may not be the healthiest of my pancake recipes, but Shrove Tuesday is not about that. These rascals are not the healthy, dense ones that I also make with protein, oatmeal, or cream of wheat and other nutritious ingredients. These are by far the lightest, fluffiest ones that will ever melt in your mouth! Enjoy them anytime you feel like eating a pancake! The leftovers are even delicious later, cold and spread with butter (real organic butter) and topped with homemade jam!

By the way, pancakes and crepes need not be sweet. Nor must they always be served with syrup or jam. They can be accompanied by just about anything you choose. Of course, they're healthy with sliced fruit on top, or you can add blueberries or chopped banana to the pancake mix, but if you're going to spread any fat on the hot pancakes, you must use real organic creamery *butter*.

Here's some fair warning! There's no margarine or fake butter allowed on my pancakes.

The thinner variety of crepes (recipe not included here) lend themselves well to encasing savory fillings such as mushrooms and chicken or ham and veggies. So it's your choice—savory or sweet! And enjoy pancakes whenever the spirit moves you, but for goodness sake, *do* eat pancakes on Shrove Tuesday.

Anthea's Buttermilk Pancakes

2 eggs slightly beaten
1 cup heavy cream
1 cup milk
2 tablespoons white vinegar
1 tablespoon freshly squeezed lemon juice
2 tablespoons butter
2 cups sifted all-purpose organic flour
2 tablespoons sugar
1 teaspoon baking soda
2 teaspoons baking powder
1 teaspoon salt

Combine milk and cream. Stir in vinegar and lemon juice (which makes a creamy homemade buttermilk), and set aside to mature. Next, sift together the flour, sugar, baking soda, baking powder, and salt, and set aside. Meanwhile, melt the two tablespoons of butter in a small container in the microwave, and then set aside. Heat your skillet to 375 degrees Fahrenheit.

Lightly beat the two eggs, and whisk in the milk and cream combination. Drizzle in the melted butter while continuing to whisk. Pour this liquid into the flour mixture, and stir until barely mixed. Don't beat or overmix, or else the pancakes will be tough!

Consistency of batter may be thick, light, and slightly lumpy. That's good.

Pour one-third of a cup of batter for each pancake onto the lightly buttered griddle. Cook until bubbles barely form, and then gently flip over. Pancakes will be light golden brown and very fluffy! Serve immediately with your favorite accompaniments. Makes ten to twelve pancakes.

Not Just Any Day—Sabbath!

Sunday is coming!

It's not like I always leap out of bed early every Sunday with a spring in my step, a smile on my face, and a song in my heart. Hardly. Many Sundays, I emerge from the depths of sleep, squint my eyes to see if it's light, peer at the clock, quietly sigh, and ponder the luxurious idea of sleeping longer.

In my weakness I'm tempted to skip church on some Sunday mornings.

I could do it, you know. I could stay in bed and pray to my Lord and just as easily listen expectantly for any words of wisdom He might whisper back or place in my mind or on my heart from the cozy vantage point of my bed. What a privilege it is to have direct access to the Almighty wherever and whenever the Spirit moves us.

As a Christian with a personal relationship with God, I can seek Him anywhere at any time. Indeed, I do partake of that gift He's freely extended. Not a day goes by that I'm not calling out His name, frequently wondering how He will answer. Sometimes I'm frustrated or confused. Other moments I'm seeking forgiveness for failings and disobedience. At other times I'm asking for guidance, praying for a friend in need, praising Him for blessings received, requesting strength and comfort, or thanking Him for His faithfulness and grace.

And I am ever mindful of His infinite love.

So why then do I go to church, even when I don't feel like it, especially since I have access to God anywhere at any time? Do I seek the fellowship of like-minded people? Do I go to connect with my church friends seated around us? Is it for the pastor's message? The motivation? To praise and worship God? Could it be for the inspirational music that stirs my soul? Is it to receive biblical information or to learn more about the nature of God? To draw closer to Him?

If I'm honest, it's a little of all the above, but it's also so much more. It's deeply personal and meaningful each week. No matter how I feel on the way to church, whether I'm bright and happy to go or I'm dragging myself there in reluctance, it's always worth the effort. I leave church more joyful than when I arrived.

It's the Sabbath, not just any day but the day when you stop what you're doing and rest.

In the present times, we face many challenges. Even when all is well on the surface, the run-for-your-life-all-the-time rat race and routine demands from people drain us. All the while, life's unexpected sideswipes pile on stress and fatigue, which wear us down. Frustrations in the workplace exhaust us physically, and worse still, they leave us spiritually depleted. The emotional roller coaster of today's world can empty us of joy.

Our spiritual cups are sucked dry, and our souls are crushed relentlessly.

How, when, and where do we replenish what the worldly thieves have stolen? How do we recapture what we've freely given of ourselves to others as we strive to become broken bread and poured-out wine in service to those around us? Of course, we can immerse ourselves in nature and soak up a new supply of strength and soul food in the solitude of green pastures by a babbling brook, filling our lungs with deep breaths of mountain air. Nature can refresh us spiritually and deepen our intimacy with God, so it's helpful, but there's also restoration in attending church on the Sabbath.

Worshipping among a throng of like-minded people is very powerful and somehow more meaningful than being alone. It's about giving and receiving. It's about being encouraged and encouraging others. It's gaining a greater understanding—why I exist, who Christ calls me to be, how He asks me to serve and give to others, and how He challenges me to love my neighbor.

Sunday morning church contributes significantly to my much-needed spiritual growth. When I allow God to challenge me, I find I can stretch beyond borders. I am compelled to seek a deeper understanding of His ways and His plan for me. So I find my way to church on Sunday mornings because I need it and because I want to be there on the Sabbath. It's God's chosen day for rest and renewal. It sets the tone for my week, helps me place my priorities in order, replenishes my soul, and restores my trampled spirit.

And so I go. It's always worth the effort. God always shows up.

I will give you thanks in the great assembly;
among the throngs, I will praise you.
—Psalm 35:18 (NIV)

Give Joyful Thanks

Thanksgiving Day, as proclaimed by President Lincoln on October 3, 1863, is one of my most favorite holidays. It's one of the high days in the year for our family. I'm guessing it might well be the same for you, and since it's one of the busiest travel days in the nation, it's fair to say that you and I are not alone in our mutual love of Thanksgiving. Families everywhere head for home to be with those they love, anxious to show gratitude for one another and their many blessings.

Since Thanksgiving is the last Thursday in November, it often fell on the same date as my mother's birthday when she was still living. Over the phone I'd wish Mum a happy birthday, and she and my dad would wish us a happy Thanksgiving. There's no Thanksgiving Day celebration (as we know it) in England, although there is a Harvest Festival, during which we give thanks for a bountiful harvest of food. This festival is celebrated traditionally on the closest Sunday to the harvest moon, so the date can vary, and it's often in September or early October. It is unrelated to our Thanksgiving here in the United States.

In 2015, I wasn't sure how I'd feel about Thanksgiving Day as it was also November 24, my mother's birthday, the first without her, and I missed her. I sometimes I felt like I had one foot in the

United Kingdom and the other in the United States, straddling the massive body of water we call the Atlantic Ocean. That weird apparition brings a smile to my face. I picture me looming into the air like some enormous human bridge! What an interesting vision, to say the least.

One country owns my birthright, and the other has my allegiance through naturalization. While I had chosen my home in one place, the United States, my roots beckoned me to return to my country of birth, so I would travel at least twice a year to visit my parents in their home in England. It was our home away from home in the enchanting town of Sturminster Newton on the winding Stour River, set in the beautiful green, pastoral countryside of Dorset.

That year our family was on my mind. It's not easy to be miles away from loved ones, but at present we are all so scattered. That's true of many families. On that specific Thanksgiving, our immediate family was strewn from coast to coast here in the United States. I thanked God for the blessing of modern communications. Yes, the very ones that I often denounce during the inevitable technology challenges with iPhones, Skype, Facetime, and WhatsApp!

There's no denying that modern technology can bring families closer. Daily telephone calls with my parents would close the gap, connect our lives and magically transfer me into their home and bring them into ours, while calls, texts, and photo-sharing between family members here in the United States bring us closer. What a blessing!

Since I raised the idea of one proverbial foot on either shore of the Atlantic, you're probably wondering if I ever felt torn at times, so I explored that thought and am surprised to discover I didn't! The truth is that I counted myself fortunate and privileged to experience the best of both worlds. I think the mind-set makes all the difference. I didn't view myself as torn between the two countries miles apart. Instead I imagined straddling the ocean with a foot on each shore. In my mind, I saw myself as the virtual bridge that closed the gap and united the two worlds. The mind is amazingly powerful.

It's all in the way we view things. Perspective is everything! I wasn't sure how I'd feel about Thanksgiving 2015. My mother's birthday fell on Thanksgiving Day again, but this time she wasn't at the other end of the phone. While she was living, the two occasions coincided periodically, but now she was gone. That changed things for me.

On the one hand, Thanksgiving Day is for giving joyful thanks for our many blessings; however, on the other hand, it was Mum's birthday, and I missed her with all my heart. I wanted to hug her and wish her happy birthday. I felt a flood of sadness that she was gone.

I wondered how I would reconcile the conflicting emotions of joy and sadness.

The answer came to me in a flash! I'd *bridge* the gap. I would close the divide with *gratitude* that Mum was in heaven and that she no longer had to suffer from dementia. I expressed thanks for having had the opportunity to celebrate so many birthdays with her, including her ninety-fifth. My cup overflowed as I pictured her with God. After a while, any sense of loss and grief was replaced by deep joy at the vision of where she was, frolicking with loved ones in heaven, floating across the landscapes. She was as free as a bird, her hair flying in the breeze as she breathed in what must be indescribable beauty, the magnitude of which we can only begin to imagine. I envisioned her rejoicing with her reunited heavenly family. I pictured her happy. Presently, I felt joy deep down in my soul. Gratitude for the blessing of my loving mother had replaced the sadness of her absence. I constructed a mental bridge, and in doing so, I reconciled my conflicting emotions.

Where gratitude resides, happiness thrives.
—Anthea Tripp

Gratitude changes everything! Whatever our circumstances, let's always seek gratitude. Surely, each one of us can find some little blessing for which to be grateful, even though we must dig deep at times. Each day we wake up to a day the Lord has made, so let's strive to rejoice and be glad in it. Thanksgiving Day is a time for giving joyful thanks for family, good health, faithful friends, a free nation, the majesty of nature, and a bountiful harvest from a loving Creator.

Let's not reserve our gratitude exclusively for the high days and holidays or for the times when we catch a lucky break. Instead, let us all make gratitude a daily habit—something we genuinely feel and express to those around us. May we each demonstrate it in our daily actions in appreciation for the gift of life. We're blessed to be a blessing.

No human counsel hath devised nor hath any mortal hand worked out these great things. They are the gracious gifts of the Most-High God, who, while dealing with us in anger for our sins, hath nevertheless remembered mercy. It has seemed to me fit and proper that they should be solemnly, reverently and gratefully acknowledge as with one heart and one voice by the whole American People.
—Abraham Lincoln, "Thanksgiving Proclamation"

Christmas Is Coming

Let the beautiful craziness begin. Another holiday season is in full swing.

With Halloween dead and buried—save for the remains of a few not-so-popular leftover candy bar rejects—and Thanksgiving Day already fading into another fond memory, the next big holiday approaches like a bolt of lightning!

Christmas Day is coming; however, for many *Christmas* is already here, and it's been here for a while. Have you noticed that every year the carols start playing a little sooner and Christmas trees are lit up and decorated before Tom Turkey even makes it into the oven on Thanksgiving? What's with that anyway?

I'm in no position to judge though because I'm usually one of those enthusiastic *start-it-early* folks. I love Christmas on so many levels, so I'm eager and happy to get a jump start. But then I wonder, *Why am I in such a rush to bring on one holiday before we've even started the one before?* I know the reason, but I'm going to keep you guessing for a little while longer.

Recently, I got to thinking about the holiday season, especially the short space of time between Thanksgiving and Christmas. Oh, what a wonderful, crazy, busy, stressful, emotion-packed, joyous time of year it always is. It's enjoyable and joyous because of the reason we celebrate the holiday in the first place, but it's crazy and stressful with the bazillion activities we stuff into that short amount of time.

We get busy decorating the house inside and out, assembling and dressing the tree, hoping all the bulbs light with that first flick of the switch. Then there's the Christmas card fiasco of choosing that one picture-perfect photo … or two or three or more to adorn the annual greeting cards. Then that's followed by addressing, stamping, and mailing them. And how many cards are going out this year?

Oh my! Are you hyperventilating yet?

But I'm just getting started! There are the family's favorite goodies to bake, gifts to buy and wrap, stockings to stuff, and toys to assemble often in the wee hours after Christmas Eve festivities. There are parties to attend where the delicious food and drink captures our attention, and the inevitable overindulgence steals our precious energy. Energy desperately needed to fuel our crazy, self-imposed schedules.

We fight endless lines of traffic on the roads and madding crowds of frazzled, frantic shoppers in the stores. Let's not forget the airport runs to collect relatives if we're the ones hosting. If it's our turn to visit them, we must endure the tedious, stressful travel conditions on our way home to the family. But it's all worth it, right? They're our loved ones, and being with them is paramount. Speaking of the family, emotions can run high at these times. The truth is that our relatives bring us the greatest joy in life, but at times they can also bring pain. Sometimes it's because they're with us, and sometimes it's because they aren't.

Does the very thought of extended family get-togethers cause you to hold your breath?

You're not alone!

Having lived through seventy-odd Christmases as a child, an adult, a mom, a grandma, and a great-grandma, I can say with assurance that no two holidays are ever the same. They may share similarities, but each one is uniquely different. Some of our holiday seasons have been meager, others filled with abundance, while a few were indulgent to the point of being ridiculously over the top! In retrospect, perhaps those were my irrational attempts to compensate for an earlier time when a restricted budget bound my exuberance with restraints and constraints, leaving me with pangs of guilt for being financially unable to provide my family with an experience I thought they deserved and wanted.

Nowadays I think back and remember that no matter the state of our other resources, love was always present in overabundance, and that's what matters most. After all, Christmas trees wilt, tinsel tarnishes, lights go out, gifts are quickly forgotten, but love lives on forever. Can I get an amen to that?

How are your family celebrations over the holidays? Some years our family celebrations are quiet and peaceful while others are loud and crazy. Sometimes we're blessed by the gathering of the entire clan, which fills my heart with joy. Other years we've felt the absence of a loved one called home—home to the Lord. Then there are times when one or more members of the family are visiting in-laws. Occasionally, one of the dear ones is all alone. Sadness and loneliness are never easy to endure, but during the holidays they're unbearable.

Being surrounded by family and *feeling* alone isn't easy either. At times, though not alone physically, some of the family may be overwhelmed by loneliness as they struggle inwardly over troubling personal circumstances or private matters, about which the rest of the family may know nothing. We may sense their anguish and observe their preoccupation as they visibly withdraw into themselves and shrink away from those closest to them. Seeing them pull away is painful. It's painful to be the troubled one and heartbreaking for the loved ones who recognize the suffering yet are helpless to ease the pain. I pray for all who are alone and all who are lonely at any time, but particularly over the holidays.

When it comes to celebrating Christmas, it's not the what, when, and where of the season that matters. It's the who and the why. It's who we're with, why we're together, and the reason that Christmas came into being in the first place. As we become embroiled in the season, let's remember that the most valuable gift of Christmas is not purchased with money, wrapped up in a fancy package and placed under the tree, stuffed into the stocking, or stamped on a gift card. The real treasure is the gift of our loved ones, their time and their presence wrapped up in hope. Hope is everything. The hope of the world is in our Savior, Jesus Christ.

My prayer for you during the Christmas season is a heart filled with gratitude, joy, faith, hope, peace, and love.

> For to us, a child is born, to us, a son is given, and
> the government will be on his shoulders.
> And he will be called Wonderful Counselor, Mighty
> God, Everlasting Father, Prince of Peace.
> —Isaiah 9:6 (NIV)

Breathe through the Holidays

My most favorite holiday is Christmas. Having survived and thrived through many years of holiday seasons, I'm happy to share what I've learned about relationships, family dynamics, life, and breathing through it all.

As I reflect on past holidays, I am reminded how much I cherish bygone Christmases and their accompanying memories. Indeed, the vast majority have been amazingly joyful celebrations and harmonious family gatherings. However, some were marred by unexpected and stressful circumstances, uninvited drama, or emotional outbursts. But I appreciate even *those* because they challenged me, changed me, and molded me.

Personal growth is not a destination but an ongoing journey. As we travel the winding path of life, many experiences influence us. Some are wonderful, others painful, but if the heart and mind-set are right, we can learn and benefit from them all.

As I was tested to the max while facing some of life's most difficult challenges, I thankfully acquired more skillful coping mechanisms, a greater understanding of human nature, and a stronger, deeper faith. Life teaches us valuable lessons. As we each journey along the path of life, we must choose our way. The twists and turns, ups and downs, and resulting experiences shape us into who we are and who we will *become* tomorrow because transformation and growth are not single events but an ongoing process.

Surviving many a roller-coaster holiday has taught me much about life, relationships, and family dynamics. My personal growth has been tremendous. Through life's delightful surprises and its hard realities, I have mellowed as I've grown in experience and wisdom. I feel very grateful for the many lessons I've learned. I honestly would not change a thing because each experience impacted me significantly for the better.

Here are five important and meaningful lessons I've learned and applied. They have helped me through many wonderful holiday seasons. Perhaps something you read will resonate with you, touch you, provide comfort, and/or give you encouragement or hope. I pray something you read in the following blesses you where you are on *your* journey.

Be intentional, and breathe!

Go into the holidays with a sense of intention. Decide to be joyful. Resolve to respond to people rather than reacting to what others say or the situations you encounter. Breathe through anything and everything—whatever life throws at you. That includes the excitement, the joy, the stress, and the roller coaster of heightened emotions.

Breathe deeply and slowly in and out to the count of four! Relax and breathe through it. I promise it helps. As you approach this beautiful holiday, be prepared, especially mentally and spiritually. Adjust your attitude, pray, set your mind to one of gratitude for what you have, and flatly refuse to pine over what you don't have!

Seek out the good qualities in those around you, and decide right now (before you're in the throes of it all) to overlook and forgive any past transgressions—both yours and theirs.

Less rush, more hush!

One reason we early birds start off the Christmas season before Thanksgiving is to secure a head start. I've learned that when you pace yourself, you can avoid that last-minute, crazy, stressful mad dash to the Christmas dinner finish line. When you begin early, you can maintain a slower, steadier pace with less stress. You can accomplish more when you plan to space out the activities. A slower, controlled pace is more sustainable, and you remain calmer. Then life is more enjoyable for you *and* those around you. Avoid the rush, and enjoy more of the *hush* of the season. Aim for tranquility.

Breathe. Breathe in deep. Breathe in the peace of Christ.

Speaking of peace, try to silence the meaningless noise. Shut off those cell phones, and shut out the external distractions of the endless incoming alerts, dings, and beeps. Resist all temptation to jump on social media at the expense of those dear ones right beside you. Make sure you're fully in the moment with your loved ones. One of the greatest gifts you can give them is to be 100 percent present with them.

Expect less, accept more

When we expect people or circumstances to be or behave in a certain way, we're looking through our *own* lens and thinking, *This is the way it ought to be.* The problem is that we've not taken their wants, needs, and feelings into consideration, which often leads us to bitter disappointment. On the other hand, when we accept people and circumstances for who and what they are, we have fewer letdowns, we're less frustrated, and our reward is greater happiness. And we achieve a whole lot more peace for all.

The higher the expectation, the greater the potential for disappointment. In my younger day, I envisioned Christmas Day as a picture-perfect fairy tale complete with snow, the log fire crackling, and the family gathered around the tree. Everyone is laughing and loving on one another with carols playing nonstop as we open presents. Christmas dinner is on the way, the turkey and trimmings cooked to perfection, and fun games and happy family togetherness follows the best meal ever.

Hmmm! And elephants *do* fly! Well, it's always good to dream.

Of course, it was *my* dream Christmas setting with the emphasis on *my* expectation, but theirs might have looked somewhat different. Boring football games weren't even on my horizon, but some of the family eagerly looked forward to and expected football games. Ugh! Did that mean we would have to turn off the beautiful, soothing Christmas music? How disappointing!

Others, having gorged on the full Christmas dinner, were not inclined to watch football *or* play board games. They had a snooze in mind. What? You're kidding me! Did they expect those dirty dishes to magically jump into the dishwasher and clean themselves?

Do you see what I mean about expectation? You can fall hard as I did a few times before I learned to turn expectation into acceptance, and I exchanged righteous indignation for unconditional resignation.

Let's say that the more varied the personalities and ages in the extended family, the happier everyone is when we expect a little less of what ought to be and we learn to be more accepting of the way things are in terms of circumstances and family members. It is what it is! Accept reality. Embrace each person's individuality and all their traits—the commendable ones, the quirky ones, and even the annoying ones too. The latter is not easy, but it's doable. I've learned to do it, and I know you can too.

Lastly, acceptance is not being complacent or dismissing all hope. It means having *positive* expectations but also knowing what to do when they aren't met. So dream big, expect good outcomes, but stay flexible and learn to let go and go with the flow.

Breathe through it! Condition yourself to become a master of acceptance.

Ditch the drama, and embrace humor.

Life was so much simpler when the kids were little. Ask any grandparent.

When your kids grow up, marry, and have children of their own, life becomes a whole lot more complex and complicated in an ever-escalating manner, especially around the holidays. And when your children's children have children, it's crazier than ever. Holidays turn into a zoo in a jungle. A sense of humor is not only essential. It will save your life and theirs.

Yes, my friends, we *do* have to share some of that premium holiday time with the in-laws. It's only fair. And yes, I know full well that the time and times are not always fairly and evenly distributed. Do you think I don't know? I've lived it! The expanding tribe brings a boatload of complex circumstances that will sideswipe even the most intuitive, loving, and worldly ones in the family and can knock us to our knees if we're not warned. Let's face it. No class or manual can teach anyone this. For most of us, it remains uncharted territory. I'm giving you a heads-up to prepare you before *your* turn arrives.

The changes and challenges that accompany this chapter of life can charge emotions and quickly spark family drama. The gene pool runs very deep. When you combine DNA differences with personality variations, add learned behavior patterns, and stir in whatever the family members are personally dealing with in their lives, you end up with a volatile concoction. When you throw someone new into the family mix with a vastly *different* set of DNA, upbringing, and personality, you've got a perfect recipe for misunderstandings, differences of opinion, and conflict! If you inject unrealistic expectations into the brew, ideal conditions appear with the potential for a category-five storm. Be prepared for an all-out war!

Please not *this* Christmas!

There's another element to take into consideration. Be aware that all families know the exact triggers to pull and buttons to push for each relative, so here's a word of warning. When they reach for one of your triggers, don't fire a shot! Do not go off on them. And don't even think about touching one of their buttons! Hey, I know tit-for-tat exchanges can be tempting, but don't go down that road. Rise above it.

When emotions run high and sparks begin to fly, take it upon yourself to be *the one* in the family who brings calm to the situation. Be the unifier, not the divider. Don't fan the flames of conflict because someone pushed a button that rang your chimes. You're stronger than that! Don't allow yourself to get sucked into the trap. You're bigger than that. Hard as it is, you must shake it off. If you feel tensions rising within, ditch the drama.

Walk away, and breathe through it!

Focus on the reason for the season.

The only reason for *Christmas* is because of Jesus Christ, God's greatest gift to humanity. December 25 is the day set aside to celebrate the birth of God's Son, our Lord and Savior. Like it or not, He's the reason there is a Christmas holiday at all. And if I've lost you at this point, please understand that it's entirely up to you whether you believe in Him or not, but the fact remains that either way, this specific holiday is rooted *in the birth of Christ.*

The world has received no greater gift, yet in the current times, each year our culture drifts further from the true meaning of Christmas as the secular people among us eagerly embrace the seductive worldly attributes of what's become the winter season.

It's so easy to get caught up in it all, trapped in the hustle and bustle and so enthralled in the glitter and glitz. The dazzling, flashing, worldly lights can so mesmerize us that we become blinded to the only light of the world. Christmastime is the season of giving, and as we're all wrapped up in the exchange of presents, let us not forget that the greatest gift has already arrived and that it's ours to receive and accept.

I love everything about the Christmas holiday—the decorations, the tree, Santa, and the light show too. While all these things are shiny, fun, and uplifting, they may brighten us for a while and lift our spirits, but they can never satisfy the yearning in our hearts that only Christ can fill.

There is no substitute for the Prince of Peace.

As we lift a glass of cheer at Christmastime, let's clink our glasses to the King of Kings and express gratitude for His birth. Let's honor Him by loving one another. Let's appreciate our families, whether they are whole, wounded, or broken. Let's give thanks to and for our loved ones near or far, and let's take time to express our love, whether it's in person or over the phone to those far away. The gift of time and attention is priceless and meaningful. Give love freely and unconditionally to others as God has given it to you.

Breathe through the seasonal holidays from Thanksgiving to the New Year. Start planning early. Promise yourself to be of good cheer. I wish you the most harmonious and joyful of seasons every year. Blessings to you and yours!

> But the angel said to them, "Do not be afraid.
> I bring you good news that will cause
> great joy for all the people."
> —Luke 2:10 (NIV)

Easter! Easter! Easter!

One word repeated three times can make an impact! As my daughter responded to a question that drove her beyond any reasonable level of patience, she fired a string of words at me in rapid succession. She's a straight-line sort of woman who doesn't take kindly to going around in circles, and the four of us had played ring-around-the-rosy in this conversation way too long, so when I asked, "How about this?" pointing to a date on the calendar, she blurted out, "Easter! Easter! Easter!" Frustration was written all over her face!

It was a Wednesday evening a few years ago following our weekly family-night dinner, and all four of us were a little on edge, weary from challenges of the day. My husband and I were frustrated from running our in-home business, and Chandra and Dany were exhausted from the stress of their demanding corporate jobs. Chuck sat at his computer in the upstairs office, scouring the airlines for available flights for five people. Meanwhile, the rest of us gathered around his desk, throwing out various dates that might work for our spring vacation to the United Kingdom.

We all agreed it would be essential to avoid Easter weekend. Previous trips that included this popular holiday taught us how hard it was to find inexpensive flights with five good seats together, and it was practically impossible to secure cottage accommodations for Chandra and Dany near my parents' house, where Chuck and I would be. Easter is a big holiday in England. Schoolchildren are on vacation. Workers receive a four-day weekend. And the time often signifies the start of spring with warm, sunny weather, which means that traffic on the roads is heavier than usual, causing congestion and delays. All in all, we had good reasons to avoid travel over Easter weekend.

Twenty years ago, it was easier to plan a family vacation, but now things are different. Life is more complicated for many reasons, and that's why the four of us deliberated about our travel dates for at least an hour. For every combination of dates suggested, one of us had a valid reason that *those* dates wouldn't work for us. It was one of those circular conversations going nowhere.

You wouldn't think it would be *that* hard to arrange a holiday for four people and a child, but when you factor in our various work schedules, flight times, accommodation, and car availability, it can get tricky. If you rule out travel over the Easter weekend and reject the seats on the planes by the toilets, it is even trickier. The growing list of conditions added to the complexity of our planning session.

It's a good thing we all love one another and have a moderate amount of patience because after many failed attempts to nail down dates, the atmosphere in the room that night was growing tenser by the minute. However, we all persevered. A good challenge is refreshing, and it was imperative we book that night for the time was running out to find *any* flight. I find it's easy to overlook essential criteria if I have no checklist in my hand. In this case, the growing list of restrictions and conditions was flying around my head, so without looking at a calendar, I thought I'd happened on just the right combination of dates that would work, so I blurted out, "How about this?"

That's when our daughter reached her limit and opened her eyes wide, and with her hands gesturing vigorously, she loudly proclaimed, "Easter! Easter! Easter!" In my desperation to secure dates agreeable to all, I'd completely overlooked the most crucial consideration—Easter. The look on Chandra's face along with the heightened frustration in her voice as she rapidly delivered the word Easter three times was so hilarious that the four of us fell apart in raucous laughter.

There was a happy ending. We managed to coordinate the dates, book flights and accommodation, and enjoy a wonderful holiday, and we were home for Easter. Now whenever Easter approaches, we have a good laugh as the memory of that night returns.

It's Easter Sunday 2019 as I write this story, which completes the chapter "High Days and Holidays." Easter's significance transcends the humorous little tale I've just shared. It's how God saved humanity from sin by sacrificing Jesus, His only Son, so all who believe in Him might be forgiven, be redeemed, and receive life after death. The time represents the spilling of Jesus's precious blood, His death by crucifixion, and His resurrection to life, which was all done to save you and me. Now that's significant.

It was a beautiful sunny day this morning, and I awoke with a joyful heart. It's Easter Sunday! I made my way into the kitchen to brew a cup of early morning tea, and while the water was on the boil, I opened the back door to inhale a few deep breaths of fresh air as I'm accustomed to doing most mornings. Then I saw it sparkling in the sunlight and gently swaying in the breeze. The majestic, orange trumpet flower had burst from its bulging bud and was now in full bloom. I was beyond excited to see this beautiful amaryllis.

It was a Christmas gift from my friend Judy in 2017. When it finished blooming in early January 2018, I had relegated it to the back garden, and there it remained, sadly forgotten, neglected, and mistaken for dead, hidden among some bushes, abandoned in the busyness of my life last year. I rediscovered it recently while rummaging around in the bushes. To my astonishment, I saw that it had survived, and it had green leaves and new shoots. It wasn't dead; it was alive. I planted it in a bigger pot and watched with interest as a tall stalk with triple buds reached for the sky.

Then today on Easter Sunday, the most joyful day of the year, the first of its three magnificent blooms delighted me. It was God's subtle reminder of the resurrection of our Savior. He is risen indeed. And the triple buds in the crown of the flower signify the Trinity. Oh, joy! What an amazing God is ours. He speaks to us through His beautiful creations in simple ways that we might overlook in the busyness of a crazy life. But if we're tuned in, if we believe in His goodness and take quiet moments to reflect on Him, we will hear His whispered messages of assurance. We will see His love everywhere.

Today has been a fabulous day, and as I retire for the night, my soul joyfully sings, "Easter! Easter! Easter!"

> He isn't here! He is risen from the dead! Remember
> what he told you back in Galilee, that the Son of Man
> must be betrayed into the hands of sinful men and be
> crucified, and that he would rise again on the third day.
> —Luke 24:6–7 (NLT)

CHAPTER 5
Life's Lessons

A lesson learned is a bridge to wisdom.

The Life and Times of Now

We live in an era of rapid economic, cultural, and social change, and we also live in a world constantly evolving and revolving at what feels like breakneck speed. Many people tell me their lives have become so demanding, fast-paced, and fragmented that they feel as though they're spinning out of control. They feel like they're on a merry-go-round that flies off its axis and hurtles into space. Do you sometimes feel giddy from life's twists and turns and the pace at which we live? Our schedules are so full that we never have enough time in the day. Our days pass like hours, weeks like days, and months like weeks. Time appears to accelerate exponentially. It's almost as if it's gaining on itself, causing us to wonder if God has increased the speed of time.

Welcome to modern life.

The world of today requires us to stretch ourselves in many directions, including thinking above and beyond the norm. To survive and thrive in the shifting state of our current age and to defend ourselves from the social, cultural, and spiritual attacks hurled at us like sharp arrows with ever-increasing frequency and intensity, it behooves us to be intentional about the way we think, who we're becoming, what we're doing, and where we're going. How will we manage all that life deals us?

Independent thinking is a must!

Transition is sweeping this great nation and other countries around the globe. If you glance at any newspaper or tune in to any form of media, you are bombarded with newsworthy information on a variety of topics from world news to health to politics and what my dad always referred to as the three Ds—death, disaster, and destruction. You'll hear it all in a matter of minutes, reported from every corner of the globe accompanied by graphic images within seconds of the occurrence. More information is fed to you than you ever desired to know or could ever digest.

Thanks to technology, we can now track unfolding world events firsthand from the comfort of our living rooms. We're all interconnected and affected by these events, good or evil, over which we seem to have little or no say. At times we feel powerless as individuals to make our voices heard over all the noise from the many devices at our disposal. Media sources bombard us with widespread problems, social and cultural challenges, and political ideology. Everyone has a strong opinion on every single topic. Often their views differ from our own. Everything seems to be *topsy-turvy*. Right is wrong, and wrong is right. It's as if our world has flipped upside down. It feels illogical and confusing, and that's troubling.

To survive in the life and times of now, it takes discernment and independent thinking! With that in mind, please understand that I do not intend to force-feed you what to think, feel, and believe, although I have strong opinions on worldly and spiritual matters. Instead I hope to inspire you to think independently. Don't just go along with the flow of rhetoric you see and hear on TV, radio talk shows, and newspaper articles. If we're fed the same information or misinformation long enough, we tend to accept it, and whatever we accept, we begin to believe as truth. Please don't be misled.

Here's the big challenge! Many of us don't think at all. And some people don't care what's going on so long as they're not personally affected, so it doesn't warrant their time to think about. Others are overloaded and so preoccupied with the overwhelming stresses of daily life that they have no time to contemplate and appraise the state of the world in which they live, how it's affecting them personally, what's behind it all, and ultimately, where it will lead them, their country, and humanity!

Heaven forbid that anyone invests time to examine their spirituality or ponder the existence of unseen forces in the spiritual world where an ongoing battle is raging and where evil is working diligently to present lies as truths. We're in a world where the devil is intent on capturing unsuspecting individuals and only too happy to profess wrong as right and right as wrong, all the while employing distractions that are hidden in seductive wrappings to lull and lure vulnerable souls into complacency and deception, all leading to a path of destruction.

I am blown away at the widespread naiveté regarding the existence of evil forces. Satan is alive and plotting destruction. He hates God. He hates anything that reminds him of God, especially those created in the likeness of God. Yes, my friends, that means you and me! The evil one is prowling the earth, devouring souls, and using any tactic available to him and his fallen cohorts. Be aware that we all have an enemy bent on destroying us, deceiving us, hiding from us, and attempting to convince us he's not even there. He's a master at cunning and deception.

> Be sober, be vigilant; because your adversary
> the devil, as a roaring lion, walketh about,
> seeking whom he may devour.
> —1 Peter 5:8 (KJV)

I am convinced that we *must* learn to be discerning, independent thinkers.

I'm not speaking of a passing thought here and there about something you see or hear on social media, TV, or the news. I'm not suggesting a cursory glance at the newspaper. The thinking I refer to is deep, soul-searching, independent thoughtfulness and consideration as to where you are going, where you are leading your family, and the direction in which our country and the world are heading.

The present times require that you examine where you stand in today's world. Ask yourself these questions and others. Think seriously about your answers. Activate independent thinking. Be deliberate. Be purposeful in your thought process.

- What thoughts dominate your life?
- How easily are you influenced?
- Can you discern truth from lies?
- Do you believe everything you see and hear in the media?
- Do you believe there are good and evil forces at work (and at war) in the world?
- Do you think an evil force can fool, seduce, convince, deceive, and influence even those who are intelligent and well-educated people with good intentions?
- Are you able to define the set of values to which you ascribe?
- Which freedoms would you defend with your life?

These are important things to think about for the future of you and your family. But there's even more at stake. There's your community, your country, and the world. Today we need empowered people who can discern the truth, people who can think for themselves and influence others to do likewise.

As you read this, you may wonder where you can find enough time to sit and think. I urge you to *make* room. Creating space requires you to stop the busyness of your life for longer than five minutes. Schedule a time. Make it a priority. I believe there is an urgency facing the world today. There's something more significant at stake than what we each see in our separate lives.

What is independent thinking?

- It's a process learned over time.
- It's learning to make sense of the world around you by employing your observations and experiences instead of relying on words and opinions of others.
- It's *taking* action, not just reacting.
- It's the ability to trust your judgment, even if that judgment disagrees with what others say or believe.
- Independent thinking means acting by what *you* believe.
- It's detecting flaws in arguments and questioning unsubstantiated claims.
- It's diligently discerning the truth supported by relevant evidence.
- It's seeking to be informed. It's researching based on proven facts.
- It's evaluating, looking at things from different angles and perspectives.
- It's drilling down behind the words, delving into the legitimacy of inferences.

As a race, we humans have become complacent and lazy where reasoning is concerned. It takes time, effort, and rationalization to cultivate independent thinking, but it's worth developing. It's a desirable skill for you and a gift to the world. People who know their values and have strong beliefs will always stand for something, and they know the reason they stand for it. Those who stand for nothing will fall for anything. They may also fall prey to those who would lead them into destructive ideologies and behaviors.

Think about it! Your time is here to step up. If you're an independent thinker, you will transcend the economic, political, and cultural shifts, and you will lead and influence others. You will own the ability to reason, to solve problems, and make sound judgments. Lies will not deceive you. You will recognize and expose those who would lead you astray.

Employing these critical thinking skills will ensure you're grounded in your values. A reliable belief system guides you and equips you to withstand challenges, whether they are economic, cultural, social, or spiritual.

The life and times of now are here. Are you prepared for the challenge?

Beware the barrenness of a busy life.
—Socrates

How Many Life Lessons Does It Take?

I gazed through my open bedroom window, longingly staring into the carefully manicured back garden where my parents were relaxing together after mowing the grass, weeding the flower borders, edging the lawns, and trimming the hedges. Long, lazy shadows stretched across the newly mowed lawns, announcing the arrival of evening. The sun was sinking fast but had enough power left to reflect beams of flashing light and little sparkles up at my window as its rays danced on the water, bringing my attention to the two fishponds beyond the terracing.

It was midsummer of 1952, and daylight savings was in full bloom in an unusually warm English summer. It would have been close to nine thirty in the evening, approaching sunset, but it was light enough to keep a seven-year-old wondering why she was supposed to be asleep when her parents were laughing and enjoying the evening.

The truth is that I yearned to be down there sharing their magical moment.

I had been told numerous times throughout the long summer nights to get back into bed and try to sleep. I was strictly warned not to climb on that precarious three-legged stool to sneak a peek over the unforgiving window ledge, made of grey slate. "Not one more time, Anthea!" they had warned me. I'd already tipped the stool over two or three times, landing on my young derriere with a thump. Fortunately, I had come to no harm on any of those occasions!

The temptation of the outside world was just too overpowering for this curious, high-spirited child, and try as I might, sleep was as evasive as the butterflies I'd chased all afternoon. I tiptoed across the carpeted room, succumbing to my compulsion. I merely *had to* look out the window one more time, which meant climbing up on the milking stool and parting the curtains to peer furtively into the garden below, hoping no one would catch me.

They say curiosity killed the cat! Maybe not always. According to William Arthur Ward, "Curiosity is the wick in the candle of learning."

Feeling very self-satisfied, perched on the stool, knowing full well I was naughty and disobedient, I figuratively patted myself on the back and congratulated myself for getting away with something. I rested my chin complacently on folded arms, sprawled across the narrow slate windowsill. I settled in to observe what was causing all the merriment down below, straining my ears to hear the conversation. What was making them laugh? I couldn't stand not knowing what fun I was missing!

Then it happened. Life delivered another lesson. The great teacher stepped in one more time! As I casually shifted my weight from one foot to the other, the stool tipped over. My feet slid downward and backward. My chin hit the rough slate windowsill with a thud. During the slide my throat received long scratches from my chin to my clavicle as it contacted the unforgiving window ledge. Ouch! It not only scared me half to death but hurt like the dickens. I let out a bloodcurdling scream of anguish, which caused both parents to fly into the house and race up the stairs two steps at a time and dash into my bedroom faster than I'd ever seen them move, both arriving white-faced and breathless in anticipation of the calamity they might find.

Once they established I was not seriously injured and after I initially received their hugs and was comforted, I received a severe tongue lashing and reprimand for disobedience. I was humbled by the fall and knew their words of disapproval were well-deserved.

I believe I learned *that* lesson.

How many times did I repeat that same lesson before finally learning not to climb on precariously balanced three-legged stools? Well, on several previous occasions, I had teetered on its seat, close to falling off, and a couple of times I toppled over landing gently on the carpet, but please note that it took some real pain, a little blood loss, a considerable fright, and a great deal of injured pride before I learned the lesson once and for all.

Do you think I continued to steal glances out of the window on long lazy summer nights after this experience? Of course, I did. Kids will be kids, especially those with more curiosity than good sense! I found other more stable pieces of furniture to climb on so that I could peek over the window ledge. I learned the one specific lesson about the stool but still had not learned obedience. Nor had I yet learned to listen to my inner voice and heed the early warnings that could have saved me from future mishaps. Yes, I had a rather adventurous naughty streak as a child, but let's get back to the topic of lessons learned.

There have been so many lessons in my life, both personal and business, that I've had to learn as a student, friend, daughter, wife, mother, grandmother, entrepreneur, and mentor. Sometimes I learned because of pleasing results or rewards; some lessons I learned from pain, disappointment, embarrassment, or necessity. Occasionally, life dealt me a hand with a treasure of an experience that I understood right away, so repeat circumstances were unnecessary! But then there were also life's huge meaningful lessons that for some reason I didn't grasp the first or even the second time. I had to live with and through the consequences of many mistakes, choices, and decisions. I faced the same lesson over and over until I learned it. I had to endure suffering and implement the required changes in myself and my circumstances to grow wiser and stronger.

> Life is a succession of lessons which
> must be lived to be understood.
> —Helen Keller

Here's what my years have taught me about lessons. *Life* is the best teacher in the world, and it will dish out many valuable lessons in our lifetimes, using experiences that mold us into who we are and who we become. Life is a compelling teacher that persists in its endeavors to protect us, shape us, guide us and strengthen us. Life is relentless in its pursuit to instill us with wisdom, experience, and understanding, and it is a tenacious teacher. It strives to instruct us, to effect positive change in us, and to help us to grow from lessons learned.

Life never gives up. It is the master of repeat.

Happily, most of us *do* eventually learn from our experiences and mistakes. What troubles me is those I meet who *never* seem to learn despite the resulting hardships they have endured and continue to face. They make a poor decision that results in untoward consequences. Life deals them difficulty and pain. Then they complain. Next they blame.

The pain-complain-blame syndrome is alive and well in our society. We know it as the victim mentality. People caught in this trap blame everyone else for a predicament they bring upon themselves, usually as a result of poor choices or decisions they've made. They blame other people, their circumstances, and life in general. Worse still, they may even blame God for their shortcomings or poor judgment.

People with a victim mentality speak in a language that infers they somehow had nothing to do with where they are or what's going on in their lives. They portray themselves as helpless victims of circumstance, powerless to change their lot in life. They use phrases such as "It just happened to me" or "It wasn't my fault" or "There's nothing I could do" or "I don't know why I'm having such a run of bad luck!"

To those folks, I give the following unsolicited advice: "Man up, or put on your big girl pants. Dig deep, find your inner strength, and understand that unless you experienced a major tragedy or something that was beyond your control—and yes, there are legitimate reasons too—you have the power to learn from life's lessons, to move beyond them, and to change your circumstances."

If you recognize yourself as a victim, it is vital to know and believe that it's not a life sentence. It's a lie you've told yourself, a lie you have chosen to believe. You don't *have* to stay where you are. You have the power within *you* to change your life. You can change who you are and where you go in the future. Think back at the choices you made that have caused you to be where you are. Look them honestly and squarely in the face. Then decide to change. Make a better choice, a wiser decision, and commit to empowering yourself. You can rewire your thoughts and change the attitude and activities that brought you where you are today.

Here's what I know for sure. We must *all* learn the lessons! Life will continue to place the same experience in front of us over and over and over again until we learn that lesson. Remember that if you repeatedly face the same problem, it will continue to return until you learn the lesson!

Are you struggling with something that plays over and over like a broken record? Are you reliving circumstances that return time and again to haunt you? I urge you to break the cycle. Sometimes we overlook answers to our problems because they're so simple. Stop doing what doesn't work. Learn the lesson from the undesired result. Then change what you're doing! Figure out what you could do differently, and chart your future course accordingly. Empower yourself! Change *who* you are and *what* you're doing, and your results will also change. So will your entire life!

If this speaks to you, get on it right away! Don't dawdle. Do it now. Learn from the teachings of life!

> Let the wise hear and increase in learning and
> the one who understands obtain guidance.
> — Proverbs 1:5 (ESV)

Comfort Zone Discomfort

It's such a comfortable place to slip into and so much harder to climb out. Have you ever eased into a comfort zone? Were you happy there, or did it perchance haunt you a little as well?

I have been there. I liked it, and I despised it!

Inside the fortress of the comfort zone, it's warm and cozy. It feels safe, secure, and pleasant, kind of like being in a cocoon or what one might imagine it to be. There's no agitation, no stress, and no demands of oneself, so what's not to like?

Hmmm! What's not to like? Everything, including yourself.

Years ago in my twenties to mid-thirties, I found my comfort zone was a great place to hide from public speaking. Hey, when you are a member of Toastmasters International and your speaking skill fails to improve, it's terrible! Uttering words in front of a room full of people was my greatest fear. The very thought of talking to a group (even people I knew) filled me with irrational and inexplicable terror. *That's just butterflies,* you may think. Are you kidding? I liken it more to a pack of hungry wolves intent on devouring me from within.

I declined invitations if there was the remotest chance of being asked to speak. I begged others to take my place if asked to make an announcement. When I was a realtor and Monday came along, which was when we routinely promoted our real estate listings, I hid behind my hero hubby, who gallantly shared his *own* listings and mine too. In those days while I was fine during one-on-one or one-on-two situations, I would do *anything* to avoid speaking to a group, which was strange behavior since I had won a speech contest when I was seventeen!

Whenever I escaped the dreaded request to speak, relief flooded over me temporarily. To avoid fear and stay in my cozy little zone was instantly gratifying. I could relax, and the angry wolves morphed into cute, cuddly, puppy dogs! I was calm inside once more, but the euphoria and relief were short-lived. Within minutes, an invader penetrated my fortress. An unpleasant feeling disrupted my short-lived peace.

Hello, rabble-rouser! You're disturbing my serenity. Discomfort arrived. It took up residence in my being and shook my core. The real me, namely the courageous side of myself, showed up, prepared to do battle. Oh, my goodness, now what? The fact is that deep down I despised the weakness of giving in to fear and retreating. I hated it more than fear itself. I felt like a coward. I disliked that side of myself, and in the safety of my happy place, I always vowed to conquer the fear and stay out of the zone.

"Next time I will face the fear, and I *will* speak no matter how terrified I am or how shaky my voice or how stuttering my words," I'd say to myself. Thus, I would bravely resolve until the next time when I once again retreated deep into my safe place. Then I'd be furious with myself, and I'd promise to stay out of the comfort zone the next time. And so the cycle perpetuated for years. No amount of resolve or discomfort seemed effective until ... I started my business. You see, I love people, and nothing brings greater joy than the rewards of helping them get healthier and happier. I am *passionate* about it. It gets me out of bed in the morning. I discovered that the desire to share something so good was far greater than any fear and stronger than the need to escape to my hiding place.

The discomfort was a catalyst, but the desire was my compulsion.

Passion for making a difference and love for others helped me face the wolves that stalked me at the terrifying thought of speaking to a group. Slowly but surely, I met the fear and ventured out of my comfort zone. I finally conquered it. Nowadays I get butterflies, but they flutter off when I begin to speak. Over time I have learned to enjoy public speaking.

Sometimes it's *discomfort* that disturbs your comfort zone. At other times its *desire* that compels you out!

> Have I not commanded you? Be strong and courageous.
> Do not be afraid; do not be discouraged, for the
> Lord your God will be with you wherever you go.
> —Joshua 1:9 (NIV)

Creating New Is Easy!

How often do you ponder life and all it encompasses in the world that surrounds you? Whenever you take the time to look beyond the ordinary activities of day-to-day living, do you find yourself entranced in a deep state of wonder that stirs your soul? Do you steal fleeting moments here and there in the busyness of your day to marvel at the indescribable beauty and order of nature?

For me, it's not only something I crave regularly, but it's also an overwhelming need that compels me to abandon the ordinary and to seek a place that stirs my soul. Melodious music or reading inspirational words can take me to that place sometimes, but most often I choose a walk in the woods or find a tree stump by a babbling brook or lean over a fence and watch the livestock grazing on the green grass. There amid God's creations, my soul is restored. It was during one such walk in the Cornish countryside when I happened on a magnificent oak tree.

I have no idea about its age, but it had seen many years of life. The height and breadth of its gnarled trunk took my breath away as I stared in awe. A six-foot man would be a mere dot next to it, dwarfed under its massive, spreading canopy of leaves. This tree's canopy would have provided shade and shelter to many a traveler through the ages. Its knotted and twisted branches revealed the struggles it had to endure, withstanding a multitude of environmental and seasonal challenges.

There it was, planted solidly in all its glory. It was stately, strong, and majestic. It was a testament to time itself, one of God's magnificent creations. Standing beneath this tree, looking skyward in wonder, the rustling motions of its millions of leaves engulfed my senses. I listened as they sang their enchanting song, and as I watched them dance in response to the gentle sea breeze caressing them that day, I was mesmerized. I marveled at the beauty of this ancient tree, at its power, its perseverance, and its long life!

This tree has a history! I thought to myself.

Oh, what stories it could tell, and what wisdom it could impart. How did it thrive when others that had been more recently planted had long since fallen by the way, succumbing to disease and the elements of nature or withering and dying in their struggle to survive?

How much joy has this tree bestowed over the years, and to how many children and adults who had accepted the challenge to climb its branches to new heights? How many lovers might have carved or felt tempted to carve a heart with their initials and love notes, now concealed deep within its toughened ancient bark?

This unique tree and the thoughts and emotions it evoked in me created a lasting impression, so I photographed it to capture its stature and majesty in a permanent picture that I could revisit time and again, even when I was no longer standing in its presence. Its impact on me was so intense that I recalled its image almost immediately when I happened on the following quote: "Creating something new is easy! Creating something that lasts is the challenge" (Adam Braun).

This quote got me thinking about the way of the world in present times. It's an easy-come-easy-go kind of life today. Of course, there are always exceptions, but this seems to be a trend today. The days of someone staking a claim and toughing it out to create something lasting is *so* yesterday. As a people, we tend to give up quickly. We eagerly drop whatever or whoever, and we jump ship as frequently as we change underwear. I'm exaggerating, but you get my point. As fast as time flies by and as often as things change, it seems that way.

Do *you* ever wonder about this trend?

Sometimes we aren't strong enough to withstand the challenges of life. The twists and turns in our path or the unexpected arrows aimed at us can be discouraging, so we seek asylum from the pain! Maybe we're tired of the monotony and ho-hum of a boring life, or we flee from uncomfortable situations in search of peace or reduced stress. We find ourselves unable to weather the inevitable storms of life.

Then there are times in life when we're happily trucking along, satisfied where we are and what we're doing when out of the blue appears an exciting new distraction that catches our attention and we can't resist its lure, so away we go in hot pursuit of a more exhilarating adventure.

It comes down to this.

Nowadays it's our culture to hop from one thing to another, especially when the challenges appear, which they always do in anything and everything. Shiny objects capture our attention, and we're off to the next best thing, dazzled by the new and exciting, attracted by the different, seduced by the promise of better, convinced by an expectation of more, and ever hopeful of easier.

It's so easy to create something when it's *new* because we're living on an adrenaline rush! It's like a drug! It's a new addiction! It's titillating. It's exciting and different, and for a while it gets our blood pumping and our hearts racing, so we are overflowing with a wild kind of energy, a deepened resolve, and heightened dreams that fuel us into frenetic action!

Creating something lasting, on the other hand, is not always as exciting as when it is brand new. There are times of triumph and delight, of course, but mostly, it's more of the same year after year. It's building a strong foundation, growing deep roots, dealing with the challenges of daily life, and staying the course. Continuing under adverse circumstances requires unshakable belief and commitment and the strength to face the challenges, knowing in your heart that weathering the storm and keeping on keeping on will build something of lasting value. Through the ages humanity must have learned that while the grass often appears greener on the other side, it's just as hard to mow.

Alas, all too often those who are always lured by shiny new objects are the same ones who flit from this to that, seeking the greener grass or the latest thrill. Sadly, most of those folks never build anything that lasts, whether it's a relationship, success, or power. The problem isn't what they're doing or who they're with. It's who *they* are. It's an internal issue, not a matter of external circumstance.

Kind of like joy, it's an inside job!

Some haven't learned that anything worth having doesn't come easy. Hopping over the fence and expecting things to be different on the other side is often a disappointing lure because the fence-hopper discovers the grass is not any greener. When the luster wears off—and it always does sooner or later—will these individuals make a stand and weather the storm, or will they decide to flit again?

The beautiful old oak tree teaches us profound lessons in real life if we're willing to listen and heed its advice and wisdom. Whatever your heart desires to create, whether it be a relationship or anything else, stake your claim, firmly plant your roots deep and wide, stay put, and weather the storms of life. Face those challenges head-on, and you will grow strong like our tree. You'll be a little gnarled perhaps, but you will endure.

And what you create will defy the passage of time.

> That person is like a tree planted by streams of water, which yields its fruit in season and whose leaf does not wither, whatever they do prospers.
> —Psalm 1:3 (NIV)

Faces, Spaces, and Social Graces

I watched a movie in 2009 that provoked deep thoughts that I mulled over for months. The film is *Surrogates* starring Bruce Willis. The movie description reads, "Set in a futuristic world where humans live in isolation and interact through surrogate robots, a cop (Willis) is forced to leave his home for the first time in years to investigate the murders of others' surrogates."

Although the film is more than ten years old to date, it's worth watching. It will challenge your mind. It's timely, and besides, it's excellent entertainment.

In the movie it was clear that the real humans hiding behind their surrogates could do, say, or be anything they wanted with no consequences to themselves. The proxies took the hits or the pleasure for all actions and outcomes. Humans could live virtual lives through the robots, which were exact replicas of themselves. The architects of these robot creations controlled events by hooking themselves up to a complex set of high-tech equipment in their homes, where they became inactive, reclusive, obsessive, and unfulfilled.

The robots appeared to have way more fun or pain than their human counterparts. After all, they were the ones *living* life. As

I watched the movie unfold, I began to think about the present times and our obsession with social networks, where one can live a kind of virtual life online, operating from home or anywhere you have your mobile phone.

I admit I'm fascinated by social networks, but not because I'm addicted. I don't *have* to get my daily fix, but I do stay connected. Business requires me to participate on some level, and I enjoy interacting with associates, clients, friends, and acquaintances, mutually sharing photos, activities, and life. Family and my close circle of friends are quite another matter to me. I'd prefer to connect face-to-face or phone-to-phone. Give me in-person interactions over virtual ones every time. It's pure joy when the phone rings and a real-life friend has chosen to *talk* instead of text or email.

I find it compelling that my mind associated social networks with the movie *Surrogates*. There are certain similarities. In *Surrogates*, the humans control their robot selves, and they can do, say, or be anything they so choose. On social networks, you can be authentic, or you can be that *other* person and maybe take on an alter ego. If nothing else, you can morph into and project the person you'd like to be but aren't in real life!

I have a personal profile and a business page on Facebook and Instagram, so over time I've observed some fascinating things. I am intrigued by all the dimensions of human nature, so it doesn't take much to capture my attention. Bear in mind the comments that follow are merely my observation. I don't intend to be judgmental and I am not singling out anyone in particular, but with a few hundred *friends and friends of friends,* there are adequate numbers from which I have observed trends of behavior. While I'm no expert, I have noted particular social graces and patterns of postings that fit into groups as I will illustrate in the following paragraphs.

There are those on social media who set up profiles and never comment about themselves and rarely post anything except for the occasional responses to friends' posts. I think of these people as the *voyeurs* who quietly enjoy viewing what their friends are up to, but they rarely contribute any news. Then there are the voyeur cousins. I call them the *likers*. They *like* all their friends' comments but hardly ever post thoughts or activities of their own. At the other extreme are those who post every single detail of their lives with hourly updates on their whereabouts and activities. I call them the *entertainers*, the look "what we're doing" crowd. The news feed might be monotonous without their continuous chatter.

Some social networkers prefer to download all the game apps where they can play a wide variety of games online, from building farms to creating sororities. They're always requesting an item to enhance their game or win more points. These are the *gamers*. I don't do games, so I delete the apps. I apologize to those who invite me to play. I am too busy doing other things for leisure, so I'm not much of a game player, except with family around the holidays. As a result, I simply don't participate. That's not entirely true. I do play my own solo game! It's called "zap the app."

Then the cousins to *gamers* are the *listeners*. They're the ones who provide us with their favorite music videos. Now where would we be without music to delight our ears and feed our souls?

The *promoters* convey a clear agenda. *They* are all business with a constant drip of marketing, selling their products or services in every post, some more frequently than others. I must apply restraint so I'm not one of *those* people since there's no denying I love what I do and am passionate about sharing my line of products. But I don't want to be a pest or labeled as someone always selling. Neither do I wish my friends to *hide* me, so I try not to bombard the news feed with business commercials. I use my business page for business, and on occasion, I post something interesting on my personal profile that relates to my health and wellness business.

I would be remiss if I missed the *defenders,* those friends who bravely pronounce their faith in Bible verses or continuously express their political views or share posts from others of the same political persuasion. I tend to avoid commentary on politics, even though I have my own passionate beliefs. I have no desire to be lured into heated, time-consuming discussions online. It's not that I'm indifferent. I choose to focus my comments on other matters. However, I am guilty of posting inspirational messages occasionally, some of which include scripture that reveal my faith.

The most amusing posts to me are from the *pretenders.* They often can rant or rave online in an uncharacteristic manner. They say things they wouldn't ever say to another person's face. They show pictures online they'd never think to hand to a friend to view in person and reveal private matters they'd never share at a meeting attended by hundreds of people, even if all were friends.

What about the *posers,* people who post a celebrity picture or cartoon character as their profile? The photos of posers reveal a lot about themselves! The posers often morph into pretenders in the flash of a camera. They flash exaggerated puckered lips or strike a weird pose that isn't representative of who they truly are. Isn't it great that social networks provide a forum through which we can play a game of pretend and pass ourselves off as anyone we want to be, aspire to be, or would rather not be! It's make-believe at its finest.

I must admit I am guilty of being included in this next group! I love to read inspiring books of self-help and personal growth, so I quote words of wisdom. The *quoters* cannot resist sharing their favorites from celebrities, writers, philosophers, and others. Since I have an arsenal of quotes at the ready, it would be so easy for me to post them frequently, but that could potentially drive my social network friends crazy, so I refrain from the temptations and post quotes only occasionally.

Did I forget anyone? Oh yes, there are the *whiners*. This social media group bemoans their lot in life with haunting words of sorrow, regret, and self-admonishment. But they need not fear, for one of the *encouragers* or *cheerleaders* will undoubtedly be compelled to live out their saver instincts and post words of encouragement or inspiration. I have tendencies to belong to both those categories and am always eager to shoot out a word of hope. The *whiners* might even prompt the *hiders* out of seclusion to make a phone call! The hiders are those you just saw post an entry, so you know they're around, and you make a quick call to chat. Bingo! They are nowhere to be found. They don't answer the phone and don't even respond to your voice mail message! Poof! They evaporated. You might wonder if they're avoiding you or just hiding out? You'll never know since they vanished into oblivion. Last but not least, there are the *collectors*, whose goal in social media, is to accumulate friends whether those people fit the description of friends, are barely known to them, or are mere strangers.

Social media is an unusual phenomenon. Do you agree? If I've struck a chord, I hope you have a sense of humor and can laugh if you see yourself in one or more groups. I hope you're amused by my perspective of social media. I see myself in a few categories and have a good chuckle. We live in an ever-changing online world that reveals much about ourselves, our friends, human nature, and the times in which we live. The popularity of social media affirms and confirms that we are incredibly social creatures—online if not in reality.

I've concluded we are all *inters*. We're interconnected and interdependent. Where would we be nowadays without this mode of communication? I hope you'll indulge me the next time you're surfing a social network. Ask yourself this thought-provoking question: Am I the human being behind the surrogate, or am I the surrogate behind the human being?

> To be yourself, in a world that is constantly trying to make
> you something else, is the greatest accomplishment.
> —Ralph Waldo Emerson

Do Big, Hairy Monsters Really Exist?

Monsters *do* inhabit the world today. I've seen them.

They skulk in the dark shadows, patiently waiting to entice the most vulnerable and unsuspecting among us into their seductive grasp. They're out there all right! Big, hairy creatures are lying in wait under the bed. Perhaps they're consorting with the skeletons in the closet. Monsters creep up on you. Their giant tentacles slither ever so slowly toward their prey, beckoning the next susceptible victim into their hypnotic trap. They've mastered this skill perfectly. Naïve participants can fall under their spell before they realize what's happened to them. They'll consume you one bite at a time. They're sneaky, so you barely notice them eating you alive.

Do you believe you can fall prey to something you can't see? You sure can! I've experienced it myself.

Perhaps you've never encountered any such monsters. That's not unusual. These devious creatures are cleverly camouflaged so they blend into their surroundings. They're undetectable with the naked eye, so it's not like you can photograph them or describe their appearance. But that doesn't mean they don't exist. They sneak up on you. You're living your daily routine, skipping happily along, oblivious to what's going on in the background when suddenly, *bam!* You get nailed and wonder what hit you!

That was how it attacked me a while back when it suddenly seized me and sent me into a tailspin. The ambush wasn't *that* sudden, of course. It had crept up on me in the most insidious manner and caught me unaware—the thing, the creature with tentacles, the treacherous monster, the big *it*. I had grown too complacent. I had let down my guard and turned a blind eye to the dangers of the beast and its accompanying omens. I never dreamed I'd be taken unaware by an invisible monster. No, not me. I thought I was too savvy for that.

But there I was, trapped in its evil clutches.

The monster's lack of visible physical form makes it easy to fall under its hypnotic spell. That's all part of its allure, of course. And I was too busy *doing* to pay attention to the signs and symptoms of its presence. I was innocently skipping along in life, and all the while, the hungry beast was stalking me!

Honestly, I'd felt its presence before. I was wary of its nature, and I sensed it was gaining on me, even though I didn't see it, didn't define it, and didn't admit it. It's called denial. I experienced its magnetic pull beckoning me, reeling me in ever closer to its dominance. Finally, its massive, far-reaching tentacles slowly engulfed me in a stranglehold. Consumed by its power, I felt the life breath sucked out of me. *God, help me! What is happening to me? Please let me wake up from this hyperactive, overstimulated nightmare.*

Then it captured me, but before it took me down, in a moment of horrified realization, I mustered all my strength and fought it, refusing to surrender. Gasping for breath and struggling to escape its hold, I had what I call a hissy fit for a good thirty minutes. My man, my rock of a hero husband calmly listened to my emotional rant, comforted me, and supported my decision to do what I knew I must. I had to regain control over the monster and seize back my life!

I disconnected. I killed the monster. I rendered it powerless.

What monster? you may think now. It was the monstrosity of social media and endless technology. I had eagerly invited the giant creature into my life piece by piece over time, thinking that using this or doing that through modern technology would somehow expand my business. I thought it all would simplify and enrich my life. It seduced me into its massive clutches. I was mortified. I had to admit I was a willing participant.

No, wait. It probably was I who stalked the monster. I invited *it* into my life. It was the three of us (me, myself, and I) who had created this monster together. I realized that I—and I alone—was responsible and accountable for my predicament, so it was up to me to extinguish the beast and sever its hold on me.

"Exactly what animal?" you may ask. Well, let's say I had six active websites, two of which I had built from scratch and maintained myself, two others I updated, and two more I probably didn't use, but I let those remain active for fear of missing out on something! I suffered from the dreaded FOMO that is so prevalent today. Bear with me because there's more.

I also had my personal Facebook profile, three Facebook business pages, a Twitter account, a LinkedIn account, a YouTube channel, a Vimeo account, and a webinar room to manage. Notifications were arriving right and left with chimes and dings, a menagerie of noises and music going off on all my devices. Not to mention the distraction and annoyance of meaningless emails flying into my computer and the text messages on my iPhone and my iPad every few seconds of the day. It was all happening until I thought I would scream and run for the hills! I felt as though I was ADHD on steroids.

This frantic state of affairs was insanity for a woman who loves the peaceful life! The day of the hissy fit, I broke my own camel's back by adding one more website to beta-test in hopes of expanding my business. It was the last straw. Something suddenly snapped inside me. I fled from my desk and computer and collapsed into a full-blown meltdown. My good friend Don always told me, "Whenever you have a hissy fit, baby girl, go into the corner, stamp your feet, and repeat *dirty words* three times. Then get over it." Instead I fled to the sanctuary of my man's strong arms. Those loving arms could comfort and calm my jangled nerves and rock me back to sanity.

Together, we devised a plan of action that I implemented immediately. I completely disconnected from all electronics for a short period to reel myself in. I felt so empowered. I had made a tough decision, which took a lot of courage and willpower. It was not easy, but my determination to escape from the monster's grip made it easier.

I announced on my Facebook profile page that I was reining in my activity on social media to passionately pursue the business and personal goals that aligned with my purpose. I thanked God for answering my prayers, showing me the way, and providing the strength to do what I needed to do. My family and close friends supported me through the challenges.

I could soon see clearly again. I could breathe once more. I neutered the angry attack dogs of redundant sites and accounts that hounded me. I decluttered the knot of technology that held me in a stranglehold. I organized Facebook into lists of clients, friends, and family and devised a plan to maintain a small social media presence by scheduling posts once or twice a week rather than being on tap every minute of the day.

Mastering the technology monster has cleared big spaces of time, so I can connect via phone and in person to enrich and build personal relationships, which is where I know my strength lies. I derive positive energy from those personal connections, and I believe my friends and clients are also benefitting from the interactions.

I am still learning new lessons on how to manage and control the massive monster of social media in a high-tech world, but I'm encouraged. I've freed more space for high-touch time. I was happy to cast off the monstrous burden that was weighing me down and taking me down. I'm sure there will be other battles to fight. It's the way of life; however, for now I have contained the monster, and life is manageable and enjoyable.

I have time to write. I have more time to *be*. I feel free.

All things are lawful unto me, but all
things are not expedient:
all things are lawful for me, but I will not
be brought under the power of any.
—1 Corinthians 6:12 (KJV)

I Just Want to Understand

How many times in your life have you heard someone passionately exclaim, "I *just* want to understand!" The deep-seated desire for people to *understand* one another isn't new. It's been that way since the beginning of time. Wanting to understand and be understood is an inherent part of our being.

I never cease to be amazed at what people express, especially on social media. I see posts where people are drawn into controversial topics, bantering back and forth on opposing sides. Often the discourse degrades into name-calling and personal attacks in the comments, leaving hurt feelings and frustration. Sometimes it causes a rift in relationships. And it's all aired for the world to see.

Before anyone gets their knickers in a twist (which is a British idiom), please *understand* that I'm not calling out names or referencing any specific circumstances. I'm directing the contents of this story as a note to self, and I'm hoping it may help someone *understand* a friend with a differing opinion on any given subject. With that said, let's explore some thoughts around this topic. But first, it's essential we examine the dictionary definitions relating to the words themselves. At this point I realize you may grunt, roll your eyes, tune out, and want to put the book down. I understand, but please humor me for a few moments as we refer to the *Oxford*

Dictionary for the following definition: To understand (verb) is "to perceive the intended meaning of words, language or speaker." One of the greatest desires of human beings is wrapped up in the complexity and contexts of understanding both the noun and the adjective's meanings.

Understanding (noun) is "the ability to understand something; comprehension." Understanding (adjective) is "sympathetically aware of other people's feelings; tolerant and forgiving. Having insight or good judgment."

Note that these parts of speech are synergistic and most powerful when all three words are present and their meanings implemented.

For example, if you have an *understanding* (noun) of something, you probably sought to *understand* (verb), and you reached out with an *understanding* (adjective) attitude and demeanor.

Congratulations to those of you who have hung in there with me! Thank you! With that articulated, we can move on to the heart and soul of my message on how to better understand a person, a situation, or a differing point of view.

I believe that *most* people seek peace and harmony and that they genuinely desire to *understand* one another's point of view on whatever the topic. They want a satisfactory conclusion that's free of unpleasant discord, hurt feelings, or an irreparable conflict. I'm convinced *you* feel that way too.

With that said, we live in an imperfect world. We are all human beings who think, feel, act, and respond differently. Our responses may change day by day or minute by minute based on our perception, belief system, values, and emotions at the time.

In other words, understanding doesn't always come easily. It usually comes with a price attached for the one attempting to understand as well as the person explaining his or her position. The price is patience, vulnerability, the intent to seek understanding, a willingness to accept a differing point of view, and the skill to ask questions. Then you need patience to listen with an open mind and a loving heart.

Very often discussions of a passionate nature don't end in win-win situations. The tone degenerates, and the volume escalates. Inevitably, one or both parties begin to feel angry, hurt, resentful, or silenced. Instead of acquiring more profound understanding, the lack thereof intensifies. The gap widens. The hurt feelings deepen.

It doesn't have to be that way! Here are five ways to arrive at an *understanding* where friendships can remain intact and even lead to deeper appreciation and acceptance:

Understand that some prefer to argue. Just because someone *says* they want to understand, that doesn't make it so. Their words might *say* they do, but their actions contradict them, making it clear that they want to argue their perspective so *they* can be understood. You can recognize the futility of engaging these types of individuals when they discount or dismiss your thoughts by force-feeding you theirs, arguing over you or shutting you down. Each time you open your mouth to share an opinion, they bury you alive with a barrage of what *they* think. You might as well end the conversation right there and amicably agree to disagree because continuing is futile and does not end well 99 percent of the time.

Make it a win-win situation. Always enter a controversial conversation with a desire for a win-win ending for both parties.

Be the one to genuinely seek first to understand, setting aside your differing point of view to discover why the other people feel the way they do. It's not easy to do, but it's worth it. Winning an argument rarely improves understanding. It usually means the *loser* succumbed to *bullying*, stopped expressing him or herself to keep the peace, and was left unheard and forced to nurse stifled feelings. That's never a good ending. It's so much more satisfying to openly and respectfully agree to disagree with a person after gaining a deeper understanding of why the other person thinks or feels the way they do. Arriving at *mutual* understanding is the ultimate objective and accomplishment, but it's not always achievable!

Ask questions. Telling is selling! When you ask questions and permit the other person to answer without interruption, contradiction, ridicule, or a sneering look on your face, you're projecting that you value and respect the other people and what they're saying and feeling. When you *tell*, you come across as selling or pushing your idea and point of view. Worse still, if you tell someone what *they're* thinking, it's not only rude, arrogant, presumptuous, and dictatorial but also provocative. Asking questions and then listening patiently and intently with a sincere desire to understand is more mature, loving, considerate, and the best way to *gain understanding and to be understood*. Exercising control of emotions and showing interest in the other person is empowering, and it's one of the surest ways to make or keep a friend. Every friend we have matters.

Be respectful. Shouting, eye-rolling, ridiculing, insulting, condescension, arrogance, rude gestures, and grimacing serve no practical purpose when it comes to understanding or endearing yourself to someone. And please never resort to cursing and swearing. Find different words in your vocabulary. Be respectful even if you're disrespected. Rise above the common. Be exceptional. Take the high road, agree to disagree, bring the dialogue to a close, and preserve your self-respect. Too many people today are devoid of *common courtesy and good manners*. Be the one who sets the civil tone. Be gracious. Be kind.

Be loving and accepting. Look, no one said it's easy to understand why some people think the way they do, say what they say, or do what they do. It's hard to fathom when it's so clear to you and *they* cannot or will not acknowledge your side at all. It's even more challenging to remain calm and in control of emotions when both parties are passionately convicted or when a person's comments become vicious, extreme, accusatory, or false. Be intentional. Decide to not venture over to the dark side no matter what. If the discord is on social media, you can always scroll on by controversial topics. If it's a face-to-face encounter and you feel the heat turning up, be the one to cool it down. Be strong, and tap into your loving side. Accept all differences with grace.

Understand that it's okay for friends to differ. What isn't okay is to be unloving and destroy a relationship or friendship over a difference of opinion. The much-preferred option is to respectfully accept each other's position and keep the association intact.

Always choose love and acceptance. Everyone wins.

> Nothing in life is to be feared, it is only to be understood.
> Now is the time to understand more,
> so that we may fear less.
> —Marie Curie

A Tale of the Courteous Couple

Do you remember when good manners was fashionable, and no matter where you went, this man showed up with a smile, always eager to brighten someone's day with a kind word, a good deed, or a sincere gesture? He was known as a real gentleman in the workplace and social settings.

*Manners are a sensitive awareness
of the feelings of others.*
—Emily Post

You might also have noticed that wherever good manners went, you would find common courtesy. She was a gracious lady who never failed to say, "Please," "Thanks," and "Excuse me," and she raised her children to be polite! Good manners and common sense were the talk of the town. The two were ideally suited, compatible and always found together. It seemed they were inseparable. They were quite the couple, and people welcomed them everywhere they went. Wherever they appeared, they were the center of attraction. People enjoyed their company, respected them, and strove to emulate them.

In the company of this friendly pair, people were polite, more considerate of others, and a pleasure to be around. GM and CC were so popular that one would never dream of hosting a business meeting, a family gathering, or a party for friends without inviting them because in their absence it was all too easy for rudeness and inconsideration to crash the party and spoil everyone's fun.

In the present times, it seems good manners and common courtesy have disappeared from society. Except for a rare sighting, we haven't seen them around. What in the world happened to them? Some say they ran away together to escape rudeness and inconsideration, which were rapidly gaining status and climbing the social ladder. But nobody *really* knows for sure when and where they went or why they left us!

I wonder if they will ever return. I miss good manners and common courtesy.

What do you think became of them? Perhaps they left because we started to take them for granted. Maybe we failed to appreciate their intrinsic value in our society. Some say they were forced from our midst by the increasingly popular couple, the more dominant, in-your-face twosome! Yes, *that* pair. They were the ones who used four-letter words in every other sentence and had no problem using profanity, often in the most inappropriate context in a conversation and even in the presence of children, perhaps at dinner, at a ball game, or any time they chose with no consideration for those nearby.

Rudeness and inconsideration seem to be everywhere, and you'll frequently find them together, making an impolite spectacle of themselves in a stubborn show of solidarity. Rudeness is the one who never returns phone calls, doesn't respond to emails, and makes no apology for his behavior. Unless he wants something from you, he ignores your existence. He wouldn't dream of offering his seat to an older adult, and his air of entitlement is exceeded only by his arrogance. I think he's responsible for tossing good manners out the door when no one was looking.

Inconsideration is never far away from rudeness. She feeds on his delinquent behavior. They're quite a couple! She's the one who never calls home to say, "Hi, Mom and Dad," and she rarely acknowledges a generous gesture with a thank-you. She wouldn't dream of sending an RSVP to an invitation! She'll steal your parking space at work and laugh in your face! Her kids are out of control, and she's oblivious to their disruptive behavior, pandering to their every whim and demand for attention. She's likely the one who chased off common courtesy.

Does anyone know where we can find good manners and common courtesy? Do you miss them as much and as often as I do? Let's invite them back into our midst! I'm not sure where they went, but I do know this. If we make rudeness and inconsideration feel unwelcome and shun them, they will eventually disappear from society. When we banish that obnoxious pair, I feel sure that good manners and common courtesy will make a big comeback and be the popular favorites once more.

I can hardly wait!

Life is short, but there is always time for courtesy.
—Ralph Waldo Emerson

The Reluctant Participant

I slowly opened the envelope and stared intently at the words on the invitation as a flock of conflicting thoughts flew hither and thither inside my mind, creating pure mental chaos! My first thought was to accept and go to the party, but then I thought again.

Frequently, the words that follow the dreaded *but* count more than those that precede it. In this case, an entire family of *buts* rushed into the white space in my head. Disguised as excuses and reasons to decline the invitation, these buts began to compete for my attention, talking over each other and rudely interrupting one another as they fought for dominance. Worse still, the annoying clatter from these thoughts quickly dulled my initial desire to respond in the affirmative. The buts planted seeds of confusion, causing me to rethink my decision. I was already fully booked during the holiday season. Should I commit to one more thing? Should I go, or should I not go? What would *you* do?

Life is not always easy. Nor is it black or white. It's not all good or bad. It's not all yes or no. The present times are full of many shades of grey, dozens of maybes, and lots of questions. If we're honest, each of us will admit to the running commentary in our heads. It's called self-talk, and it's always with us. It interrupts us or argues with us. It discourages, throws out buts, and makes disparaging remarks, *or* it encourages us and cheers us on as we wrestle with decisions, priorities, choices, and even voices of temptation.

In a sudden, impulsive moment, I quickly sent the buts packing and banished the trash talk in my head. I commanded the voice to cease. Poof! I silenced the internal voice that was whispering sentiments I chose not to hear. It stopped long enough for me to RSVP in the affirmative. There, I did it. I had squeezed one more event into my bulging-at-the-seams schedule, saying to myself, "I can do this!"

The day of the party arrived. It was one of *those* days! I wasn't exactly sitting around, primping and pampering or painting my nails to look pretty for the festivities. My original plan for the day had sadly gone awry, and I was on mental and physical overload. I found myself pretty much chasing my tail all day thanks to one or two unexpected sideswipes that threw me behind the power curve.

Consequently, as I was driving home from my last commitment of the day, all I could think about was getting back to sit by the cheery, bright lights on the Christmas tree. It was a comforting thought on that cold December evening. I just wanted to slouch on the couch, stare aimlessly at the flickering fire, and sip some hot mulled wine with the love of my life. That was an enchanting and inviting vision. I was so ready to relax!

As I pulled into the garage, I suddenly remembered the invitation and the party. An overwhelming feeling of pressure invaded my being! The internal conversation with myself admonished, "Anthea, you *must* show up at that party tonight! You accepted the invitation, and you can't bail out now."

And so the internal struggle with my racing thoughts began once again!

Another tug-of-war raged in my head! The battle of the yays and nays were in full force. Yay, go! Nay, stay! My gut was encouraging me to go, *but* I was tired from the numerous demands of the day and not enthusiastic about turning myself on when I wasn't in the mood. While my instinct was saying I should go, the buts tuned in and said, "But your hosts will understand if you stay home!"

The buts pressed the point. "With the day you've had, it's justifiable to call and give your regrets. There'll be plenty of other people there. They won't even notice your absence. It's a cold, windy night, and it's not a good idea to risk your health in this weather. They wouldn't want you to overextend yourself. It's okay to stay home."

Then my conscience weighed in! Thanks a bunch for yet another voice in my head. Didn't I need one more point of view? I got another opinion and this time a *should*, which is often the worst. Don't you just hate that parental tone coming at you?

The voice of authority chastised me and said, "Anthea, you *should* always do what you say. You *should* keep your commitments. It's who you are. You were raised to be responsible! You *should* step up and go." You should, should, *should*!

I screamed in my head, "Okay! I'll go."

Goodbye to my tempting vision of tranquility and a night at home, I thought. I took a deep breath and headed to my room to freshen up. I was raised to keep my word. If anything is true of me, it's that I am one to honor commitments. I knew I must go. So I bucked up, dressed up, and showed up.

You might say I was a reluctant participant. I'm sorry to admit it, but it is the truth.

The chatter in my head continued as I drove to the party. I scolded myself on the way for impetuously accepting the invitation in the first place. I denounced myself for not listening to the buts' point of view, which provided me with plenty of valid reasons not to go. I wondered who would be there and what conversations we'd have. Truthfully, my expectations for the evening were unreasonably low, not because of who would be there or what we'd say to each other. My reservations certainly had nothing to do with my delightful hosts. No, my hesitation had everything to do with *my* internal struggle and reluctance. I took a deep breath as I slowly cruised past their brightly lit home, looking for a parking spot on the crowded street.

Too late now, Anthea. You're here, I thought.

I slid out of my car with a sigh of resignation. With the host's gift in hand, I adjusted my attitude, marched briskly up the driveway, rang the door chimes, and was greeted with a warm, welcoming hug and a blast of Christmas spirit that permeated the cold night air with mixed scents of gingerbread, pine cones, and hot apple cider all mingling together. I crossed over my friend's threshold and stepped into one of the most enjoyable evenings I've ever encountered.

Have you ever experienced this? You accept an invitation, and then when the time arrives, reluctance sets in for a variety of reasons. You look for excuses not to go. You argue the pros and cons of bailing out. The argument in your head causes conflict in you. You may even succeed in talking yourself into skipping the event.

Human nature can be strange at times. If I'd not gone to the party, I'd have missed a really lively time that included meaningful conversations with friends both old and new. One never knows where one is destined to be to touch someone's heart and make a difference or to receive a blessing that impacts one's life long after the party's over.

The moral of this story is to conquer reluctance and enjoy the fullness of life. Become the eager participant! Overcome the dissenting chatter in your head, and force yourself to boldly embrace all life's invitations. You may well discover as I did that you have the most enjoyable time. In fact, it may be the best time ever because you were right where you were destined to be.

> There is a strange reluctance on the part of
> most people to admit they enjoy life.
> —William Lyon Phelps

One "Poor Me" Short of a Pity Party!

Around week three following my surgery, I had one of *those* days! I felt a pity party brewing! Truthfully, it might have been more of a full-blown meltdown. What? This happy-go-lucky, nothing-gets-her-down, strong woman, the one who always appears to be upbeat and in control, the one who lives a charmed life and is happy no matter what? Yes, that very one!

In 2014, I had major surgery, a full hip replacement. I had timed it so I'd be sufficiently healed and rehabilitated by week nine so that I could fly to England to stay with my parents. I was supposed to care for my mother while my dad was in the hospital receiving *his* hip replacement at the grand age of ninety-three years. In retrospect, my recuperation time passed quickly. I had fantastic support from family, friends, and medical professionals, all of whom contributed to my speedy recovery and helped me stay positive and hopeful despite the apparent restrictions and incapacity I faced for a while. Ninety-nine percent of the time, I managed my feelings around the daily ups and downs with prayer, affirmations, and picturing myself walking pain-free.

I reassured myself that all would be back to normal soon.

It's amazing the impressions we leave with others, isn't it? I've had people tell me I'm lucky to have the life I have because I never have any ups and downs. I never have any family drama or business challenges, and every morning I wake up full of positive energy to take on the day! In other words, I lived a charmed, magical life.

I'm chuckling at *that* one! I wish it were so.

Outward appearances don't necessarily mirror the battle raging internally. It wouldn't be fair for me to let anyone think I'm *always* super positive, so I'll be authentic and truthful and confess that my attitude plummets now and then. And when I am up, it's *not* because I'm lucky or naturally charmed in some way. It's rather because I work hard on my attitude. I recognize there are times when I'm down, defeated, challenged, sad, frustrated, angry, or feeling some other negative emotion. Yes, it's true!

I know myself well, and I understand human nature, so I work intentionally and consistently on my attitude on a daily basis! I recite affirmations. I pray, and I conduct positive conversations inside my head. I prepare myself for the day. There will be challenges and setbacks perhaps, but the key is not in the outside factors that life inevitably throws at us but how we accept and respond to them that matters. It's how we deal internally with the sideswipes of life that determines how we behave outwardly.

Let's talk about the pity party I hosted for myself the third week after my surgery and examine the lesson in it! Day twenty was the day I felt the most down in the dumps! Much like a little squirrel hoarding nuts for the winter, I had stored up a whole bunch of "poor me" complaints, and they were dragging me into a bottomless, dark pit of irrational thoughts. Foolish fears invaded my mind, and inner voices whispered untruths. I would listen to lies that I almost began to believe! Insecurities and doubts surfaced. My thoughts turned into words, and a war raged in my head.

I struggled with an internal dialogue of conflicting messages. The negative and positive sides of me battled it out in a barrage of both irrational and rational thoughts. As soon as I countered one irrational thought with a rational counterpart, another irrational one appeared.

My irrational mind would say, "It's taking too long to get my energy back!" Then my rational mind would say, "Untrue! Patience, Anthea. It's only been three weeks since major surgery."

My irrational mind would say, "I just exchanged one type of pain for another" Then my rational mind would say, "Untrue! Really? Muscle aches are no match for pain."

My irrational mind would say, "My progress is too slow." Then my rational mind would say, "Untrue! Your expectations are unrealistic. Get real, Anthea."

My irrational mind would say, "Will I ever be able to walk around the block again?" Then my rational mind would say, "Ugh! That's a dumb question! Of course, you will!"

My irrational mind would say, "What if my folks have an emergency and I can't travel yet?" Then my rational mind would say, "That's an irrational fear! Faith, Anthea. Have faith!"

My irrational mind would say, "These compression stockings are so uncomfortable!" Then my rational mind would say, "So what? It's only temporary! Get a grip!"

My irrational mind would say, "Ugh! How many more days of blood thinner shots do I have left?" Then my rational mind would say, "Stop it, drama queen! You *know* the exact number. It's eight."

My irrational mind would say, "What if I get a blood clot?" Then my rational mind would say, "Duh! That's why you're wearing compression hose and injecting blood thinners!"

Can you see what I was doing? I was whipping myself into meltdown mode using irrational fears and negative self-talk. The negative emotions kept on coming, and they appeared to be gaining the upper hand. I was on the verge of tears, so I retreated to the comfort of my bed to rest and to wallow in some "poor me" tears!

The meltdown was brief! It lasted three minutes maybe. Then I suddenly remembered the dreaded blood thinner injection. The next jab of Lovenox was due! Oh boy! This injection had been the bane of my existence for twenty days. The one I pricked into my belly fat! This procedure dominated my thoughts for at least thirty *minutes* every day for twenty-eight days, and each time I had to muster the courage to deliver a shot that lasted a mere thirty *seconds.*

I chastised myself and said, "Seriously, Anthea! You are such a wimp. Deal with it. Get a grip. Get up, and do it! Get it over with *now*! You just had major surgery and survived. You gave birth to three babies. You've got this, girl!" So I dried the tears, eased off the bed, prepared the shot, pinched an inch of belly bulge, rubbed it with alcohol, jabbed the needle into the fat, and deposited the medication, and it was over that fast.

Seriously, Anthea! Was that so bad? I began to laugh at myself as a humorous thought popped into my head. I just had to call my friend and share a laugh. "Hey, Phyllis! Guess what? The worst thing about hip surgery is the Lovenox that I have to inject into my belly fat! But there's good news too. There's no shortage of belly fat!" We both laughed loudly! There is humor in circumstances even though sometimes you must dig deep! I said farewell to the "poor me" attitude and ended what could have developed into a pity party!

I had learned my lesson. Laughter chases away the blues. Seek humor in challenging circumstances. If you find yourself heading for the dark pit, stop short of the "poor me" attitude, and thwart a full-blown pity party!

CHAPTER 6
Hope Whispers

Your spirit soars on the wings of hope.

That Which Doesn't Kill Us Makes Us Stronger!

I've been challenged many times in my life and faced plenty of crises where the experience, hard as it was at the time, was ultimately advantageous for my personal and spiritual growth. I was tested. I survived, and I emerged stronger, wiser, and more intuitive. The list goes on. Let's sum it up by admitting that when we face off against adversity, we usually emerge as better human beings. Can we agree on that?

That which doesn't kill us *can* make us stronger.

I have also lived through a couple of instances where I was knocked to my knees and my strength and endurance were tested. I recall one specific period of suffering that was beyond intense. Although I won't share exact details surrounding the circumstances, the resulting anguish inflicted both physical and emotional pain. I felt the pain on a personal level, which was bad enough, but when others you dearly love are devastated, the heartbreak deepens exponentially. You hurt yourself, and you hurt for them. The ache reached deep down into my bones and shook me to the core.

That season of life found me close to despair at times and struggling to muster even the smallest scrap of strength to carry on with my daily routine, while chaos, roller-coaster emotions, and uncertainty swirled all around. When all reserves of energy are drained, where do you go? What's next? I chose to dig deeper, searching for that last drop of energy within my being. Oh, that I might catch the slightest glimmer of hope that this soon would pass. Oh, that a deep reservoir of inner strength would magically show up if I envisioned it vividly enough or willed it into existence. Oh, that I'd be granted a miracle if I prayed more fervently to God. It wasn't like I hadn't been praying. I had prayed continually for resolution and for the endless suffering to stop.

Still, it continued.

As a human being, you sometimes run out of patience waiting for God, even when your faith reminds you that *His* answer to your prayers may not be what *you* want or expect. Even when you know it's always in God's time because He is privy to the bigger plan, our human impatience sometimes tempts us to orchestrate a compromise with God. We may believe He's in control, that He truly loves us and wants the best for us, but there are times when we try to intervene and seize power. When we're wounded and afraid, our trust and faith are shaken.

Have you ever been there? I'm sure you've had your moments. We all do if we live long enough. Perhaps your suffering has been more profound and more continuous than others you know. If so, my heart goes out to you. If you're someone who hasn't ever experienced intense suffering, be aware that at some point it shows up when least expected, usually uninvited. We may not have done anything to deserve it. It simply shows up. But when it does, we might start to question our part, turn inward, and beat ourselves up. "Why me?" we ask ourselves. "Why now? What did I do to deserve this?" Scripture reminds us that as we travel through this world, we will face trials, tribulations, and sorrow at times. That's just the way it is here on earth at present.

Perhaps at this moment *you're* engulfed in one of those chapters in your life. Tell me, my friend. Do you feel stronger in its midst? If you don't, take heart, and read on.

At those desolate times of severe distress, I didn't *feel* at all strong. I felt weak, drained, helpless, and hopeless. My heart ached. My mind deceived me with lies, and my soul lay crushed. I've always considered myself to be an unshakeable woman of faith, full of hope, optimism, and independently secure, but there were two or three times in my life when the multiple darts and arrows fired at me hit their target. My strength cracked to near breaking point. The evil one's tactics drove me to a place beyond which I could bear no more of his attacks. During those days of shattered fragments of life and moments of overpowering human weakness, I desperately sought a way out. I wanted the mental, emotional, and physical suffering to end.

If you're thinking the worst as you read that last paragraph, let me clarify. I never contemplated harming myself. But I desperately wanted *that* chapter of misery to go away, to end. I wanted the pain and suffering to stop.

Did I pray? Of course, I prayed.

I was constantly on my knees in privacy. I implored God to intervene.

And yes, I gave my utmost to be patient and brave, but sometimes when suffering is relentless and continuous, it weakens you to the point of emptiness inside. You feel you have nothing left. You wonder if it will ever end. Doubt can show up at times like that. I recited all the clichés, and I received constant assurance from others; however, that did little to ease my growing doubts. I knew all the encouraging scripture verses. I recited them to no avail.

I wanted to give up and give in. I was tempted to run with all my might into the distant mountains, seeking refuge like a terrified rabbit racing toward the safety of its warren to escape a pack of snarling predators. The thought of seclusion in the woods, immersed in the serenity of nature, and resting in the arms of an all-powerful, loving God was a compelling thought.

But I didn't run, and I didn't give up. I rallied.

I soldiered on, and I stayed the course. I circled the wagons. I cried out even louder to God in hopes of a whisper from Him. I looked for any encouraging sign that He'd heard me. I sought His reassurance that all would be well in the end. He was my giver of strength and my last bastion of hope. When answers didn't come in the timing, I thought they should, my faith in Him began to fade. I felt my light dimming, yet a flicker remained. God's written promises assure us, and He keeps His Word. Buried beneath all my pain, I knew He loved me deeply. *Where is He?* I wondered. I yearned to hear from Him, to feel His love enshrouding me, comforting me in my suffering and restoring the full force of my faith.

Have you or someone you know ever experienced an attack from evil? I pray not. But if you ever do, you will know it. You will feel it, sense it, and smell it. Powerful prayers, spiritual strength, and physical endurance are essential to battle evil powers from the enemy. This incident was the first but not my last encounter with Satan. My spiritual strength was slowly being extracted and manifested physically in the pit of my stomach right beneath the sternum. I did not imagine this sensation. It was as real as any other physical pain. It felt as though energy was being sucked and siphoned out of me. Something was stealing my life force. The intensity increased with each new extraction. It was painful beyond words, physically and emotionally, and it was rooted in my body's spiritual center.

My soul bled silently.

Satan is like that, you know. He prowls the earth, searching for souls to devour. He was after mine, inflicting pain, deceiving me with his lies, sowing seeds of doubt in my head and my heart, attacking my family and me by any means he could, and using people as his instruments. Since I believe in God, I know the evil one and his cohorts exist by scripture. However, until that moment in time, I'd never witnessed pure evil up close and personal, so it was a bewildering and frightening experience.

In some ways, Satan is a coward. He lurks in the shadows, waiting for any sign of human frailty, a vulnerability in us, and then he strikes at the heart of that weakness, all the while attempting to convince us that *he* is not the one launching the attack. He hides behind people around us and our circumstances, all the while he is influencing them. He is the master at deception, lies, and accusations. On this occasion he sensed a chink in my armor. He saw an opportunity and seized his moment. His evil intent was to take me down and laugh in the face of God. He wanted to attack us both in one hateful move. In his beguiling way, he did his utmost to turn me against God. Having experienced both worldly and spiritual attacks in my lifetime, I know the difference. This episode was an intense spiritual onslaught from the devil.

I felt my light dimming.

I longed to feel God's presence, to bathe in His glorious light of love and reassurance. What I heard was silence. Sometimes silence is golden, a welcome warm and fuzzy feeling, but this was not. This silence was icy cold like the frozen vice that gripped my guts. Darkness engulfed me, and I was seized by fear. The fear exacerbated everything. When all the emotions of pain, anxiety, doubt, and icy darkness collided, another powerful emotion exploded to the surface. Hatred reared its ugly head. If anything will destroy us internally, it is hating. Initially, I hated myself for my pathetic weakness, for letting fear replace my fading faith. I hated my chaotic circumstances. Then I began to hate the instruments of the pain and devastation.

I knew I had to shake myself loose and reverse the downward spiral, or my light would be completely snuffed out by darkness. So with every ounce of my being, I rallied. I rejected all negative thoughts. I activated my survival instinct. I decided to be more intentional. I saturated myself in emotions of love and gratitude. I thanked God for the experience, and I forced myself to *forgive* those who inflicted harm. That was the hardest thing for me to do. At first, I told myself I'd forgive them, but I didn't really *feel* it. The words were spoken but carried no power. I didn't feel authentic, but I knew it was what God wanted of me, so I persevered. And miraculously over time, the forgiveness became real. I truly forgave. Many years later any feeling of ill will has been replaced by unconditional love.

Despite the suffering I prayed for joy. I would rejoice in all circumstances, not only when life was good. I beseeched God for deliverance from the power of evil. I screamed at Satan in my car, "Get behind me, you fiend. You have already lost the battle to Jesus." When I felt doubt, I read Bible passages on faith, and I surrounded myself with positive, supportive people who were seasoned believers. If I thought I was weakening, I recited over and over, "I trust you, Jesus. You are the light of the world." I listened to praise music. I professed my love to my Lord, and slowly, my light returned. Once more I felt His Spirit shining through me. Darkness disappeared. Hope, faith, and love returned, and they were stronger than ever.

I'm indebted to all who surrounded my family and me with such great love, understanding, encouragement, and prayer during one of the darkest times of our life. When my light was dimming, what helped fan the tiny flicker of hope in me was their love, prayer, and support. Their strong faith ignited what remained of my own. Their constant encouragement empowered and sustained me until my own emotional strength returned.

We must never underestimate the power of prayer and the value of love and friendship. At times of severe suffering, those who love us lift us up and graciously allow us to tap into their strength, to borrow their hope and their faith until ours returns. Love truly conquers all.

As I look back at that dark time, I realize that God never left me. His love was unfailing. He was there all the time, fighting my battle behind the scenes, unnoticed by me. He was there upholding me in His righteousness despite my floundering faith, the fear, and the pain. In my weakness He was stronger. He loved me so much He allowed me to feel the full intensity of the suffering for *His* reasons—reasons I no longer question because He is God Almighty, Creator of heaven and earth, and it was part of His divine plan.

What I can now say with assurance is that the experience didn't kill me and that it *did* make me stronger, not through any worldly strength on my part but by His mercy, His love, His grace, and His faithfulness. I learned to question His reasons less and to trust

Him more. I also learned to never doubt that He knows whenever *any* of His children suffer because He knew the ultimate pain in the sacrifice of His own Son so that we might have life everlasting. His perspective is different from ours. He knows the plans He has for each of us, and they are good plans.

God knew the circumstances I would face in the years ahead, and He allowed or orchestrated the suffering to transform me. That period of pain was a significant tipping point in my spiritual maturity. It prepared me for yet another encounter with evil in the future, one of great importance involving the soul of a loved one. It was a battle that could have taken me down had I not learned from the first experience to be stronger in my faith, more equipped to endure suffering, and better armed as a warrior for God. I may not always feel His presence, but I know He will never leave me. For that, I am His faithful servant, His instrument, and a testament to His love and redemption. My cup overflows with love for God. My soul sings His praise.

If you are in a place of suffering right now, turn to God. He is our Father, and we are His children. He loves each one of us. Whenever we lift our eyes upward to seek His face, He is already gazing down at us, pouring out His unconditional love. Even when we don't see or feel Him, He *is* there. He sees us. He knows us. We are so undeserving of His love, yet He showers goodness and mercy upon us. He blesses us beyond measure. To Him goes all the glory.

God *is* love.

> I have told you these things, so that
> in me you may have peace.
> In this world, you will have trouble. But take
> heart! I have overcome the world.
> —John 16:33 (NIV)

If You're Standing Still, You're Not Moving!

Sometimes the simplest of things have the most profound impact on us!

For example, if you envision a forest, you will agree that the trees are standing still. If they're standing still, they are *not* moving. Kidding aside, we *know* trees cannot transport themselves. They have no legs or wheels, so they can't walk or roll away. Unless they are uprooted and physically moved by a violent act of nature or intentional human effort, they are not moving. They perpetually stand in place.

If you looked at a picture of a tree that bore a caption stating, "If you're standing still, you aren't moving," you might notice the longer you stared at the picture and the more times you read the caption, the more significant the impact on you ... and the deeper your level of understanding would be. Weird, isn't it? With a cursory glance at such a caption, I suspect you might conclude it's rather silly to put two thoughts together that virtually mean the same thing. It's *so* obvious if you're not in motion, you clearly *are* standing still. In the same way, if you're standing still, you're not moving!

That's why stating the obvious is so powerful. It is ridiculously simple, and yet it has an impact. That's my intention here. I want the statement to leave a lasting impression on you. Simplicity rules.

Humans often resemble the tree example. We go through phases in life where we stay in one place and don't move. I don't mean that we're motionless. We could be walking around in a circle, not moving from that one spot, not going anywhere, not moving forward in our jobs, our personal growth, our marriages, or our lives, and not accomplishing anything. In other words, we can be stuck in one position, going *nowhere*, rooted in place in our comfort level, frozen in fear, or paralyzed by complacency or confusion.

With a few exceptions—and of course, there are always some—most people are not happy standing still. Progress matters to us. Even a tiny little bit of progress counts. We don't take kindly to being stuck in a rut. We feel frustrated and stagnant, and we begin to dislike ourselves for going nowhere; however, even though we hope to break loose, perhaps we have forgotten or don't know how to uproot ourselves and move forward.

So how do you break out of the rut? The answer is in the story of the tree picture, embedded within the caption. All too often, we can't see the forest for the trees, or we complicate the situation. We overthink the problem. That's when stating the obvious is helpful. It's a bit like underlining capital letters. It's annoying but effective! The answer is simple and clear. *Stop* standing still, and move! It's a simple answer, but it's not so easy to implement. How do you get yourself moving again?

Word has it that what people regret most at the end of life is not what they *did* but rather what they *didn't* do, so be the one who does everything possible to avoid living a life of regret. Live life to the fullest, and pursue your dreams.

Many are willing to settle for what life hands them because it's more comfortable that way. It's easier to wish for something more or to dream about a better experience than to break away from the familiar and change the status quo. Those who genuinely desire more but settle for less are often those who end up with the most regret. Be the one who chooses to act on your goals, step out in faith, and bring them to fruition.

> If you don't like how things are,
> change it! You're not a tree.
> —Jim Rohn

Chronic procrastinators fall into the group of people who court regret. They may have the best of intentions, but because they fail to act in time, or they think there's always tomorrow, they take no action at all. Here's a note to procrastinators: Tomorrow is not promised. Don't be the person who ends up living with regret. Act on your impulses right away. Make that call to someone you love, accept that opportunity placed in front of you, hug your kids, lose that extra weight, get healthier, take that longed-for vacation, and do these things while you can. Live a life with no regrets.

It is essential to know that breaking through barriers takes desire, courage, and action. Don't be the one who has hope and courage but fails to act. Don't wait for circumstances to change themselves because they rarely do. Don't expect someone else to make it happen for you. Don't put off to tomorrow what you can accomplish today. Instead, know that you and only you are the one to achieve what you want to do, have. and become. Experience has taught me that to live a life of fulfillment, my mind-set must believe the statement "If it is to be, it's up to me."

I have never wanted to leave this earth with the regret of unfulfilled potential, so embracing my purpose is a powerful influence in directing my actions. Living a dream includes *knowing* your purpose in life. It is defining the right direction and being willing to take a risk. It's following through on ideas, no matter how lofty or outlandish they may seem. It means stretching yourself, breaking through the chains of complacency, and asking the question "What if?"

Pondering the what-ifs stimulates you, and then you can imagine possibilities and dream bigger dreams! Remember there are no substitutes for *you*, no pinch hitters in life. Only you! There's no rewind button on living either. It's up to *you* to create your fulfilled, meaningful life. So stop standing still. Uproot yourself from where you're planted, and go after your dream. Take a risk. It will stretch you and provide you with confidence to do more. Visualize what you want. Go confidently toward it and believe with all your heart you will attain it. Replace fear with faith. Then put feet to that faith and *move.*

You are destined for greatness. You're here on this earth for a purpose. God has a unique plan for your life and a reason for your existence. You're called to make a difference in the lives of others. Shine your light, and let His light shine brilliantly through you.

> For we are God's handiwork, created in Christ Jesus to do good works, which God prepared in advance for us to do.
> —Ephesians 2:10 (NIV)

My Feet, My Faith! His Will, His Grace!

I love new beginnings, don't you?

Whether the dawning of each day in the week, the first day of the month, or the new year, it's like we're given a fresh start over and over again throughout the year. I crave, need, and value these chances to begin anew.

At the start of each year, I dive deep into thought about the year ahead. How will I make my life matter this year? In what way will I maximize the hours in each day to make *every* day count in a meaningful way? What plans do I have for our business this year? What steps will I take to bring them into being? So many questions always spin around my head. The answers usually don't come as quickly—that is, except for those instant answers like the careless, snap decisions that rush in.

But I'm not seeking quick solutions to such vital questions. I like to take my time to prayerfully and thoughtfully determine my plan for the year. I force myself to listen more intently and await the right answers. I generally let intuition lead the way. And in 2018, intuition spoke loud and clear. It was deafeningly insistent.

It said, "Anthea, *this* year you must think differently, act differently, and be different!" I did sense the year would be notable. I experienced a heightened sense of urgency to pay attention to my gut. An unidentifiable, internal voice compelled me to defer to my inner compass. I recognized the source of that voice.

"Is that *You* Holy Spirit? I feel Your counsel coming!"

Have you ever felt like you merely muddled through a period of your life? That your best-laid plans were thwarted at almost every turn and you found yourself navigating curves you never saw coming or dodging arrows that appeared from nowhere? Have you ever experienced a string of minor or major disruptions to your plans, sending you careering off track in a zigzagging direction?

That's just the way life is. We can plan to the last detail, but the longer we live, the more we realize we cannot *control* life. Life just happens. What we *can* control is how we respond to the twists and turns that distract us from our impassioned goals and strategic activities. We can decide to stay the course. We can remain focused on our goal. We can be constant in our purpose. We can keep on keeping on.

That's it, I suddenly thought to myself. *Constancy will be the key difference for me this year. I must stay true to my life's purpose, wherever the path leads me.*

One of my favorite scriptures urges us to be still and know that God is in control. I do for sure seek His will, and I trust God; however, I am not always still. I can be very proactive! It's a constant struggle for me to stop striving while I wait. I give God control, and then I try to seize it again. I let go and let God, and then I attempt another takeover! The independence and humanness in me sometimes result in me going all out to maneuver things in my way and my timing.

I am humbled often. I've learned to be grateful for the humility because in the end *God's* way has always proven to be better than what I could have dreamed up on my own. His wisdom is infinite. Mine is limited. He knows the larger plan, while I see only fragments of what might be.

I decided that *constancy* would be my word for 2018—constancy to God, devotion to my life's purpose, and persistence in my business. I wondered if my plans for the year would get sabotaged. Maybe! Probably! Why, of course, they would! It was inevitable. Life throws curveballs at us and drives us off track. I vowed that in 2018, my *constancy* would not be derailed, and my scripture for the year would be from Psalm 46:10. I would tell myself to remain consistent and steadfast. I promised to listen more intently to the still, small voice of God, which would require me to be quiet and calm so that I could hear clearly.

So on January 1, 2018, armed with a collection of lofty goals, I stepped out in faith with a sense of anticipation and excitement. I envisioned writing my book. I planned to expand our health and wellness business, and I was determined to seek God's will and accept His grace consistently. According to His bidding, I would joyfully adjust course if it was needed. I decided my motto for the year would be "My feet, my faith. His will, His grace."

> Let the morning bring me word of your unfailing
> love, for I have put my trust in you.
> Show me the way I should go, for to you I entrust my life.
> —Psalm 143:8 (NIV)

God's plans crashed into my life in mid-January, barely after the New Year. Sometimes God interrupts our best-laid plans with His plan. Extenuating circumstances that are out of our control can alter the equation. Our lives can change course in the blink of an eye, so it helps to be *resilient*. We must stay focused on our chosen plan, but we must be open to moving in a new direction. Sometimes it behooves us to go with the flow.

I had hardly stepped into January when God interrupted *my* plans with *His* plan. A phone call from my dad on January 12, his ninety-seventh birthday, stopped me in my tracks. Sometimes you know without a shadow of a doubt you're called to a particular action. I knew God was calling me. I felt His summons in the pit of my stomach, and my whole being understood the bidding. When you get that strong of a call from God, obedience is the only choice. On January 17, I was on a flight to be with my dad. My funeral dress was packed. As I said, when the Holy Spirit speaks, you *know* with conviction! After six beautiful days of our togetherness, my dad passed peacefully in his sleep on January 24.

"Constancy. Be still. Know that I am God," I heard.

I buried all my sadness, disappointment, anxiety, and fears in those few crucial words. Those words of assurance and the unfailing support of my family and friends were instrumental in my making it through the challenges of the year. Only God knew the depth and breadth of how I needed those very words to get me through an epic year of highs and lows. I needed them to carry me through the grief and loss, to encourage me forward with new plans in the face of disappointment because of my inability to execute my original plan. I needed them to calm my anxiety for all required of me to settle my dad's estate and to embolden me with faith in place of the fears that would often rise to the surface during the months we spent in England, sifting and sorting almost one hundred years of belongings, shipping family treasures to the United States, readying my parents' house for sale, and dealing with the necessities of a lengthy, complicated probate. God knew just what I needed, and He never left my side. He knew what lay ahead, and He made provisions to help me cope. He gave me the right words for the year. *His words* were chosen with me in mind.

Each time I looked at what seemed an endless list of insurmountable tasks, I commanded myself to *be still. Stop fretting, Anthea,* I thought. *God's got this.* He did, and miraculously, I remained constant in my faith. Knowing the power of God kept me sane and my mind-set in the right place. Each time I felt myself stressing, I let go and let God. With His faithfulness, my family's unwavering support and encouragement, and my man by my side, we made it through the year. Lord God, what an amazing ride you gave us in 2018. All glory to You.

This past Christmas our family played a game that encourages meaningful conversations. We each had to rate the past year on a scale of one to ten. To everyone's surprise, I calculated the 2018 year a number *ten*! It was nothing like the year I had planned, but it was a year of great magnitude. It was a year of substantial personal growth and spiritual maturity, and although I was late in starting my book, at least I formulated some ideas. While our business did not grow at all and we lost traction, the blessings of the year were more abundant than I ever could have hoped for or imagined. But God knew. He knew before it happened.

It was a meaningful year of epic proportions and unexpected blessings. The year was monumental on all counts. It was not of my own doing in any way, shape, or form, but it was a loving gift from God. I received His grace, His mercy, His strength, and His infinite love. I am forever His grateful and humble servant.

The year 2019 is here. As I write this, much of the year is an unknown entity, a mystery, but I'm excited. As my vision unfolds, the associated plans are taking shape. Our family, our business, and writing my book are featuring prominently in the picture. I'm smiling as I wonder what God's plans are. Only He knows for sure, but we must wait and see. Meanwhile, I press on with my goals in high expectancy, and I pursue my dreams passionately.

I remain resilient, watchful, open, and obedient. I am full of hope for the future. The word I heard God whisper to me for 2019 is *discernment*. My scripture is "For God hath not given us the spirit of fear; but of power, and of love, and of a sound mind" (2 Timothy 1:7 KJV).

I'm ready, Lord.

Where Do Dreams Go to Die?

"Anthea Shipperlee. Principal ballerina with the Royal Ballet." My name was proudly displayed on a placard, lit up by flashing lights. The years of hard work and dedication had borne fruit. I was a sensation. I was famous.

I was *the* leading ballerina with the Royal Ballet in London. It was my dream; one of the beautiful dreams I had as a child. In my mind I glided across the stage on expert toes, and I was lifted high into the air by my leading male dancer. In my imagination the audience was applauding, the orchestra playing *Swan Lake* or *Sleeping Beauty*, and the spotlight was on me, giving the performance of my life, leaving all I had on the stage. As the curtain rose for the last time, I saw myself curtseying to the crowd who jumped to their feet, cheering, "Bravo." My leading man and I accepted those accolades from our adoring fans, basking in the moment before prancing elegantly off the stage, carrying a huge bouquet of roses.

In my dream I had reached the pinnacle of success. In reality, I owned a pair of ballet-like shoes, and for a few months, I danced all over the house, gracefully mimicking ballerinas I'd seen in live performances at the theater in Oxford. However, I had not received a single dance lesson of any kind, let alone the years of ballet it would require to be a leading dancer with the prestigious Royal Ballet. But in my child's dream, that was no problem, no stumbling block at all. Dreams can come true. I believed that with all my heart, and that was what mattered.

I quickly moved from that vivid dream to another. I wanted to be an Olympic athlete, a famous interpreter at the United Nations, and a published author. Many daydreams came and went. Call me a hopeful romantic, a dreamer, an eternal optimist, or a confirmed positive thinker, and you'd be right on all counts! I make no apologies for being this way. It's the essence of who I am. While some of the dreams never materialized and only lasted a few months, many others have come true. Big dreams have endured—the ones I vividly envisioned and pursued with determination and vigor.

Was I born to be a dreamer, a confirmed optimist? Maybe. Did I learn the mind-set from my super positive mother? Did I get it from admiring my father's dogged determination and perseverance? Perhaps. Have I become that way over many years of intentionally and habitually choosing my thoughts, solidifying my beliefs and working on my vision and attitude? Probably. But I'm sure I was influenced by a combination of all the aforementioned.

As a dreamer infused with hope for the future, I feel compelled to seek the elusive good in all circumstances, even if it requires digging deep to reveal only a tiny glimmer of light that might otherwise be hiding in the shadows or enshrouded by darkness. With that thought in mind, I have a question about dreams.

Where do dreams go to die?

I believe that dreams (as in our hopes and aspirations) reside in each of us. As a child or young adult, we know how to activate our imagination to create a vision or picture in our mind of what we aspire to be, to have, or to do. The more vivid our imagination, the more alive and real it appears, and when accompanied by a strong desire to attain the object of that dream, we're magnetized by it, drawn to it. We can almost reach out and touch it. Desire burns, and all the forces within ignite us into action, propelling us to pursue that dream.

Ah, such are the dreams of former youth!

But alas, for many of us, as the years go by and the trials and tribulations of life dominate our thoughts and daily activities, we set aside our dreams. We might even hide them away somewhere safe but out of sight.

And then our imagination falters, the once-so-vivid dream fades to nothingness. Desire and passion wane to indifference. Ultimately, we justify feeling the way we do. It wasn't meant to be. It was a childish whim. It was too hard to achieve anyway. It was too this or too that. The reasons are endless. And so another desire is lost. The beautiful vision, once so alive, passes away, its breath snuffed out, its vibrant light extinguished by the very dreamer who created it—one more dead dream.

So where do dreams go to die?

What do you think? Do they evaporate into thin air? Do they burn themselves out in the imagination that conceived them, settling there like silty ashes to clog the mind of the dreamer? Do they float off into oblivion or do they transition to a hereafter for dead dreams? Are they suspended somewhere in limbo? Do they drown in a pool of their own tears? Is there life after death for dreams, or is death permanent for them?

So where do dreams go to die?

Would you like to know what I think? When dreams die, they merely move from one place to another. They leave the imagination and transition into the heart of the dreamer, where they remain forever. They await new life or transformation into a different dream. The dreamer has only to ignite his imagination, breathe life-giving desire, love, hope, and belief into the expired dream, and it will spring to life once more.

Every dreamer has the power to resurrect their dreams. Do you have one smoldering in your heart, awaiting resurrection? I imagine you do. Your dream awaits. It's all up to you.

> **A single dream is more powerful**
> **than a thousand realities.**
> **—J. R. R. Tolkien**

On the Wings of a Prayer

No sooner had my head touched the pillow than an undefined anxiousness filled the pit of my stomach. My mind, which refused to shut down, lit up like a noisy amusement park. Or perhaps the sensation of restlessness in my gut was precipitated by my mind darting here, there, and everywhere.

I knew I had to get some rest as there would be no sleeping late the next day. I had a full day ahead! So I focused on slow, deliberate, deep breaths. I pictured peaceful green fields, and I commanded my mind to stop racing. I systematically relaxed each body part one by one from top to bottom. I envisioned myself sleeping peacefully. I prayed for sleep, but sleep did not come.

It just was not happening. Nothing helped. I did not need a sleepless night! The unsuccessful attempt to force sleep upon my tired body further fueled my overactive mind with a string of unrelated thoughts. *Okay, fine,* I thought. I had tried everything else. It was worth a try to go with the flow. I was tired of fighting it, so I lay there and succumbed to the moment. I gave my mind permission to have its way with me, and it did!

It led me to a memory from years ago, one that surfaces periodically. When it does, I sense a strong nudge to write about what happened, but I've always managed to ignore the bidding. Tonight it was more than a gentle push. It was insistent. It persisted, and I realized there would be no sleep for me until I extracted the words from my head and wrote them into a manuscript.

I left the warmth of my bed with an obedient heart and settled into writing mode at two fifty in the morning. So be it!

"You will write," said the prophet. "No matter the time of day or night, hear the call and write. Don't worry about sleep. Write down your thoughts! There's a writer in you. Express your emotions. Describe your experiences about family and life. You've got important stories to tell. Share them!"

I stared thoughtfully at the blank page on my computer, my fingers hovering over the keyboard in readiness to type a string of words that had been rattling through my mind for what seemed like hours. I wondered why my mind was so stuck on replaying the memory of this story over and over. I'd replayed it time and time again in the archives of my mind. Very few people knew this story. So why now? Why tonight? Perhaps I overthink things, but I had no idea why I was supposed to include this story in my book. I was compelled to do so, and there'd be no sleep for me until it was written. There's one thing I've learned about life's mysteries when I feel compelled or driven. It's not for me to analyze, question the timing, or demand the reason. I must be obedient to my inner voice, share the events, and leave the outcome to the powers that be.

So here is my account of a mysterious event.

It took place during that prolonged period of spiritual attack that I mentioned at the beginning of this chapter. A series of circumstances beyond my control forced me to cancel my spring trip to England to visit my folks' house. Let me interject a quick thought here. Unless you've had a close personal encounter with the spiritual realm, you might be rolling your eyes around your head as you read this. Perhaps you're wondering if spiritual attacks exist or if they are mere figments of an overactive imagination. I can understand your skepticism. I used to be suspicious about such things until I fell victim to one myself. I hope you will keep an open mind and read on.

I hope you believe in God and His goodness. I pray that you know firsthand His faithfulness, His constancy, His love, and His mighty power. I understood from a young age that unseen forces coexisted in our world, influencing people and circumstances. I hope your mind is receptive to the existence of the spiritual realm of good and evil. While I had always been happy to give credence to the *good* force, I danced around the *evil* counterpart, not wanting to admit it was real. In my lifetime I've seen evidence of both forces. The battle is real.

Thank God for the many friends and people in our church congregation who prayed for protection for our family during this challenging time. I knew we were facing some serious stuff when a friend volunteered to anoint the four corners of our property. He seemingly had *felt* the presence of darkness surrounding us and our home. We took him up on his offer. Prayer is powerful. It's strange, but during that time frame, I was less fearful for my own safety and more concerned for my parents' welfare, especially since I'd been forced to postpone my visit to England because of unavoidable circumstances requiring that I remain in the United States.

The following account details a manifestation of *goodness*. It was like a lamp that brightened a dark time in my life during a succession of challenging *bad* circumstances.

The phone rang insistently and much earlier than usual. My parents were both at the other end of the telephone. They spoke so hurriedly and breathlessly that once I established all was well, I grew more and more intrigued by their evident excitement. As the details unfolded, it turns out that at roughly one in the morning Greenwich Mean Time, something awakened them from a deep sleep. Their bedroom window was rattling loudly and vigorously. Something was right outside the glass. Simultaneously, a blinding bright light of epic proportions shone through the curtains into their bedroom, lighting up the entire room as if with sunlight.

My mother, who was nearest the window, bolted upright in bed, while Dad crept around the foot of the bed and very slowly pulled the curtain toward him, creating a slight crack to peer outside, hoping to determine the cause of the commotion. He recalled that it initially sounded like a helicopter with the whirring and whirling of its rotating blade, but it was not. The light was brilliant, so he couldn't see the source, but he was adamant. It was not a helicopter. I can pretty much concur. It would have been impossible for such an aircraft to get that close to the house without taking out the surrounding trees or structures. It would have left an unmistakable trail of evidence.

I questioned my parents further as we all tried to make sense of what they had seen and heard. It's important to know that my father was a clearheaded, no-nonsense kind of man with an analytical mind. He was a doubting Thomas in terms of the spirit world, and he certainly was never one to dream up fantasies or fairy tales. No, not *my* dad. He knew there had to be a logical explanation, and when none was forthcoming, he lay awake for the remainder of the night, his brilliant mind exploring the possibilities of what might have caused the apparition. He was stumped. It was all so mysterious. In the morning he scrutinized the back garden beneath the bedroom window, searching for tangible evidence of the disturbance. He visited all the neighbors around them. Surely, they had heard or witnessed *something* unusual from the night before. Nothing!

Alas, no one else had been disturbed, and there was no trace of anything to raise suspicion. No evidence that *anything* unusual had happened at all. There was nothing at the window, on the window, or in the garden below. Did they both dream it? It was highly unlikely since they were wide awake within seconds and both witnessed the very same series of events. Whatever it was, it left my father puzzled, and the whole occurrence remains an inexplicable mystery.

Or does it?

Perhaps my mother's description of what she saw, heard, and felt provided me with the most convincing evidence as to what I believe they experienced. Here's what Mum described: "The window was shaking and rattling loudly, and a piercingly bright light was shining through the window, lighting up the entire bedroom. Dad pulled back the curtains, but we couldn't see what it was. It *definitely* was *not* a helicopter or any mechanical contraption. The whirring noise was deafening. It sounded more like a flock of large birds flapping their wings so fiercely that the draft resounded against the window, causing the glass to vibrate."

I asked my mother if she was afraid or fearful. She said brightly, "Oh no, not at all!"

I find that response quite astounding. My parents had seen and heard something unusual, powerful, and mysterious, and yet neither had been fearful. If it were me, I'd have been scared if not terrified. But then it occurred to me that in any manifestation of goodness, fear might be absent, which comforted me and led my mind and heart to the same conclusion. God is an amazing God! He found a way to protect my folks while sending a strong declaration across the Atlantic to us in California. Fear not. He had my parents in the palm of His hand, and so like our heavenly Father, He chose a mysterious way to convey it.

My parents were sheltered under the wings of many prayers. God answers prayers in His way, in His own time. Who are we to question what God chooses? In this instance they experienced brilliant, piercing light and a thunderous flapping of wings that bore no identifiable source or left no visible trace in the morning. Don't you think it's a spiritual manifestation? A host of angels? One mighty angel? With God, *anything* is possible. According to scripture, some of God's angels do have sets of wings, and they have been known to shine brilliant light. Whatever showed up that night long ago transmitted a mystical message, yet in its midst there was a clear understanding accompanied by a whisper of hope.

We'll never know or prove what made an appearance to my parents' home that night, but I believe without any shadow of a doubt that *hope* is the anchor of the soul and that it is God who can create a door of *hope* from a valley of trials and trouble. And now I leave you to draw your own conclusions! I'm merely the messenger.

Prayer is powerful. Good things come on the wings of a prayer.

> "For my thoughts are not your thoughts, neither are your ways my ways," declares the Lord, "As the heavens are higher than the earth, so are my ways higher than your way and my thoughts than your thoughts."
> —Isaiah 55:8–9 (NIV)

Some Things Remain a Mystery

An unusual experience a couple of months after my mother died left me speechless. For someone who loves to write, being at a loss for words is rather humorous, so I am chuckling at myself now. In today's world of concrete thought, too often we gloss over the supernatural possibilities and brush them off as inconsequential. I've been guilty of dismissing the unknown and mysterious for years. While writing this book, I vowed to stop sweeping these experiences under the rug, so I'm obliged to write yet another story surrounding the mysteries of the universe.

This one involves technology.

Those close to me must understand that I'm a spiritual woman, tuned in to God, and I believe in the existence of many inexplicable mysteries in the universe, so that's nothing new. However, there is another side to me. I am a logical thinker, and I love rational explanations, especially where computer technology is concerned. I figure if I can create something once, I can surely recreate the same circumstances, right? That's a logical deduction. I seek concrete answers to puzzling problems. When something weird happens, I strive for a *reasonable* explanation. I *need* an interpretation that makes complete sense to me.

A couple of months after my mother died, I was journaling about the range of emotions that surfaced as I sorted through treasures from my mother's effects. I felt a wave of grief and a delayed sense of loss, a sad emptiness that I intentionally dismissed by deciding it was dinnertime. After all, food solves everything!

On entering the kitchen, I noticed my iPad on the counter. Since mastering my smartphone, the iPad took a back seat among the electronic devices, and I relegated it to occasional use. I used it only to pair Pandora with my Bose speaker to play music while my house cleaner was here. She was due the next day, so I stopped to check the charge, ensuring she would have music while she cleaned. It was okay, so I thought I'd use it to surf the internet for a few minutes. It refused to connect to Wi-Fi for some reason, and when I discovered an update was available, I thought that might solve the issue, so I began to download the latest IOS. I was bored with the time it was taking, so I left it to its own devices! No pun intended. I let it sit there on the couch to install the update while I cooked dinner, and that's where it remained, forgotten, out of sight and out of mind.

I awoke the next morning feeling groggy and stumbled out to the living room, looking for a morning cup of tea. Chuck was already *on* it! Mr. Amazing Stud Hub was up making the tea. I sat down to await its arrival when what should I espy but the blacked-out iPad. I reached for it and fired it up. I'm always happy when technology works! The new IOS had installed, so I decided to check out the Wi-Fi situation. I clicked on Safari and hit the URL for my blog website to test how fast the site might load.

That's when it happened—the weirdness!

I expected to see the tree-lined English country lane graphic, which is the default banner in my blog template. This graphic only loads on the home page along with the most recent post. There are no banners on the individual page posts. The familiar tree-lined lane, a picture I'd taken during one of my visits to Dorset, did not appear. There was a different picture in its place. What I saw startled me so much that I couldn't stop staring at it. I could see, but I couldn't believe what I was seeing. I was dumbfounded. Yes, I was shocked and speechless!

What did I see? I saw my mother.

There in the banner was a photograph of my mother taken on her ninety-fifth birthday. It was up close and personal. Her beautiful bright blue eyes were staring directly into mine, and they were piercing. Yes, it was a close-up showing only two-thirds of her face. When I regained my composure, I held up the iPad and showed it to Chuck.

"How in the world did this get there?" I exclaimed.

I think he thought I was suggesting he put it there because he interpreted my startled tone as accusatory. I knew he would *not* have done that. He couldn't have. First, he wasn't an Apple fan, and second, Stud Hub was not technologically savvy with my WordPress template, so he definitely couldn't have made that happen! I was frantically trying to wrap my head around how *that* graphic of my beautiful mother got in the banner because I knew the steps required to replace a graphic in the template. To position a photo correctly so that it fit in the banner without distorting the picture required some skill and practice.

I have never liked feeling stumped, but this was inexplicable. What in the world? It occurred to me that I'd somehow published the post with Mum's photo in with the text by mistake. That sometimes happened if a graphic's pixels were higher than the required parameters. It would show up in the banner as well as placing the graphic within the text, but that was not the case. I'd examined the published article, and it hadn't been there the day before. When I had last checked, the three graphics in the post were pictures of memorabilia, not people. Perhaps the photo got mixed in there somehow from the photos App in my iPad? No, that picture was not amongst any iPad collections.

"I know," I thought aloud. "I'll check on my iPhone to see what it looks like there."

The iPhone revealed my article precisely as I had published it the day before with the tree-lined country lane there in the banner as big as life! I ran to my office and pulled up the blog on my Dell desktop and laptop. They were both consistent with my iPhone, displaying the tree-lined lane in the banner. That was when I gasped in disbelief. There must be a logical explanation! As I returned to my iPad, I half-expected to see the tree banner back in place, but my mother's face was still there.

I took a photo of my iPad with my iPhone. Don't you love technology? I noticed Hero Hubs tearing up and emotional (I love sensitive men) as he said, "Your mother wants you to know she approves of your writing! Honey, some things just can't be explained." He was right.

At that point I refreshed the browser again, and it disappeared. The banner returned to the tree-lined lane. I have often wondered how I could logically explain this mystery, but I cannot, so I will graciously accept it as a beautiful sign from God that my mother approved of what I'd written about her the day before!

I remember that day well, and I thank You, Lord, for blessing me in such an unexpected way. Lord, I am humbled by Your power and Your capacity to love each one of us intimately. You know us better than we know ourselves. You grant us the desires of our hearts. I delight in Your magnificence. You are Lord of the universe.

> Behold, these are but the outskirts of his ways,
> and how small a whisper do we hear of him!
> But the thunder of his power who can understand?
> —Job 26:14 (ESV)

CHAPTER 7
Dementia Daze

Touch is the unspoken language of love.

Peace of Mind

I thought long and hard before deciding to insert this chapter into my book. I can't begin to express how greatly I struggled internally in making a choice. Should I, or shouldn't I? It's important that I do the right thing for all concerned, that what I express is truthful and consistent with the memory of my mother and father, and that it meets the approval of my family. Most of all I questioned if it would be pleasing in His sight. If I were to share this painful chapter of my life with the world, would it glorify God?

Selfishly, I was reluctant to transport myself back through the painful memories and sadness that consumed me as I accompanied and supported my mother's journey with dementia. It would mean feeling the complete range of emotions once more—deep, raw emotions I never wanted to feel again. All the frustration, the sadness, the fear, and the helplessness would resurface, and I'd have to live it again.

If you have a loved one who has Alzheimer's or any form of dementia, you will understand the depth and breadth of emotions that seize the one afflicted and their loved ones on any given day through the entire progression of the wicked disease. Dementia has evil tentacles that grab and squeeze its victims and all their family members. When my dad announced that Mum was officially diagnosed with dementia at the age of eighty-seven years old, I had no idea about the seriousness of the implications or how widespread the impact would be.

At the time I thought I knew, but I didn't.

It is much more far-reaching than I imagined. I knew dementia inflicted the elderly with forgetfulness and memory issues. However, fifteen years ago as I looked into the sparkling eyes of my mother and marveled at the beautiful vibrancy of her physical appearance and the alertness of her bright, witty mind, it was impossible to imagine. I had no idea what lay ahead for her, for me, but especially for my dad, who continued to care for her through all the remaining years of her life.

Living miles across the Atlantic Ocean was perhaps one of the hardest elements for me. The two trips a year to visit my parents, while the best we could muster, were not nearly enough. The daily phone calls helped, but calls were not quite the same as being there in person. I was thankful for the blessing of a phone chat every day, but I longed to be there more often and for more extended periods of time in order to brighten my mother's days and to be more supportive to my dad. He persevered unceasingly but was degenerating under the severe strain, even with the outside help coming in several times a day. Physically it was demanding, but I believe the emotional stress of seeing the love of his life fade away was the hardest for Dad to bear. He busied himself in many activities that I eventually realized were respites to him, not avoidance of the condition but welcome escapes from reality. It was how he protected his sanity from the sharp emotional pain of seeing my mother slip away.

My heart broke for them both.

Prayers, my faith in God, and intentional gratitude for the many blessings sustained me through the journey—a journey I hope I never have to take again with any loved one. We were very fortunate that my mother lived ten years with dementia, and at first, it was a slow progression. She ate healthy food and took natural supplements and later took prescription medication to help retard the advancement. I learned firsthand that while dementia was forgetfulness and memory loss, it is much more about *not remembering*. You see, in my naivety, I understood that Mum would forget about things and that as the disease progressed, she'd also lose memories.

I had not bargained for her to forget how to remember.

She didn't just forget where things were or people's names. She forgot how to do the simplest of things. If you choose to read forward in this chapter, I write in more detail about this topic. I wish to emphasize I am thankful beyond words that my mother never forgot me, who I was, and what I meant to her. She never forgot how to love. I thank God for that mercy.

As I said at the beginning, I thought long and hard about including this chapter. After soul-searching and praying, I feel compelled to share this personal journey alongside my mother. Alzheimer's and dementia are prevalent diseases in modern times, impacting so many families. Thus, I feel it is a story I must share. I pray it will help someone in some small way. Perhaps it will encourage a relative of someone with dementia or provide them with hope or at least increase their awareness of this severe degeneration of the mind.

As you read, you will discover that while dementia is devastating and incurable, there are also many hidden blessings, moments of great love, pure joy, and even some humor in the journey. Keeping copious notes in my iPhone, journaling about my experiences, translating my deepest feelings and emotions into words is the way I dealt with dementia's impact on our lives.

As dementia crept in and slowly attempted to steal my mother's mind, I fought harder to stay mindful of the one who is ultimately in control. I worked diligently to hang on to my peace of mind under the strain of all the pain, heartbreak, and fear of the unknown. Sometimes I failed miserably. At other times I conquered my emotions. Occasionally, my faith faltered, but mostly, faith was my saving grace. My belief in God, His infinite love, and His strength along with the support of family, friends, caregivers, and the Sturminster Newton community, where my parents resided, were the ongoing blessings that uplifted me and carried me through this time of severe testing.

The stories in this chapter are taken directly from entries in my journal, written as I walked the painful path of dementia with my mother. What I refer to as the dementia daze ultimately led to her death.

Set your minds on things above, not on earthly things.
—Colossians 3:2 (NIV)

I Wish I Could Wake Up

My beautiful white-haired mother stood by the bed and froze ever so slightly. As I guided her closer to the bed, I kept my arm around her, gently steadying her. I *felt* her body tense against mine before I noticed her stiffen just a little. It was a subtle motion but detectable to me. Only a few seconds earlier as I eased her weak and weary frame off the chair from the stair lift on the landing just outside the bedroom door, I had sensed her hesitation to pass through the doorway. My husband stood by discreetly, giving us space, but he was right there if we needed him.

My dad was downstairs, awaiting his turn to ascend in the stair lift. I knew what was coming next. It happened the night before, the night before that, and every other night for the previous twenty days I'd cared for my mother.

"Where have I to go, Anthea?" she asked pleadingly.

Mum had been eager to get into bed. She was tired, even though she had catnapped a lot of the day. For a good half hour before bed, she had whispered continuously, "Is it time to go to bed?"

"Soon, Mum. Soon," I'd say. I had responded to her twenty times or more in thirty minutes. I honestly didn't mind the repetition.

God provided the patience. He gave me understanding. I knew if I were ninety-five and confused, I'd be grateful for kindness, understanding, and patience from my loved ones.

But now as we stood together by the bed, something was different from the other nights. When the previous bedtimes came, we walked together toward the bed, Mum saying, "Where have I to go?" and, "What should I be doing?" Up to that point, she had accepted my responses. "We're going to get you into your nice, warm bed," I'd say. She heard me this time too, but it didn't register. She seemed to be preoccupied.

Yes, I could see tonight would be different.

Mum stood rooted in place beside the bed. I unfastened the soft, warm crimson dressing gown she'd received from us one Christmas and gently slipped it off and folded it at the end of her bed. She remained standing, frozen in place, just staring at the mattress. "What's wrong, Mum?" She slowly gazed at me with those light blue eyes that have shown their love for me from the day I was born. She had this look of puzzlement and despair as she touched her lips with shaking fingers. With one glance I knew there was no need for words. I didn't need words to tell me how deeply she loved me. Those expressive eyes revealed all.

But there was more than love staring at me. It was confusion and fear. I could see it. I could feel it. I didn't have to ask, but I sensed she wanted to express what was bothering her. I encouraged her again by asking, "What's wrong, Mum?" I put my arms around her, reassuring her. "I love you, Mum, no matter what," I said. I wanted her to feel my unconditional love, my acceptance, and my understanding as she struggled to make sense of what she was feeling, frantically trying to recall how to translate her emotion into words. I could see and feel her trembling, and she let out a faint little wail and said, "Oh, dear! Anthea, I want to get into bed, and I don't know how! I'm sorry!"

So there it was. Mum had managed to express the inexpressible.

The words reached in and grabbed my heart like a vice. Not only was my mother confused, but sadly, she was fully aware she was confused. She knew there was something wrong, and she didn't know what to do about it, what to call it, or how to make it go away. And of course, deep down inside she must have known—as we did—that it was not going to go away or get any better. Times like that must have been terrifying for her.

"I can't bear it! Oh, God, please help us all get through this," I prayed silently. "Dastardly dementia! You have my beautiful mother in your grip. I hate you!" It's at times like those when I wanted to change places with her. Seeing a loved one suffer is brutal. I'm sure it is this way with all families where dementia or Alzheimer's has invaded the mind of a loved one.

"I'm here, Mum," I said. "Just sit on the side of the bed." I helped steady her on the bed and removed one slipper at a time.

Mum said, "Now what do I do?"

"Just lie down, Mum. Put your head on the pillow." I snuggled the soft, warm duvet around her as she struggled to turn onto her side.

She lifted her head off the pillow slightly. "Now, what have I to do, Anthea? I don't have to go anywhere tomorrow, do I?"

"No Mum, don't you worry about a thing. You're not going anywhere tomorrow."

"What now, Anthea?"

I said, "Dad's on his way up to join you, Mum. Just close your eyes. It's time to go to sleep. Say your prayers. Sweet dreams, Mum. God bless you, and I'll see you in the morning. I love you, Mum."

Mum responded to love. Love was the language she fully understood. She had freely given so much in her lifetime to me and my dad. She recognized the look and feel of unconditional love. "Oh, thank you," she said, tears of gratitude welling up in her eyes. "I love you too, darling!"

I stroked her hair until she closed her eyes. Peace came over her, and she would sleep all night. "Thank You, God, for the respite, for the blessing of sleep, for resting my mother's mind through the night," I prayed. "For Your divine mercy."

We would rise in the morning, feeling refreshed. Mum awakened to confusion. First thing in the morning appeared to be the most confusing time of day for her. It was the same scene every morning as I served Mum her medication followed by a cup of tea in bed. It was déjà vu. What happened the day before, even though we followed the same routine for years, was all forgotten. It was nonexistent for Mum. "What have I to do?" she'd ask. "Is it time to get up?"

I'd respond, "Not yet, Mum. Sit up, and enjoy your tea in bed. It's a lovely hot cup of tea, just the way you like it."

"But what have I to do, Anthea?" she insisted. And with those beseeching eyes piercing mine for reassurance, she'd ask, "I don't have to go anywhere today, do I?"

"No, Mum, you're staying at home. You're not going anywhere." I glanced over at her bedside table at a card with the words written in capital letters in my dad's handwriting that read, "NOT GOING ANYWHERE."

It was my dad's desperate attempt to answer Mum's question before she could ask it. It was his preventive care. He wanted to satisfy her questions and help his sanity. I guess he thought if she asked the question, seeing those words on the card would help her remember she wasn't going anywhere. He thought she could reason. Unfortunately, all reasoning was forgotten, replaced by irrationality. After eight years of dealing with dementia, I can understand how he would try everything to help Mum, his soul mate of seventy-one years. It must have been very trying to answer the same questions over and over. Dad had scattered cards like those around the house in various rooms, some drawn with his artistic flair or a comic character smiling back.

All were to no avail. Dementia prevailed. Mum's insistent questions would persist in her futile attempt to bring order to the confusion within her mind. It's not that any of this was new to me. It's just that it gripped me tighter than ever before. It hit me like a ton of bricks. We had known Mum was experiencing short-term memory issues eight years earlier. We saw the signs, and it was later confirmed. Thankfully, it progressed slowly but gradually worsened despite all attempts to halt it holistically and with prescription medication. The deterioration had escalated in the previous two years, especially in the last six months.

My dad had devoted his time to care for Mum. He would help her shop, cook, clean, dress, and deal with personal hygiene. It was a massive undertaking for a man of his age. I was and still am filled with admiration for my dad's love for Mum. His extreme sacrifice, his stoic determination to do his best for her, demonstrated his devotion. There came a time when he needed outside assistance to help with Mum's care, so in the latter years, caregivers provided personal support, house cleaners came in weekly, and gardeners mowed lawns and weeded the borders. Then came the necessity for a live-in caregiver to look after Mum and provide Dad with a much-needed break. The good news was that through it all they were able to live in their own home in familiar surroundings, and they had each other too.

The hospital scheduled Dad's hip surgery for October 24, and he asked me to be there to care for him and Mum during his operation and the first part of his recovery process. Thus, my husband and I took a three-week trip to England. At first, I must admit the idea seemed like a daunting task for Chuck and me to take on the responsibility of caring for two parents in their nineties, both disabled in different ways, both on walkers, and both very dependent on us. But Chuck and I went with hearts full of love, intending to bless my parents at their time of need. Ultimately, it was *we* who were blessed—blessed beyond words.

What a privilege it was to care for them. I am so grateful for the time invested in my parents and the opportunity to return the gift of love. Dad came through the surgery like a champ. At three weeks after the surgery at the grand age of ninety-three, he was walking with a stick and doing fantastic. His physical recuperation was astounding, and he was mentally as sharp as a tack. Mum was not so fortunate.

Dementia doesn't heal. It doesn't get any better, and it doesn't loosen its grip on the mind. It is a devastating disease. It torments the victim of the disease and the family members too. It's not as simple as forgetting what happened a few minutes before. It's not like forgetting where you put your keys. We all could and probably have chuckled about that at one time or another. No, it's more like *not knowing* what to do with those keys.

It is looking at your clothes and *not knowing* how to dress or to feel the urge to go to the bathroom and not knowing how to do it or to look at your plate of food and not understand how to use the utensils or how to eat food. It's like my mother standing by her bed, wanting to get into bed but not understanding how because she'd *forgotten* the process. And she also *knew* she didn't know how.

That's the worst. Dementia is heartbreaking and gut-wrenching for all concerned.

Thankfully, my mother continued to recognize me and call me by name. She knew my voice, and she understood who I was. Praise God for that. When I first learned Mum's diagnosis, I had decided that if the disease ever reached the point of her not knowing me, all would be well because *I would know her*! That is what mattered.

There is laughter in the dementia daze too. It is helpful to see the humor in certain things and to laugh about circumstances together. I want to share a few moments that made us laugh. As I said, Mum asked the same questions over and over. "Where have I to go? Are we going anywhere? What have I to do? Please tell me if I should be doing anything." She also made statements over and over that described the way she would feel. Here are a few of her favorites: "I'm a real goner today! I've gone with the wind, and I'm waiting for it to blow me back. I think I'm going around the bend. I'm away with the fairies. I wish I could wake up!"

That's what I call the dementia daze.

One day I asked her what it was like to be a real *goner*! She thought for a moment or two, rolled her eyes, and replied with a big smile, "It's really quite lovely. I haven't a care in the world." It was so like my mother to always look for the positive in all circumstances, even in the devastation of dementia.

Another time I asked her where the fairies were, and she replied, "They went home to tea."

"Why did they go home to tea, Mum?" I asked.

"They saw me coming!" she said with a cheeky smile. In the latter years, I spent a lot of time in her world!

On another occasion I had to run into the village to get some meat for dinner, so I left my dad and Chuck with Mum. "Where are you going, Anthea?" she asked.

"I'm going to the butcher's to fetch dinner!"

"He'll make a tasty meal," said Mum. She could still manage wittiness through it all, and she loved to make us laugh. Making us laugh brought Mum joy. It compensated for her inability to bring us happiness in the ways she was accustomed to doing in the past, such as waiting on us, cooking for us, and the numerous other ways she demonstrated her love.

We could be in the middle of a conversation or eating a meal, and Mum would start reciting poetry. I have no idea where she got this, but one of her favorites, which often appeared randomly, went like this: "It was a dark and stormy night. Two men sat on a rock. One said, 'Jump,' and he did. And he was never seen again." We tried to find out which of the men jumped or what happened to the one left behind, but Mum either didn't know or wanted to keep us guessing.

Such was her world. I would venture into it where I could. Toward the end I could rarely bring Mum into my world, but I could always choose to enter hers. And I did fairly often. She loved it, and so did I. Our togetherness made it a beautiful place. I spent much time in her world, just being with her, keeping her company. Living in the present moment was enough. She blessed me so much with her positive outlook and incredible moments of dry humor. We laughed, and we loved. I know that my presence made a difference. She most definitely impacted me significantly. One thing I know about dementia is that while words are forgotten, feelings remain. Mum always responded to laughter, physical touch, and expressions of love.

It's all about love. Love conquers all.

My mother always believed in the power of love. She instilled that belief in me. She modeled it for me, and I embrace it. I feel it. I hope she felt my love for her, and I pray that she glimpsed the face of God shining through me and that she felt God's touch through my hand on hers. I pray He reached her in a way that brought her lasting peace and instilled in her a sense of the clarity awaiting her when the time would come for Him to call her home.

I had to believe that. I know God is good.

> The LORD make his face shine upon
> thee, and be gracious unto thee:
> The LORD lift up his countenance upon
> thee, and give thee peace.
> —Numbers 6:25–26 (KJV)

It Was a Dark and Stormy Night

In her last eighteen months, my mother's dementia worsened noticeably. I guess it was to be expected—the natural progression of an insidious, incurable disease. If you're like me, you will remain ever hopeful, and you might even look for a small sign of improvement, knowing all the while in your heart of hearts, you won't find it. It's not there. There's no denying Mum's dementia advanced significantly, so we had to embrace it for what it was, and we made the best of a challenging and heartbreaking reality.

Humor helped. Not that dementia is funny, but having the ability to laugh and to find the lighter side of things in life (no matter how hard you must try or how deep you must dig) does help ease the pain, the sadness, and the frustration that accompanies this affliction of the mind.

When I was with Mum, I found myself intentionally looking for those moments. I would search for a few seconds of shared happiness and an opportunity to laugh with her. I looked for any amusing little gesture or a glimpse of her wit, which occasionally would sneak into the light through the darkness of confusion, and it triggered smiles that lit up our faces. It could so quickly escalate into raucous laughter! Trust me. It helped!

I want to share this with you. It's about that curious story Mum would recite, a strange little story that puzzled me for months. I often wondered where it originated and why Mum recited it over and over and over again. She always had an aura of mystery hovering around when she narrated it. The tone of voice and the facial expressions intensified to match the mood she was creating. It was kind of like her very own whodunit! "It was a dark and stormy night. Two men sat on a rock. One said, 'Jump,' and he did. He was never seen again."

We would press her for the ending but to no avail. Who jumped? Who was the man never seen again? What happened to him, and what became of the one left behind? It remained a total mystery. One time she got close to my face, looked me in the eye, and told the story in the eeriest tone of voice. Then she got a mischievous look and asked if I wanted to know the ending. I was so excited that I blurted out, "Of course! Do tell!"

She smiled secretively and whispered, "I don't know!"

As I said earlier, not knowing how she came by this was frustrating. Was it something she knew as a child? Was it something she learned from school? Did she fabricate it? It had a familiar ring to it, but it was nothing I could pinpoint. So I did some investigating on the internet, and it appears Mum didn't dream it or fabricate it. It was a *funny* endless story or poem that people would make up as they went along. They would also add amusing variations.

I found insight on booksie.com and in Wikipedia. It seems that the opening phrase "It was a dark and stormy night" was very popular at one time because of English novelist Edward Bulwer-Lytton in the opening sentence of his 1830 novel *Paul Clifford*. The story began that way. Some considered it to be the worst opening sentence in literary history! So the "dark and stormy night" game was made up in a way to ridicule the author and his book.

I believe that my mother was reciting something old and familiar to her, or it was a game she played in the past that provided her with a great deal of fun. Can you see me smiling as I write this? It would be so like my mother to do something humorous and whimsical like this. How could I have missed that it was her way of being playful, making light of a sobering condition? I vowed to play the game next time I was with her.

Fortunately, there was a next time, so I played along and added a version of my own, and then we tried to keep it going. Sustaining humor and frivolity during the ravages of dementia is a saving grace. I thank God for endowing His children with the gift of fun, laughter, and merriment in the face of adversity.

A merry heart maketh a cheerful countenance:
but by sorrow of the heart the spirit is broken.
—Proverbs 15:13 (KJV)

The Rambling Mind

"What have I to do? Where have I to go?"

These are simple questions from a sound mind. We ask ourselves these inside our heads as we go about daily life, planning our day, directing our activities. In contrast, these same queries from a confused mind are complex and disturbing to hear. At least they were to me. These two little questions haunted me for a long time. They still do to some extent. It's not easy to shut out their echoes inside my head.

If you read the previous stories in this chapter, you may have a feel for the intensity of these repetitive questions from my beautiful mother persistently asking the same two questions a hundred times a day. Sometimes these were so softly spoken that they were barely audible, a mere whisper. At other times they were sorrowful or blurted out loudly in frustration. And then sometimes they were even angry and demanding. But they always had a pleading undertone accompanied by an equally beseeching look in her eyes, piercing at times and continuously searching my face for an answer with her expressive ice-blue eyes.

It was not the words alone and what they suggested or revealed. It was the tone in which she asked, the ever-changing emotion attached to her questioning plea that touched me profoundly and lingered with me long after I was home in Texas with the vast Atlantic Ocean dividing us.

I so missed my mother on those visits. She was there, but she was not there.

Even when I was with her, I missed that part of her that had wandered off into oblivion. I longed for our mother-daughter talks. I yearned for her quick wit and her humor to surface. I knew it was still there in some ways, and we occasionally caught a fleeting glimpse of drollery, but it mostly just vanished into the bottomless pit of dementia that had stolen her memories and rational thoughts.

Missing her was one thing! What was harder to tolerate was the anguish that flooded over me knowing *she* missed *me* when I had to leave for home. She was incapable of expressing it rationally. Texas seemed far removed from her level of understanding. I could tell she felt the loss of my company even before I left, not by her words but by the look in her eyes, her heightened emotion, and increased agitation. She *always* knew when it was time for me to go home. She sensed it with a powerful intuition that had remained intact.

It took all I had in me and all the strength God gave me to hold myself together as we said our goodbyes and sadly bid farewell to her and my devoted dad. I know Mum experienced intense emotions. She felt a severe sense of loss when I had to leave. Though unable to express it, the emptiness was there. It was extremely distressing to her. I guess that's what disturbed me the most. She was not able to identify or express it, but she felt it profoundly, at least at that moment.

Did the sense of loss she felt at our parting linger with her, even after I was out of sight? I don't know. I hope it didn't. I pray she quickly forgot the sadness of parting. I understand how she struggled to make sense of all that happened amidst the fog of confusion swirling around her mind. I cannot even begin to imagine what transpired inside her head—being unable to string two thoughts together; having no real memories to connect people, places, and events; knowing who I was yet not grasping that I live in Texas. She didn't understand why I wasn't always *there* with her. I think she had regressed and was living back in the day when I was there with her as a child or teenager and the three of us were a family unit.

I often wondered what Mum thought as she stared out the window. Did she even have thoughts? Was it blank inside her head? Did she see pictures in her mind's eye? I believe she did because I heard her describe the fairies, pretty little things that would fly around and carry her away to where they live. "I'm away with the fairies," as she put it. I wonder if Mum's fairies were God's angels. I like to think they were. It gives me comfort … and hope.

Mum's dementia began to progress rapidly. I saw it. I felt her confusion and lack of understanding of what was happening to her, and yet in so many ways, she revealed that she was aware that all was not well. She clearly understood her incapability of caring for herself, not knowing what happened only two seconds before or what to do or where to go at any given moment.

"What have I to do? Where have I to go? Oh, please don't leave me, Anthea. I won't know how to get home!" she'd say.

I think it was good that Mum slept a lot during the day and all night toward the end. With sleep came a sense of peace, and the bewilderment quietened, at least for a while. I'm grateful for that to this day. My soul rests in that knowledge.

A pastor friend reassured me that God would be conversing with Mum in dreams and communicating with her during sleep. In quiet moments He would whisper to her in a language she could understand. And she would transmit messages back to Him. It was comforting to believe that God knew my mother's mind before she thought or spoke. God did not need her words. The thought of Mum having real conversations with God in a language they both understood was heartwarming! When His timing was right and He had fully prepared her, I knew He would take her home to be with Him. Peace would reign in her mind, and her physical body would be healthy and whole again. I believe that. Thank You, God!

I was so grateful for my dad's depth of love for my mother. Mum expressed her appreciation often by saying, "Dad takes good care of me." That he did. He showed indescribable love and devotion to and for the love of his life. It's what kept Dad going forward. His passion for art and other activities were reluctantly set aside, surpassed by a relentless desire and determination to be at Mum's side until the very end. To her last breath. That was unmatched love in action—agape love.

In that chapter of life, I was never closer to God. I trusted Him, and I entrusted my mother into His care. I placed all my hope in Him. When worldly circumstances weakened me and overwhelming emotions threatened to consume me, I leaned heavily on His strength. I accepted the offer of His yoke. It was indeed easy. With the burden lifted, I could rest. Peace replaced agitation and worry. I could go on. I could face another day with joy in my heart. One hour at a time, one day at a time, I cast my cares on Him. I trusted Him implicitly.

"Lord God, I give it all to You. You've got this!" I would pray.

And of course, He did have it. Even so, I never stopped struggling with a full range of roller-coaster feelings, especially during Mum's last days, when she neither ate nor drank anything for ten days. During that time I learned more about the end of life than I ever cared to know. It was traumatic yet beautiful. I hit mountain highs and valley lows several times a day, sometimes in the same hour. Hard as it was to experience, I would not have missed being there at her side. The time came when I knew I had to go to her. There was no stopping me. The Holy Spirit left no doubts in my heart or mind that her time was at hand and that she needed me. When you're in tune with the Spirit and open to His bidding, you know when He summons you.

The remainder of the accounts in this chapter concerning Mum's final days and transition to the other side are from my journal, which I wrote in real time during the exact moments. I wrote many of the words as I sat quietly by her bedside. I was in a state of just being, and I felt a heightened sense of every emotion. The language is sometimes written in the present tense because I wrote in real time, as I experienced each moment. I considered rewriting all of it in the past tense since it was more than four years ago, but I have chosen to leave it as originally written.

Thank you in advance for walking this path with me. Thank you for understanding how sacred and sorrowful as well as how wonderful death is. How meaningful the transition can be from this life to the next! When God is present, unbridled joy bursts through the sorrow.

> May the God of hope fill you with all joy and peace
> as you trust in him, so that you may overflow
> with hope by the power of the Holy Spirit.
> —Romans 15:13 (NIV)

God Pours Out His Favor

I must confess that the last few days have been among the saddest yet most joy-filled times I've ever experienced—sad because my beautiful mother is fading away from life as we know it on this earth and I am heartbroken. I feel joy because her spirit is about to take flight and she will transition into the most glorious state of eternal life with her Lord and Savior, where her body will be whole again and there will be no dementia.

It was Sunday yesterday, a beautiful sunny day, and if that wasn't enough to raise our spirits, God favored us in a delightful way that makes my heart sing with joy and gratitude, a beacon of light in a sorrowful time.

Dad had expressed a desire for a roast chicken dinner, so I strolled up to the local grocery store to buy one. Mum was resting peacefully, so I felt I could confidently leave her in the capable and compassionate hands of the live-in caregiver and my dad.

Halfway up Bridge Street, I heard them ringing.

I heard the beautiful bells. The sound of church bells pealed out joyfully, summoning the faithful, the weary, the broken, and the thankful. I changed course. I followed the sounds and heeded the beckoning call of the bells drawing me ever closer as the chimes rang louder and louder. My heart beat faster. I quickened my pace. The pit of my anxious stomach alerted me that I must hurry to God's house and flood my soul with the beautiful music coming from the bell tower of St. Mary's church.

Very quickly my walking turned to a slow jog. I was running for fear the bell ringing would stop before I caught sight of the church, so I started filming a video clip so I could at least capture the audio. That was when God favored me with my heart's desire. I was suddenly standing at the front door, gazing longingly at the arched entrance while the bells rang melodiously, revitalizing my soul. For a few seconds, the music from the bell tower surrounded me, and then there was silence. The service would commence. Had I not heeded the Spirit's bidding to pick up the pace, I would have been too late to capture this meaningful and special moment to record the bells and the sense of peace that accompanied their ring.

My mother loves church bells. She always enjoys being in church, and she loves her maker. I am filled with gratitude at God blessing us so meaningfully at a distressing chapter in my family's life. When I got home, I played the video for Mum so she could hear the call of the bells and see the church. It brought a big smile to her face and joy to my heart.

Thank You, dear Lord, for Your faithfulness, and for Your special favor on our family. It's so like You to give Your children the desires of their hearts.

> Call to Me, and I will answer you, and show you
> great and mighty things, which you do not know.
> —Jeremiah 33:3 (NASB)

Swans by the River at Sundown

Yesterday was a particularly distressing day. Mum's peaceful state changed rapidly to one of agitation and anxiousness. She was wide awake, her pale blue eyes darting back and forth in an almost childlike way, asking questions in rapid succession and in a frantic, obsessive manner, rubbing her eyes and clutching at her face. She was clearly in a very disturbed state.

We tried everything we knew to calm her down and lull her back into serenity, stroking her forehead, playing music, softly reassuring her that all would be well, professing our love for her, and reassuring her that soon she would be happy and whole forever. We reminded her we would all be united again in eternity.

My dad even hummed the tune he used to sing for Mum during the war. It was their secret melody, alerting her that he was back from flying a mission. He would whistle it as he darted by the door where she carried out her duties as a WWII Wren. Alas, nothing would calm her agitation. I think there's nothing worse than seeing a loved one suffer and feeling helpless to assist. I must confess those three hours challenged me in a way I've only experienced once before a long time ago.

I felt hope fade as my faith faltered. Fear and doubt began to creep in. How much longer would my sweet mother have to suffer? My thoughts were running rampant now. I was searching for answers as my spiritual strength slipped away. I called the nurse to come to the house to administer a sedative. It seemed to help very slightly but only temporarily. I called the reverend from the local church, and he came right away to visit with Mum. His gentle touch on her forehead and hand along with a reassuring blessing and prayer settled Mum a little and certainly calmed me.

I hated to leave her side, but by eight thirty-five in the evening, I felt emotionally and physically spent. I needed to regain strength for what we would face today. I declined generous offers for a ride to the B and B. I welcomed the solitude of the fifteen-minute evening walk alongside the green pastures in the setting sun. I coveted that time alone to decompress, to restore my battered soul, and to pray for serenity for my mother.

My faith floundered, and my senses reeled from the trauma of the afternoon. *How much longer must Mum suffer?* I wondered. *Why must she linger so? My God, where are You in all this? Why are You not taking her home to rest?* I was frustrated and saddened, and my faith was beginning to fray. And there was my dad in emotional pain, watching the love of his life wasting away yet still clinging to life. I hated to see my dad so stressed and suffering in his helplessness. I was exasperated to the point of wailing! *She's ready to go. What are You waiting for, Lord?*

The questions came tumbling out. They were rhetorical questions because I knew the answer full well. It would be in *God's* timing, not mine, not my dad's, not anyone's! *You, Lord, and you alone have the power to call her home.*

It was a beautiful, balmy summer evening to stroll and soak up the spectacular scene. The sun was sinking behind the wooded copse radiating its beams upward and painting the sky shades of yellow and pink. As I neared the bridge at the River Stour, I came upon a beautiful scene. The still waters by the bridge were reflecting the dappled sunset-lit clouds amongst the lily pads. Circular ripples slowly pooled from the center outward in multiple rings, ever widening as they danced across the river water. I stood there for a moment to admire the scene and breathe in the beauty of God's artistry when a movement on the riverbank caught my attention.

I was captivated by the picture.

There in the reed were two beautiful white swans with their cygnets, making their way toward me. I cannot remember seeing swans there before and never a family, although I'm sure they lived there year-round. They'd just gone unnoticed by me in past visits. What a treat it was. I felt my spirits rise, and I snapped a photo and a short video. I lingered and enjoyed the swans for about ten minutes, watching the family interaction.

It was dusk now, and the sun had disappeared below the horizon, so I walked back to my lodging. I didn't think much more about the swans until a couple of hours later as I was sending the pictures to our family back home, answering their supportive WhatsApp communications as they attempted to boost my low spirits with their love and encouragement.

Then suddenly, it came to me! I remembered hearing somewhere that swans signified serenity, purity, faith, and transformation.

Could this be a sign from God? God speaks to us in many ways and often in simple ways, using signs and symbols we can comprehend. It would be so like Him to deliver a comforting message through one of His magnificent creations. A family of swans could have been sent to assure me of serenity, faith, peace, and transformation.

When I arrived to visit Mum at seven thirty this morning, I found her serene and peaceful. My faith restored, I await God's time for her transition to heaven.

Okay, God. Thy will be done.

> Do not be anxious about anything, but in everything,
> by prayer and petition, with thanksgiving, present
> your requests to God. And the peace of God,
> which transcends all understanding, will guard
> your hearts and your minds in Christ Jesus.
> —Philippians 4:6–7 (ESV)

Gentle Rain from Heaven

I so love the rain. I *feel* the rain. Of course, sunshine on my shoulders makes me happy too, but there's something about the rain that penetrates my spirit. It inspires me to pour out words of soulful expression. Today I awakened to the pitter-patter of raindrops gently tapping at my bedroom window in the bed-and-breakfast. It was music to my ears and food for my soul.

I will especially enjoy my walk along to Mum's bedside today. The river, its surrounding green pastures, and the stately trees along the route are adorned in shimmering, flowing teardrops from above. There is a quiet beauty found in nature when heaven weeps. It comforts me to know that God understands our sadness and uses heaven's tears to reassure us of His love and understanding of the human soul. I welcome the soft raindrops kissing my face as I walk over to sit with Mum on this grey, rainy day, which very well could be her last one here with us. I'm mesmerized by the falling rain splashing on my face, mingling with my salty tears of joy and sadness.

Oh, God how great Thou art. You know the desires of my heart before I speak.

I am so happy that Chuck, the love of my life, the north on my compass, will soon be here by my side. I am beyond grateful for the overwhelming support and love pouring from family and friends. It means the world to me. I want to share something beautiful about the tears today. They are different from the hot, salty tears of sorrow from last night. Today as the tears roll down my cheeks, they comingle with the raindrops, and a powerful sense of peace slowly sweeps through my body. I am suddenly aware that the new tears are of a different origin. They are fresher, not as salty. These tears are tears of love and joy, and they are overshadowing the sorrowful ones.

Articulating this emotional experience is impossible. Sometimes words fall short as the stronger emotions supersede the power of a word. I accept it as a gift from a living, loving Father calming the storm in His child.

Yesterday Mum was partially awake for a few hours. Dad and I sat by her bedside, taking turns holding her hand. She uttered no words. None were needed. Our hearts have expressed our love for one another a million times over the years. Mum knows she is loved. Dad and I know she loves us. Words of endearment spoken over years of immeasurable expressions reassured me.

Love understands touch as clearly as any spoken word.

As I sat and marveled at the love between Mum and Dad that lasted for more than seventy years together, Mum gently pulled her hand out from under Dad's and very slowly raised both arms upward as she turned from Dad toward the direction that compelled her. Something had captured her full attention. Her lips barely moved as if to whisper and mouth a few words. Her countenance relaxed. She looked so beautifully at peace.

Mum was staring in childlike innocence. Her facial expression resembled that of an infant's. Imagine a baby lying on her back with little arms stretched upward, hands and fingers in continuous expressive motion, her eyes gazing heavenward, enthralled in sheer wonderment at her discovery. A sensation of love and peace surrounded me. I almost forgot to breathe. I was transfixed in the intensity of the moment. The look of love and wonder in my mother's eyes and on her face was nothing short of great joy. Whether she saw members of her family who had passed or a glimpse of heaven or angels, I don't know. I do know that whatever held her so spellbound was spiritually awe-inspiring and amazing. It spilled into my space, *and* it flooded over me, into me, and through me, penetrating my soul. This experience was a life-changing moment that will forever impact me. I'll never forget the emotion that permeated my being as the peace that was transposed on my mother's face also encompassed me. It was a pure delight, and I translated it as assurance from God.

Because of it, I can embrace whatever the day brings.

In the wee hours of the next morning, Mum passed peacefully in her sleep with Dad at her side. Only a couple of hours previously, unable to contain his anguish, my dad implored God to intervene in a gesture of submission.

"Take her, or heal her," he pleaded.

The suffering ended. The wait was over. Mum was in the arms of God.

And this is what he promised us—eternal life.
—1 John 2:25 (NIV)

Surreal Sojourn

My dearest Mum,

I've been thinking of you today as I always do. How could I not? You are in my heart forever.

Today I'm especially immersed in you. We're planning a grand celebration of your life. We've chosen one of your favorite dresses, the one with the bright purple and pink splashes of flowers, the one that is so you! Your earthly body will look beautiful, a perfect extension of your sweet spirit, which is alive and well in heaven but lives on here with us.

We've ordered a beautiful spray of flowers to adorn your temporary resting place, flowers of many shades, hues, and fragrances that you will love. The flowers are the same colors as your dress, and they will be majestic, charming, and graceful just like you.

Your celebration of life will hopefully capture the essence of your free spirit, your generosity, your unconditional love, your passion for living life each day to the fullest, and your eternal optimism, which never falters, not even in the daze of dementia.

This sojourn in your journey is so surreal. It seems so betwixt and between! While your earthly body is at peace in the chapel of rest, I envision you frolicking in heaven with your loved ones, your mum and dad, and all the siblings gone before you. I like to think of you running through the purple braes of heather in the Scottish Highlands, your body whole and young again, your familiar joyful laughter echoing through the glens. Your hair is streaming in the wind, your arms outstretched to the sky, so perfectly reflected in the beautiful lochs you love so much. I'm sure you're enjoying every moment of your long-awaited, newfound freedom. Take flight, sweet spirit!

Mum, I want you to know that Dad, all our family, and I are faring well, and while we're sad and we miss you desperately, we hear your voice loud and clear urging us to live each day to the fullest until we meet again. We're trying!

We are confident you are surrounded by love divine, all loves excelling. Everything is as it should be. All is well!

God bless you, Mum. I love you, and I am so happy for you.

—Anthea OOXX

Verily, verily, I say unto you, He that heareth
my word, and believeth on him that sent me,
hath everlasting life, and shall not come into
condemnation; but is passed from death unto life."
—John 5:24 (KJV)

Roses of Devotion

My dearest Dad,

Unknown to you, I captured a vision of you in the garden amongst the fragrant, delicate colors of the roses.

My heart melted to see how you gazed so thoughtfully up at the beautiful blood-red ones, those that were Mum's favorites, and I immediately knew you were thinking of her. Forgive me for intruding on your moment. I'm happy you weren't aware I was standing back quietly out of view. It was a special moment, a private one.

I want to thank you, Dad, for your devotion to Mum, especially during the last few years when her dementia grew heart-wrenchingly worse. I can't imagine the pain you endured to see your bright, beautiful bride slowly deteriorate mentally and later physically before your very eyes. And it must have been hard for you, who have always been so in control of your life and in command of all situations, to find yourself completely helpless to prevent the progression, unable to fix the circumstances or make it all better for Mum.

But Dad, you did. You did make it better. You made it better in all ways humanly possible under the circumstances, and you sacrificed so much of yourself for Mum. While you would claim you only did what you had to, that's not true at all. Your devotion to Mum kept you going when many others, including me, would have despaired and given up.

You embraced the challenge of caring for Mum as diligently as any other project you've ever tackled in your long life. I so love you and respect your courage, your endurance, your perseverance to keep Mum at home at all costs, and your dogged determination to keep yourself alive to "see Mum safely out," as you so often stated.

You can rest assured, Dad, that no one could have done more or loved more. Your devotion to Mum has shone brighter and stronger than the fragrant beauty of the roses of love you grew and tended for Mum's pleasure and enjoyment. The love you openly expressed in her last few days was so evident to her and me, and with a little smile here and a hand squeeze when weak whispers failed her, Mum confirmed her love and gratitude to you. She knew you were there with her to the very end. She clung courageously to life, waiting for you, hopeful you'd acknowledge God, giving her assurance that she'd see you again. God heard your voice, and He granted your fervent prayer. He released her spirit.

Mum will be with you every day in your heart. You'll see her when you least expect it in the little joys and beauty of life. You'll feel her love embracing you from above. Whenever you feel sad or low, look to the beauty of the roses. On the coldest day in winter, think of them in full bloom as they are today, and Mum will come to warm your heart, raise your spirits, and confirm the lasting love you've shared for seventy-one years. She will let you know she's waiting for you just around the corner, not far away. You are soul mates forever. All is well!

God bless you and keep you, Dad. I love you.

—Anthea OOXX

> The King will reply, "Truly I tell you, whatever you did for one of the least of these brothers and sisters of mine, you did for me."
> —Matthew 25:40 (NIV)

CHAPTER 8
Farewell Is Not Goodbye

Fare thee well. Good wishes until we meet again.

Parting Is Not Sweet Sorrow

I awaken with a jolt, my eyes adjusting to the darkness, trying to focus on the shapes and shadows in an unfamiliar room, one that doesn't smell like home. Reality hits hard as consciousness kicks in. I feel my heart sink as I recall what's about to happen. My hand wanders slowly and quietly across the bedsheet, looking for a sign of warmth from my husband's body heat, not wanting to disturb him, searching for his hand, reassurance that he's still here, tangible proof that he hasn't left yet. I feel his warm, familiar touch as his hand grasps mine in response to my reach. He's still here. I'll steal every second I can get and do anything I can to keep him here a little longer. I had sensed he wasn't sleeping. He'd been as restless as I had. I catch a glimpse of the clock radio in the motel room. It's one o'clock in the morning. I'm thankful and sad—thankful we have three more hours together but sorry that at four in the morning, the alarm will signal it's time to … *Stop, Anthea*, I say to myself. *Don't think about it.*

Chuck moves toward me and enfolds me in his arms, holding me so tight I can hardly breathe. At this point I don't care. I think, *Just don't ever let go of me. Please, please don't go. Don't leave us.* Our hearts are beating fast. Hot, silent tears are falling on each other, his dropping on my hair, mine running down his chest. I resist the urge to sob out loud. It'll only make the pain worse. And

I mustn't wake up the kids. Oh, Lord, I can't imagine how painful this is for Chuck. I know his heart is breaking. He feels as though he's abandoning his family. How will he live through this alone? At least I have our three beautiful children. Oh, how both our hearts ache for our little kids. They must be so confused, not fully understanding this emotional upheaval. How will we help them through this? Will we all come out of this unscathed, stronger, and closer, or will the time and distance cause us to drift apart? Thirteen months is a long time. A lot can happen.

There is no need for words at this point. It's all been said over and over in the weeks leading up to this dreaded moment. We've made the professions of love and stated all the hows—how we'll get through the forced separation with the letters we'll write *every* day, the photos we'll share, the cassette tapes we'll mail back and forth; how we'll communicate with *no* access to phones; how desperately we'll miss one another; how I'll keep him up to date with the little fun moments with each of the children; who their friends are; how they're doing in school; how they're dealing with life without their dad; and how I'll convey to the kids how much their dad loves them and hates being away from them. But duty calls, and this is part of the mission of military life. We had discussed how Chuck would keep busy on the base when he's not on duty and how he'll work extra jobs to make the time go faster and how he'll join us for R & R in Australia, where we'll be with my parents for the thirteen months he's in Thailand on a remote tour of duty.

It's two in the morning. Parting is a living nightmare. We only have two more hours together. Part of me wishes it was five in the morning. At least the torture of the parting moment would be over. I thought, *Let's get on with this now. Say the gut-wrenching goodbyes, go our separate ways, and the sooner the year's done, the sooner we are back to life again as a family. I project myself into the future. Life will go on, not as before, but it will go on. And we will make it better than ever.*

I glance around the room. Chandra is in the small cot close by, and the boys are in the other double bed. Our beautiful little kids are finally sleeping soundly, exhausted from the late night. It hasn't been easy getting them settled in the motel after the trauma of leaving most of their belongings behind, saying goodbye to the empty house, which is to be rented by a new family in our absence. David and Stephen are seven and eight years old and know what's coming down, even though they can't possibly grasp the extent of it. Chandra is only two years old and just senses that something is different and not quite right. Anxiety is in the air. My heart goes out to these adored children, and I wonder if I have it in me to be Mom and substitute Dad for more than a year without the physical presence and support of my strong hero husband, my rock, my soul mate, my all. Even with my parents to offer their loving support, it seems like a daunting task ahead. How will I manage? And our beautiful car, which is only ten months old, will be sold to a new owner. Ugh! There's nothing sweet about the sadness of a remote military deployment.

My eyes settle on the small shadowy stack of suitcases leaning against the wall. Beautiful little hands lovingly packed those cases with guidance from me as I checked the contents, making sure there were enough clothes and a few of their treasured possessions to lend comfort and familiarity amongst the imminent upheaval.

Lord, please give me Your strength and bear this burden for me, for us. The tears flow freely again as fear and uncertainty wrestles with the faint little bit of faith and hope I've managed to muster from deep within. It comes in painful waves like the ebb and flow of the tide. I feel fear and sadness followed by whispers of hope that this won't last forever and then the faith that God will see us through and give us the strength we need. I snuggle even closer to the love of my life as if to try to infuse myself into his very being, breathing deeper as if to inhale every part of his being into my soul. It is going to have to last me thirteen months. Well, almost. We would at least get a short R & R break over Christmas. I'll think about *that*. I only have nine months to endure … then another four.

Then it happens. The obnoxious clock radio sounds off, signaling the dreaded hour—the time of departure. Shakespeare, you were wrong. Parting is unbearable. It is *not* sweet sorrow. Parting is gut-wrenching misery. The anticipation of the separation and the actual moment of farewell is painful. The emotions linger long afterward, prolonging the torment.

There's a knock on the door. One of Chuck's crew stands in the doorway, looking forlorn and dejected. He has volunteered to provide the transport. It's no fun for him to take Chuck off to the base for his flight to Thailand. He's been like family during our time together at Castle AFB. He played with our kids, ate at our table many times, and even spent Christmas with us. He knows how hard this is for us all. He forces a smile at the pitiful family huddled together in the middle of the room, clinging to one another, wishing it weren't so but knowing it has to be. There is no avoiding the inevitable. It is all part and parcel of being in the military. Duty calls one and all—the ones in military service and all the family members.

One last hug, one more tear-stained kiss, one last longing glance, and my love is gone. The door closes softly on a chapter of our life. We stand frozen in place. We are alone—just the kids and me. They're sad and bewildered, and I'm trying to quiet my pounding heart and pull it together, to be their strength. It's now time for us to get ready. Next it will be our turn to leave for the long flight to Australia. The year lies before us, an unknown entity.

We all survived the thirteen months. It wasn't easy. It was extremely challenging, but we made it back together as a family. We were intact. I thank God for that and feel so very blessed that my man came home and that we all readjusted to each other again. Yes, there is a transition time after a year of being apart, but we realized the experience caused us to grow stronger and closer than ever. My heart goes out to those whose loved ones didn't make it back—not just during the Vietnam conflict but from any war. War is brutal.

I know that some may be thinking a year apart is not such a big deal, and I agree that it's not like the finality of losing a loved one to death, not even close. I wanted to share our moments of parting because it's not just our story. It's the story that needs telling for the thousands of military families who go through this every day. Being away from one's family is brutal for the one who is leaving home and for the family left behind. It's not just the parting either. It's the entire year of a life that is changed forever, and our military families endure this every day with dignity. If you've never served your country, been part of a military family, or experienced the hardship of a long, forced, isolated separation, I pray this post touches your heart and brings a deeper understanding to the realities of military life.

I dedicate this story to all our courageous men and women in the armed forces and their supportive, loving families who endure hardship and separation nobly, all in support of the mission and in the name of honor and duty to country. We owe a debt of gratitude.

May God bless them one and all.

If I rise on the wings of the dawn, if I settle on
the far side of the sea, even there your hand will
guide me, your right hand will hold me fast.
—Psalm 139:9–10 (NIV)

Mysterious Moans and Groans

It was the first night back in my father's house, and I was exhausted after a long flight across the Atlantic to visit my dad. After a four-day stay for observation of what the doctor diagnosed as heart failure, he was released from the hospital the morning of my arrival. He had expressed his determination to beat me home at all costs. I could tell that his mind was set on that when we spoke on the phone the day before I flew to England. He would move mountains and stop at nothing to get himself discharged from the hospital only three hours before I arrived. It was so like him to insist *he* be the one to open the front door and greet me rather than have me welcome *him* back into his own home. My dad was the master of his domain until the very last.

When I arrived at the front door, true to form and despite his weakened condition, there he stood, pale and frail, leaning on his walker, a little short of breath but full of courage. He mustered a warm smile, a hug, and a kiss and greeted me with a sigh of relief. "I'm so glad you're here!" he said.

Nothing would have stopped me. Not even a team of wild horses could have prevented me from being there because I was compelled to get there as fast as possible to be with Dad. I sensed with every ounce of my being that this was his time to transition from this life to the next. Of course, I didn't know the details of what lay ahead. I didn't know the timing. I only knew in my heart of hearts that this was *his* time. He was ready to go, and he sensed it too. Sometimes you know that you know, and this was one of those times.

My intuition had spoken loud and clear, so much so that I had packed the dress I would wear to Dad's celebration of life. I had experienced the same conviction when my mother had died two and a half years earlier, so although the journey with her was different, the reasons prompting me to be at Dad's side were the same. I was there to pour out my love. I was there to administer whatever care and comfort would be required of me, particularly emotional and spiritual support since the caregivers were already in place for most of the physical tasks. Most importantly, I was there to bid farewell to my beloved dad in word and deed, and given the opportunity through God's grace, I would assure him this would not be our final farewell, but a temporary parting of the ways until we meet again.

By the time I crawled into bed after forcing myself to stay awake until ten at night and having tucked Dad safely in for the night, I fell instantly into a deep sleep. I fully expected to get a restful eight hours of quality sleep so that I'd be ready to face whatever tomorrow would bring, and I figured that after four sleepless nights in the hospital, Dad would sleep soundly through the night. It was not meant to be.

Maybe the story I'm about to relate contains something you've witnessed yourself with a loved one, or perhaps you've heard a friend share a similar experience; however, I had never encountered anything quite like this, which was not surprising really. Having been present only for the passing of my parents, I am no expert on all that can occur during the end-of-life phase. Whether what happened is natural or weird, to be expected or a rarity, I don't know. I can only write what I witnessed during the final six days of Dad's life and leave the rest to your interpretation. Let's say I am compelled to share this account to enlighten you and others who read my book. I had no handbook on the dying process. To all accounts, each passing is unique, so perhaps none of us can ever be fully prepared, but at least when—and if—your turn comes to face the death of a loved one, you'll be forewarned that mysterious things can happen. Expect the unexpected.

The following story is my encounter with the mysterious moans and groans: I awoke from the depths of sleep with a jolt at what would have been roughly two in the morning. I must confess that the sounds I heard had startled me and sent chills up my spine. As I lay there frozen in place, listening intently and frantically trying to focus my attention on where the sounds originated, they ceased, and my mind chalked the experience up to disorientation from being overly tired and jet-lagged. I convinced myself that I had either been dreaming or that I had imagined the sounds. I felt my body relax in compliance with that comforting thought and focused my attention on the sleep I craved. It was not meant to be.

It was only a few more minutes before the intermittent eerie wailing broke the silence of the wee hours yet again! But this time I was not dreaming, and my imagination was not working overtime. I was wide awake. Presence of mind kicked in, and I realized the sounds were wafting across the hall from my dad's bedroom.

Startled and with my heart racing, I leapt out of bed and ran to his side, fully expecting to see him writhing in pain. I made that assumption because of the severity of the loud moans and groans, sounds of someone in distress. The small lamp in the hallway, which stayed on at night to help Dad see his way to the bathroom, shone just enough diffused light on his bed to reveal he was stirring from a deep sleep. He had a befuddled expression on his face. Evidently, I had just woken *him* with my panicked inquiry.

"Dad, are you all right?" I said, and before he could answer I breathlessly continued, "Are you in any pain?"

With bleary eyes and slurred words, he responded, "No, no pain. I'm fine. Why? Was I talking in my sleep?"

"No, Dad, you were moaning and groaning loudly. Were you dreaming?"

He replied "No!" I scrutinized him for signs of pain or angst, but there were none. He seemed fine aside from being genuinely puzzled at the depth of my concern. I asked him again if he hurt anywhere, and he reassured me that he did not. We said good night once more, and I urged him to call out for me if he needed anything.

Uttering sounds in his sleep was not *that* unusual for Dad. As far back as I can remember, he would snore, mutter incoherent words, grunt, or even make soft whimpering noises while sleeping. The family was used to a few such sounds, but these mysterious moans and groans were like nothing I'd ever heard. Anyhow, satisfied that Dad was all right, quiet, calm, and as reasonable as can be for a ninety-seven-year-old just home from the hospital, I retired to my room, filled with relief and the expectation of much-needed sleep. It wasn't meant to be.

No sooner was I drifting off than the bone-chilling wailing started up again. The periodic moans and groans were lilting and somewhat melodious, while the volume fluctuated up and down; however, there was no specific rhythm. For goodness sake,

I thought my dad *must* be in severe pain to be crying out in such a strange way. I took it very seriously because I knew my dad well. He had always been a proud man with a great deal of courage. He would not have voluntarily shouted out in such a manner, so I concluded he had denied admitting he had severe pain so as not to alarm and disturb me. I rushed toward his room. As soon as I got to the doorway, the sounds stopped. I stood there fearful but fascinated, awaiting more of the cries, but he continued to rest calmly on his side, sleeping soundly—no writhing in pain, just deep, peaceful breaths. I quietly approached him thinking he might be pretending, but that was not the case. So I tiptoed back to my room, avoiding the creaky floorboards in the hall, and then I closed the bedroom door. This time I slept until morning.

Downstairs, I found my father making a cup of tea in the kitchen. He smiled affectionately and offered one to me, which I happily accepted. I asked how he was feeling, and he replied, "Ancient, worn, and weary, but at ninety-seven, what can you expect?" I told him he was quite amazing. I'd always admired my dad, so it was the truth. He was doing as well as could be expected and made no reference to the night's disturbances, so I chose to say nothing about his moans and groans. Better to let go of the incident, which I did. The truth is that I brushed it off as one of those inexplicable occurrences that I had probably exaggerated in my mind during the middle of the night in my exhausted state. I find everything seems worse in the darkness of night and much less intense in the light of day. Have you noticed that?

We proceeded through the day with the routine activities of daily living with lots and lots of father-daughter conversations, memories, and instructions from him as to where this was and where I could find that. He indicated it was important that I should know these things before "I leave the planet," as he phrased it. We enjoyed breaks for morning coffee, lunch, afternoon tea, and dinner, with Dad taking several short naps in his reclining chair. At one point I left him napping while I went to make the afternoon tea. That's when it happened again.

While I was in the kitchen, I heard the mysterious moans and groans coming from the living room. My heart sank and beat faster if it's possible to experience the two simultaneously. These indescribable utterings flooded me with mixed emotions of sadness, compassion, and bewilderment. I quietly peeked around the living room door almost afraid of what I might find. Would Dad be writhing in pain on the floor and having a heart attack? I had been praying for him continually, and I prayed another quick prayer. Thankfully, I found my dad just where I'd left him, sitting in his reclining chair, but this time he was awake, staring at one of his paintings on the wall. He was wailing and moaning loudly.

I'm ashamed to say it crossed my mind he was doing this to get my attention, but that was a ridiculous thought since he already had my undivided attention twenty-four seven. I even group-texted my family about this mystery and insinuated that my dad had discovered a new trick to capture my attention and keep me on my toes. Shame on me. I didn't understand.

Once I tried to record Dad's utterances secretly, but as soon as I touched the app on my iPhone, the cries stopped. Silence reigned. Whenever Dad was moaning and groaning while wide awake, I can assure you he was not suffering pain, and I am equally convinced that he was not even aware of the moans at all. Whenever I mentioned them, he appeared baffled. Each time he profusely refuted any knowledge of uttering anything himself. Dad emphatically denied hearing *any* sounds.

These moans and groans continued on and off night and day until the day before Dad passed peacefully in his sleep. For six days I had listened to the distressing utterances. And yes, they did haunt me for a long time. These mournful lamentations puzzled me and shook me to the very core, yet it never crossed my mind as to the power source of these soulful pleas. I don't know why I didn't, but I should have known. I was familiar with Romans 8:26–27. In retrospect, my failure at the time to connect the groaning with this scripture remains as mysterious to me as the elusive sounds Dad had denied uttering.

It was several weeks after my father's death that I had a revelation and a deeper understanding of the mysterious moans and groans. Sometimes it takes a while to connect the dots! I had been overwhelmed for nine weeks dealing with the aftermath of his death, clearing and selling a house filled with almost a century of stuff, so my mind was preoccupied with settling his estate. On the other hand, perhaps we're not meant to have answers when we think we should. Life is often *not* about our timing. However, despite all these rationalizations, I was still haunted by the moans and groans three months later.

Maybe patience is called a virtue with good reason. After returning home one quiet morning during my daily devotional time, a thought came to me to read the scripture about groans in Romans 8:26–27. Why it took me so long to read it is beyond me, but while reading it, an understanding flooded over me. It was as clear to me as the sunlight streaming onto the page in my Bible. The moans and groans originated from the Holy Spirit, interceding on Dad's behalf. I am convinced. "In the same way, the Spirit helps us in our weakness. We do not know what we ought to pray for, but the Spirit himself intercedes for us through wordless groans. And he who searches our hearts knows the mind of the Spirit because the Spirit intercedes for God's people in accordance with the will of God" (Romans 8:26–27 NIV).

My father, although raised to believe in God, was conflicted about his faith for many years. His WWII experience combined with the discovery at age twenty-six that he was adopted devastated him … *and* his faith. Dad had searched for concrete answers to his questions about God, wanting to believe but also demanding absolute proof. For many years he had initiated intense discussions with family and close friends about faith and God as he struggled within himself. Happily, in the last few months of his life, I realized the scales were tipping toward him believing, and the previous three evenings as we bid each other good night, he was the first to say, "God bless you!" Hallelujah! It was music to the ears of a loving daughter who knew she was about to lose her dad. The closer to his time of passing, the more peace I sensed within him. It was beautiful to see.

There is no doubt in my mind that God is relentless in pursuit of our souls as told in the parable of the lost sheep. He'll leave the ninety-nine to save one lost soul.

Perhaps God had good reason to blind me to the source of the moans and groans during the time Dad was dying. It is not for me to question the mysterious ways and timing of the Almighty. His ways are beyond our human understanding. It is for us to believe in Him, to have faith in Him, to love Him with all our heart and soul, and to know that it is by amazing grace alone He saves us and that His Spirit within us can intercede on our behalf. God's love is overwhelming and never-ending in pursuit of each of us.

I am so grateful for the understanding I now have in regards the moans and groans. What a blessing in my life. I am thankful for the opportunity to share this story with you. Everything happens for a reason and in God's timing. I hope that this story will help to serve as the reassurance of God's love for you.

Suppose one of you has a hundred sheep and loses one of them. Doesn't he leave the ninety-nine in the open country and go after the lost sheep until he finds it? And when he finds it, he joyfully puts it on his shoulders and goes home.

—Luke 15:4–6 (NIV)

Farewell Is Not Final

I could sense the emotion rising to a crescendo. It revealed the undeniable intensity of pain as tears welled up in my eyes and threatened to roll down my cheeks. I rarely cry these days unless it's tears of joy or a reaction to something that truly touches my heart and soul. This particular day I was overwhelmed with sadness, but even in that brutal, gut-wrenching moment, I knew it was imperative to find the strength to pull myself together, to control my heightened emotions. My mind desperately tried to process the reality of what I'd just heard. My throat choked with unspoken words struggling to express the depth of my feelings, all of them surfacing from deep down in the pit of my stomach, that familiar place where I sense profound spiritual encounters and the center of my being where intuition resides. I have a spiritual intuition that informs me, guides me, and never fails me when I listen. You might say it's where my soul lives. Some say it's my gut instinct. I believe it's where the Spirit resides.

Somehow I reined in my burgeoning emotions and miraculously regained a semblance of outward composure and inner peace as I silently prayed for strength for myself and my dad. At that moment I had to consider him first and foremost. There would be plenty of time for me to cry later, but that day I had to be fully present and calm for his sake.

He smiled weakly and patted my hand lovingly, fully understanding the implications and unselfishly attempting to comfort me by saying, "I don't want you to be upset. I've lived a great life. We've had lots of good times together, haven't we?" Yes, my dad was right. We did indeed have many years of shared happy times, but even though anticipated, expected, and inevitable, parting from loved ones is never easy, and I've learned no two farewells are ever the same.

In this case the doctor had just left after delivering the news to us that my dad was in heart and kidney failure and that this was his body's natural way to shut down. It was part of the dying process. He couldn't predict how long it would take, but it was imminent. It's not as though I didn't know what was happening. I had sensed it weeks before. Just twelve days earlier when we talked on the phone for his ninety-seventh birthday, intuition told me this was the beginning of his journey to be with the heavenly Father. My dad had expressed he was ready to leave this planet on numerous occasions.

Four days after that phone call on his birthday, I was on a flight to England to be with my dad for whatever time he had left. I am so very thankful for the six days we shared leading up to this moment of truth. Those few days were not the easiest, but they were glorious in so many ways. I feel grateful for many quality moments. I cherish those memories with my dad.

During those final days, the telltale signs of heart failure were all there—the badly swollen right leg, the difficulty emptying his bladder, his diminished appetite, and undeniable physical decline. What I was unprepared for and what impacted me most were the haunting moans and groans that he frequently uttered out loud, especially at night but often during the day—the ones I described in the previous story.

So here we were—Dad and me, face-to-face with the harsh reality that his amazing life would soon end. The time was near for us to bid farewell but *not goodbye*. We would meet again. "It's Mum all over again, isn't it?" he asked, meaning that on the doctor's orders, he was about to retire upstairs to his bed, never to come down again just like my mother, who lay dying for ten days before God took her home.

"I'm afraid so, Dad!" I whispered as an unexpected strength and calm flooded over me, dried my tears, and granted a voice to my words. It was helpful to observe my dad was relieved that his time was at hand. He became excited at the prospect of leaving the planet in hopes of joining my mother for eternity.

While raised as a Christian and churchgoer, my dad had fallen away and doubted his faith some years after WWII. He struggled with his faith for the rest of his life, occasionally in complete denial of God, sometimes desperately searching, often argumentative on the existence of God, and always demanding concrete proof. As my mother lay dying two and a half years earlier, Dad's anguish at her years of dementia and the final days of her suffering turned into anger at God. He lashed out at me and demanded that I refrain from speaking of God as I attempted to offer spiritual comfort. Imagine my delight as I tucked Dad into bed the last few nights before the unavoidable moment of reckoning when he wished me good night and said, "God bless you." Praise God!

The surprising strength and sense of peace that came over me encouraged me, and as we sat there after the doctor's news, I offered Dad the following words: "Dad, heaven is a beautiful place, and you'll see Mum again."

No objection came this time. He smiled and said, "I hope so."

I chose to bring some humor into the severity of the moment. "Well, Dad, I believe that with all my heart, and I want you to remember this moment and my words. At some point when you're in heaven with Mum, you'll turn to her and say, 'That daughter of ours, she's not as dumb as she looks!'" He laughed, and so did I.

With help from one of his faithful caregivers, we headed up to his bedroom, Dad on his stair-lift chariot one last time. A nurse arrived with a welcome little tablet to calm him. A few friends visited that evening. One played his favorite music by Andre Rieu on her cell phone, to which he hummed and conducted the music with the biggest smile lighting up his face. He was mentally present and in good spirits. I saw years of hardship and doubt fade from his countenance. What a joy to behold. My dad must have been very anxious to be with his beloved wife of seventy-one years because early the next morning he passed peacefully in his sleep.

Thank You, dear God, for Your mercy, faithfulness, grace, unconditional love, and salvation through Jesus Christ, our Lord. I'm so grateful for the promise of life after death that makes a farewell *not final* but "until we meet again."

> He will wipe away every tear from their eyes,
> and death shall be no more, neither shall there
> be mourning, nor crying, nor pain anymore,
> for the former things have passed away.
> —Revelation 21:4 (ESV)

Back to the Future

When life hits hard, you do what you must to navigate through a maze of challenges and emotions you've never experienced before, to survive unscathed, and to emerge stronger and wiser than before hopefully.

There's no going back, or so the saying goes, but I beg to differ. I've found there are times in life when you must back up to free the space required to move on from where you're stuck. I've found myself in that very place a few times in life, where I desperately needed space to maneuver upward and onward. It wasn't physical space like a parking spot but rather that coveted, precious white space in the mind and soul where peace and understanding abide.

A clogged mind has no clarity. A traffic jam of thoughts in the brain results in confusion and paralysis.

I've given a lot of thought to the past since January 2018. Memories of all kinds dominated my waking moments, crowding out the present at times and forestalling any plans for the future. I'm not saying that was bad or that it was time wasted. I'm merely stating reality. I eventually reached a crossroads of time. The past and future collided with a resounding realization in one word—now!

It's time to leave the trappings of the past and go back to the future.

I was once again ready to plunge into the life and times of now.

I've always been a forward thinker and very future driven while striving to live in the present. But in the aftermath of my dad's passing, I was unwillingly swept back into the past, and despite the desire and effort to extract myself, circumstances held me captive. I was powerless to escape the magnetic pull of all that belonged in yesteryear.

How could I free myself? The physical reminders engulfed me like a shroud. All the artifacts, photographs, books, letters, the old familiar inanimate objects, scents from long ago, and of course, a bazillion happy and sad memories all sucked me into the vortex of the past. I fought the allure for a while. Then I finally succumbed. I decided to let go and see where this sojourn back to bygone days would lead.

I let go and let God. There's peace in surrender. It's not human weakness. It's the strength of faith in His plan. Sometimes patiently going with the flow will get you where you are destined to be faster than fighting it.

This last visit to my parents' house, when I would empty the few remaining contents in readiness for its new owners, was freeing in a way I never anticipated. I thought it would be hard, that I'd be sad to leave. I even half expected my jangled emotions to lay strewn all over the map in full view, but to my surprise and delight, a few days before leaving England, I found myself eager to move into the future and to enter a new and exciting chapter in the book of life.

I don't know what precisely changed. Perhaps it had more to do with timing, or maybe I had reached a level of acceptance. Perhaps something magically released me from the hold of the past. Some things are meant to remain a mystery, so it's not for me to always question how or why. It happened, and I was grateful for it.

What matters most is I'm thankful for today and for my life. I look back to the past with love and gratitude for my parents, and I will carry forward loving memories of beautiful bygone days. My spirit sings with joyful hope and expectancy. It's time to bid farewell to the past until we meet again!

But now it's time to go back to the future.

> For I know the plans I have for you," declares the
> LORD, "plans to prosper you and not to harm
> you, plans to give you hope and a future"
> —Jeremiah 29:11 (NIV)

CHAPTER 9
Be Still, My Soul

Be still. Let silence stir your soul.

Time for a Selfie Check

Today we all know what a selfie is. The images are all over social media. These are pictures of yourself taken by you! Most of us have snapped at least one selfie photograph, even if we never posted it. But what about a selfie check? How many of us regularly set aside time to be introspective and to perform an *evaluation* of ourselves? Get in touch with who you are and what you truly stand for. Then verify that your actions (what you think, say, and do) are congruent with who you are.

I sent a coaching email to our business team today encouraging each of them to seriously think about what they want to achieve through their business, starting with the end goal in mind. As a mentor and business coach, I believe self-discovery is a great teacher, more valuable than someone providing a pat answer. It is much more memorable and meaningful when one has aha moments through answers given to him or herself via thought-provoking questions. The ability to ask oneself hard and provocative questions is a tool that equips a person to get on the right track, stay on it, or get back on it! It's one of those survival tools that can arm us for life. I challenged my team to ask themselves and honestly answer the following two questions:

- Will you achieve the outcome you desire by what you are doing today?
- Are your desires, actions, and motives completely aligned with *who* you are?

As I wrote the email, I was reminded of an experience long ago during my schooling as a late teenager. It was what I call one of those life-changing moments. One I hope I'll never forget because what I learned by completing the exercise equipped me with an invaluable tool and a simple process that has guided me through many difficulties. It has served me faithfully during a million decision-making twists and turns of life, helped me stay the course, and at times been instrumental in helping me change direction or change something about me.

I was asked to write a story with the end in mind.

I'm not talking about envisioning an ending to just any story. I'm talking about *the end* as in the end of my life as I know it on this earth. I'm talking about my death! You're kidding me! I was to write about my funeral or memorial service and allow my imagination to run amuck. The story would be for my eyes only since the purpose of this exercise in self-discovery was to shape my future.

The story guidelines suggested that I include detailed descriptions of the music, flowers, church service, cremation, and/or memorial service. In other words, I was to paint a vivid picture of what this celebration of life would resemble. Would the organ be playing, or would there be a piano, a soloist, or a choir? What would be the fragrance from the flowers, or would the incense overpower all other scents? Would I have a simple casket or an elaborate one? Or would I be cremated and my ashes scattered so that no physical trace of me but a memory at the service remained? Where would this event take place? A complete description of all surroundings was encouraged.

It was a formidable assignment for a teenager, but it forced me to go deep in thought and ask many hypothetical questions. The accompanying instructions directed me to place my emphasis on *who* would attend and most importantly, *what* attendees would say about me! It was most intimidating. This assignment was to be a selfie check that would stretch my imagination beyond barriers and send me into recesses of my mind that I'd never thought to explore. I thought about who I was and what I wished to be remembered for at the end of my time here on earth. I was to be accountable for who I would become and what I would do with my life.

In other words, how would I spend the *dash* between my birth and death dates?

What would people say about me? How would I want to be remembered? Hmmm. That got me thinking. Would I want to be known as poor little Anthea who had so much potential but led a life of mediocrity and died unfulfilled, never living up to her potential? What about a woman who accumulated wealth, kept it all to herself, and died happy in her greed? Or would I want to be remembered by many as having given freely of my time, talents, and treasure? Would I want to be known as a woman of conviction and integrity who stood up for what she believed? Would I be thought of as a woman who loved people and touched countless lives in meaningful ways? I did lots of soul-searching before I completed the essay.

Once I decided what memory I'd want to be associated with me, the rest was more straightforward. I had more questions! If I continued in the same direction, will it lead to the remembrance I'd want? What would the words on my gravestone say? What must I change about *me* to become the individual I aspired to be? Who is the person I most want to be, and how would I make my life count in the time I had before me? What if I died tomorrow?

There were lots of questions that demanded answers.

It was a worthwhile exercise in self-examination and self-discovery. I highly recommend everyone complete this evaluation. It does wonders for reawakening one's life purpose and furnishes a clear understanding of who we are and all we can become.

I encourage you to set aside the selfies for a few days. Take time to evaluate your state of self. Think of it as an investment in the rest of your life.

> Who in the world am I? Ah, that's the great puzzle.
> —Alice, Lewis Carroll's *Alice in Wonderland*

This New Addiction
Crushes the Soul

Unless you're lucky enough to live in a bubble or if you haven't noticed, you should realize the world has gone mad. Right is wrong, and wrong is right. Common sense has flown the coop. Nonsense is touted as good sense, and good sense is labeled as nonsense and inconsequential. So too, common courtesy and good manners are rare and scarce. People are blowing themselves and others into oblivion as war is waged by enemies that have changed the rules, weapons, and strategy of battle. But I'm not referring to this kind of insanity. There's a different kind of crazy in the present times. There's a *new* addiction on the block! Dictionary.com defines addiction as "the state of being enslaved to a habit or practice or to something that is psychologically or physically habit-forming, as narcotics, to such an extent that its cessation causes severe trauma."

This *new* dependence is a three-in-one obsession—*doing everything, knowing everything, and fear of missing out.* This latest addiction is rampant in modern society. I call it a syndrome because the addiction appears to reside more in the *relationship* with the object than in the object itself. It is as severe and destructive as chemical substances, food, sex, shopping or any other dependency. It affects its host physically, emotionally, and mentally just as the others do. This new kid on the block has the ability to crush souls.

How do I know? I've felt it pull on me from time to time. I've sensed it trying to steal my soul. I hear others express their frustration and helplessness to release themselves from its grasp. I see its insidious negative effect on many people around me—people I love, business associates, peers, and others with whom I'm barely acquainted. So what is this syndrome? How does it feel?

You're busy, busy, busy. You're doing, doing, doing. You're going, going, going, and you have obsessive FOMO. It's all about living in the never-ending rat race of endless activity, unable to be still, overwhelmed by life. If this describes *you*, you're in the rattrap. You're that little mouse held captive in the never-ending spinning wheel. You might even be afraid to get off because as much as you hate where you are, it's familiar. You may laugh but pause to look around. Everyone is busy *doing*, and they're self-absorbed too. Many complain about having no time but don't seem able to change course. Time is the most valuable, finite, and sought-after commodity in today's world. It is the great equalizer. We are all given the same number of hours in a day. How we choose to spend those hours makes the difference. Most people say they yearn for more free time, yet they keep squeezing in one more activity, piling on one more commitment, saying yes to one more request, and spending precious time on one more want!

The thirst for constant activity then evolves. It expands its reach from one rush or high to another. It migrates from the rush of busyness to the adrenaline rush, which then brings the mental rush into action. This a brutal, unhealthy combination. These habitual surges will drive a person to the point of helplessness, not knowing when or how to stop. These people may not be *able* to stop, even though they may want to and they know it's best for them. Addiction is an inability to stop doing or using something. If you suspect this addiction has you trapped, it's time to face it and make some changes.

There's another factor to consider. As if you need one more! You seize a chance to catch your breath, jump off the merry-go-round, sit down for five seconds, and you discover you're still trapped! It's a trap in a different form. Now you're engulfed by *guilt.* You feel guilty for being still. You become restless, agitated, and anxious. Your mind is so stimulated it never shuts off, and relentless in its persistence, it demands you *do* something! The *addiction* compels you to cut short your restfulness and find something to do because endless activity is the new norm for you. In constant motion you crave the sensation of being *on,* and you need to be doing something *all* the time!

Now here's the second part of the addiction—the need to *know* everything. Your obligation to be a curious busybody is insatiable. The desire to know what's happening around the world or in the life of your friends, your family, your business associates, and even your competitors is overpowering. Thanks to modern technology, you have immediate access to information on any subject any time you want it. The access lives in the palm of your hand, on your nightstand, in your car, in the middle of the night, and even in the bathroom! I pray this isn't you. Yes, it's a main line to this part of the addiction. It's your smartphone.

The seductive attraction of receiving information is on tap twenty-four seven. Just log on, and you're lost for hours gazing at places, people, and things, wandering from one browser to another, scanning post after post on social media, learning about this friend and that one, and becoming what I call a "like addict."

Like. Like. Like. Like. Like. Like. Like. But why?

Then you add FOMO (the fear of missing out) to the mix. Congratulations! You've just created a disaster waiting to happen. The fear of loss is powerful. It can capture you in a stranglehold! What if you miss that one article that guarantees the secret to your success? What if a friend shares a post that reveals the one magical tip that can make a difference in your performance, your productivity, your personal growth, or your family life?

So you pile more information into your already overloaded mind as you subscribe to more and more. You like more sites and more pages. You sign up for more email information, blogs, success tips, health articles, and videos. You join more social media platforms! You invite an excessive amount of stuff into your life that consumes *more* of your precious time.

Why one *more* activity? Why one more yes? Is it essential when you know you're falling further and further behind in life because of the added distractions? Are you learning more and accomplishing less? In attempting to do it all and know it all along with the compulsion to not miss out on anything, you sacrifice productivity, success, and valuable time. Now you're frustrated and feel a sense of worthlessness and hopelessness. You begin to wonder about the meaning of life. You feel it in your soul.

There's one more thing! It's not just what *you* invite into your world now! There are so many portals of direct access to you that people are inserting themselves into your mind, your private space, each vying voraciously for your time and attention in their attempt to consume a fair share of *you*! They want to steal a piece of *you*! It's an out-and-out attack on *you*!

This assault is real. It's complete and utter madness. Constant stimulation bombards you from within and without, from both invited and uninvited sources. The noise is deafening! The uncontrolled input from every direction. Plus the self-imposed list of activities is hammering your very being. It's controlling your output, and worse still, it's seizing your joy and squeezing the life out of you.

Now your soul is crushed.

Suddenly, one day you realize you have no time to be. There's no escaping to a place of peace and serenity—not even a moment to think. The world of today loudly proclaims you have morphed from a human being into a human doing. The applause and rewards are more significant for what you *do* than for *who* you are. If you're like many people today, you are so consumed with *doing* life, and you have nearly forgotten who you are. Let me remind you. You are a human *being*. You may feel something is missing. You sense life is not the way it's supposed to be, yet what can you change? You're in perpetual motion. You realize that your life is not your own and you've done it to yourself or allowed it to happen *to* you. And if I'm not mistaken, it's the same thing.

If any of this resonates with you, it's time to stop obsessing! It's time to disconnect, time to pull back and pull the plug on saying "yes" to everything that crosses your path in a desperate attempt to have it all. And for what? Is it for fear of missing out? If so, it's time to kiss FOMO goodbye and crush the addiction before it consumes *you*.

Your soul needs you, and *you* need your soul.

I can imagine what you're thinking! You think you *must* stay connected, that it's noble to keep busy, that you *can* handle it all and have it all. It's in pursuit of happiness, so it must be good for you. Know that it is the addiction talking. While all of those things may be okay in moderation and within reason, when you have no time to yourself to be and your life is out of control, it's time to stop.

May I switch on the parental tone for just a few seconds? You *do* know what to do, and *no*, you *don't* need all that stuff. It's distracting and mostly unfulfilling. You *can* shut it off! And I'll bet you *do connect* to real live people around you and by phone, people who love and care about you and want to be with you. The greatest gift to your loved ones is your presence in the *now*.

What you need more than anything in the present is to gain back control of *yourself* and your life. Pay attention to *your* world, not *the* world. Shut out all the demands of outsiders and the distractions that compete for your attention but have no significant meaning in or to your life. Limit who and what you allow into your world, including what enters through all portals of media. Control your time on social networks. Unsubscribe to all the mindless apps, sites, and any redundant email subscriptions not in line with your life's purpose. They're choking you to death! It's time to clean house and find white space in your email in-box! Hey, listen! If I can do it, so can you!

Focus your attention on what matters most in your life, namely *your* life! Did you hear that? It's *your* life! You don't need to know what's happening with everyone else at any given minute of the day. Reject those thieves that are stealing your valuable time and attention. The clock of life is ticking away. Assess *your* part in the craziness. Rein yourself in with self-control. Do you have to commit to *everything*? Are you addicted to busyness and don't know how to escape?

What you need most in your life *is your soul.*

Give some time to your soul. God created you in His image. You are a spirit with a body. You were born to be creative. To develop and fulfill your purpose, you must be able to think. To think clearly, you need an uncluttered mind that can focus, which requires time to be still. Serenity is music to your soul. In moments like these, you hear the still small voice of God speaking to you, flooding you with love. He restores your peace. Your soul sings!

In the crazy world of busyness and continual distraction, do you schedule time-outs to reflect on life, to search your mind for answers, to revitalize? Dear friends, stop the constant doing for a moment and take a time-out to be still.

Invest time in yourself and your peace of mind. Nourish your soul. Take a few minutes each day to catch your breath, to quiet your rambling mind, to ponder the meaning of life, to marvel at nature, to acknowledge the miracle of you, to open your heart to possibilities, to feel gratitude, to sense the will of God, and to hear Him whispering His love and calling your name.

He yearns for your presence.

My prayer is for you to know the joy, peace, and restoration of *being.*

> For what will it profit a man if he gains the
> whole world and forfeits his soul?
> Or what shall a man give in return for his soul?
> —Matthew 16:26 (ESV)

The Quality of Mercy

There was a tense silence between the two. I silently gritted my teeth. It wasn't my place to speak. Nor did I have any right to interject with my two cents.

I was a mere bystander in the park when I recently encountered an interesting discussion between a father and daughter that grabbed my attention and drew me to the conversation. In a way I found it a fascinating study in human behavior, and simultaneously, I was flooded with a sense of melancholy.

Evidently, the father was a man with a kind heart toward animals. He had a higher regard for some than others, and it seemed his depth of compassion varied in intensity according to whichever species happened to be the underdog at the time, his sympathies always favoring the defenseless creature. Let me expound.

Empathy went to the poor worm gobbled up by the hungry bird or to the small bird attacked by a more aggressive or greedier bird. At one point the father indignantly chased off an intruding cat in defense of the little birds on the grass mound near their park bench. All the while, he was providing his daughter with his take on the food chain in nature. He repeatedly noted the cruelty in it all. He finished the lecture by asking the rhetorical question, "If there is a God and He created all of nature, how could He be a compassionate God when He permits such cruelty?"

The daughter didn't answer. She was contemplating her feet, which were shuffling nervously in the loose gravel by the bench. I wondered if she decided not to enter the conversation out of respect for her father or if she had a differing opinion. Perhaps she just chose to remain silent and savor the beauty of the surroundings.

I was highly tempted to come to the defense of God, whom I believe to be a loving Creator, but I refrained and kept my point of view private, as I am known to do when I am not invited to give my opinion.

Sometime later a new conversation sprung to life, one precipitated by something the daughter had done to displease her father. I listened more intently, fascinated, trying to make sense of what was rapidly evolving into a severe scolding. It appeared the daughter had twice broken the rules. I heard the father say, "Was that the only time? Were there other times?"

And she replied, "I only did it twice!"

I thought to myself, *Oh no! Double the trouble now!* The dialogue continued.

The daughter said, "I'm sorry, Dad."

The father said, "I told you not to do that."

The daughter said, "I'm sorry. It was a mistake. I didn't mean to upset you."

The father said, "But I've told you and told you. We talked about that very thing just yesterday."

The daughter said, "I'm really sorry, Dad. I guess I wasn't thinking!"

That's when the silence intensified, and I clenched my teeth tighter as if to will the father to graciously accept the apology. It didn't happen. Neither was there any apparent evidence that the transgression would be forgiven any time soon. Meanwhile, the young woman persisted, "What can I do to make it better, Dad?" *Surely, he will take a kinder tone now,* I thought.

I could hardly believe the response. "Nothing! There's nothing you can do," he said.

The daughter gave her father a third opportunity to show mercy. "Dad, I'm sorry. I feel terrible."

The father's terse response was, "So do I!" Wow! He held her feet to the fire to the very end. There was no reassurance. He didn't say, "It's okay. We all make mistakes." There was no further indication that a kindly response was imminent. My heart sank.

I wondered if he would ever forgive her. Would he tell her she was forgiven? Surely, he would. My heart went out to the daughter's inner child, and I wondered how a father who was so concerned and compassionate about the feelings of a worm could be so unmerciful toward his flesh and blood. I prayed he would forgive her. I knew she would accept lovingly.

This encounter reminded me of a paragraph from Shakespeare's *Merchant of Venice,* which so beautifully describes the meaning of mercy in this way. The paragraph reads,

The quality of mercy is not strain'd,

It droppeth as the gentle rain from heaven

Upon the place beneath. It is twice blest:

It blesseth him that gives and him that takes.

I thought about God, His amazing grace, and His capacity to forgive each of us. As I lifted my eyes away from the discord and gazed into the distant green hills, I whispered a prayer of thanks to the Lord for His infinite love and unrestrained mercy.

Be merciful, even as your Father is merciful.
—Luke 6:36 (NIV)

I Feel Rain

There's something about rain that stirs my soul and stimulates my senses to a heightened level of awareness. I've always been fascinated by the sights, sounds, and smells that accompany falling rain! When I venture out in it and taste the raindrops on my lips, my thirsty soul feels refreshed, and my spirit revived!

What I most love about the rain is that I *feel* it! When I see rain falling, I yearn to encounter it, to be *in* it! I covet an experience with it. Do you *feel* rain like that, or does it just leave you cold, grumpy, and wet? Do you savor gentle droplets pitter-pattering on your face? Do you welcome it, embrace it, or throw on your raincoat and rush outside to greet it? Do you crave the sensation from wind-driven, lashing rain hurling down on you so hard it stings your skin and awakens your senses?

I wonder if you're moved emotionally and spiritually by the rain and if you notice how it forms little droplets on your skin that attract another droplet, merging into a single sizeable drop. Then they collide with more raindrops until little rivulets of rainwater trickle down your face and roll off the end of your nose or run down your arm and drip off the tips of your fingers. Rain is beautiful when we see it from a new perspective and when we pay attention to how it touches us physically, emotionally, and spiritually.

In the life and times of now, few people have the time or inclination to jump off the busy racetrack and enjoy a shower of rain. Most people see it as an annoyance that interferes with their life and makes them wet and chilly. They view it through their windows from the inside where they're warm and dry, so they never intentionally encounter it in a new or different way. Don't be that gnarly one who complains. Be the exception. Next time it rains, run out to greet it, and play in it like a child. Yes, even as an adult! Your inner child will love your newfound playfulness. Let loose and enjoy yourself. Explore the way it moves your emotions and touches your soul.

As a child, did you fall over yourself to don your Wellington boots, raincoat, and sou'wester hat so that you could puddle-jump with your friends? Did you and your friends laugh and scream together as the gritty rainwater splashed over your boots and some inevitably trickled down your leg into the well of the boot?

I wonder if you have ever stood in a swiftly moving stream and felt the pull of the water flowing ever faster, ever stronger at your boots, flattening the rubber to your legs until you jumped onto the muddy grass banks, fearing you might lose footing and get carried away like the stick that disappeared downstream, tossed about like a toothpick? Was it thrilling? Did you throw your head back and let the raindrops pound your face? I'll bet you closed your eyes, opened your mouth wide, and stuck out your tongue to soak up the drops falling from the sky! Do you remember how freeing and invigorating that was? I do!

In childlike wonder I recall the simplest of things on wet days, such as dancing with the raindrops and launching a matchstick boat in a torrent of water flowing down the street gutters. I remember laughing hysterically when my umbrella blew inside out, exposing me to a flood of rainwater, flattening my hair to my head. I couldn't have cared less because I lost myself in the moment, and it was the coolest thing ever!

I have known lots of rainy moments. Of course, I grew up in England, where weather dominates the beginning of almost every conversation. Small talk often revolves around the topic of precipitation! Rain is a common occurrence there like every other day in one form or another. It could be the damp, mysterious, misty, tiny droplet variety, the bone-chilling drizzle kind, or the steady, soak-through-to-your-skin kind of rain!

Then there's the heavy-duty-lashing, side-driven rain propelled by high winds. The stormwater pounds on the roofs and gushes down from the gutters, saturating the ground, flooding the streets and gardens, and causing rivers to overflow their banks. If you get caught in that kind, you run for the shelter of a café, or a doorway or even seek cover under the canopy of a massive ancient tree. Any port in the storm will suffice until the worst is over. Rainfall can bring many unexpected and pleasurable moments.

My dad was not a fan of rain. He disliked the English weather so much that we moved to Africa in search of sunshine. Then later he and my mother moved to Australia for much the same reason, namely a warmer climate and sunnier sky. Dad kept a diary of the weather for years to prove how bad it was in England. He was quite the character! When it came time to go on holiday, the weather dictated when and if we traveled or not and what day and time we left. Since it rains so much, our travel plans were disrupted frequently, leaving this anxious little girl disappointed, sadly watching the raindrops roll off the panes of glass in the front windows, chanting, "Rain, rain, go away. Come again another day."

It wasn't that I disliked the rain. On the contrary, I loved it from a young age, but I was eager to go away on holiday to the seaside, and I knew my dad full well. The rain needed to stop before we could get on the road and head to the sea. Of course, I did not influence the rain, but I always hoped it would stop when I sang the song so we could start our holiday; however, it always seemed to take its sweet time before pausing and giving way to a dry spell just long enough for my dad to give the okay to leave. I would always pray for the rain to stop and the blue sky to appear, as that was the cue to pack up the car and go. The funny thing is that once on the road, if it started to rain, we didn't turn back and go home. We kept on driving!

Having heard that little tale, you'd think that I would dislike the rain, that I'd blame it for past disappointments or associate it with unpleasant feelings. But that's not so! I admit it's inconvenient at certain times, but I don't allow the rain to ruin or change my plans—with exceptions, of course—or affect my mood adversely. I try hard not to get mad at the weather, over which I have no control! But that's just me, and I know everyone's different.

I wonder about the rain's fluidity and how it's always different. It's sometimes gentle, drenching now and then, but continuously wet, fascinating in the way it falls, and ever inviting me into its embrace. It calls me to experience it, to lean into it, to go with the flow of it. I yearn to understand its nature. I'm so thankful for the beauty of the rain and its provision to us and our planet. I love that it refreshes my spirit and inspires me to explore my thirsty soul for deeper meaning, for a greater understanding of who I am and *whose* I am.

I feel the rain. I feel God.

Ask the LORD for rain in the springtime; it is
the Lord who sends the thunderstorms.
He gives showers of rain to all people,
and plants of the field to everyone.
—Zechariah 10:1 (NIV)

The Shape of Grief

Why now? Why today? The emotion is overwhelming.

I feel this internal emptiness, an inexplicable sadness, a deep yearning for someone I love, for someone whose essence encircles me, whose presence is near, but he is not here.

I miss my dad, and I find myself gripped by grief today.

How does one define grief? How does it look? What shape does it take? Can words possibly do justice to the depth of loss one feels at the death of a loved one? It's like trying to capture the shape of a wave. How can mere words depict the poignancy of its undulating swell as the ebb and flow of its liquid form transforms its appearance? A wave is ever changing! One cannot do justice to it with mere words. It's too elusive.

Grief is like the wave—deceptive, fluid, and indescribable. How can words validate the poignancy of grief, the deep, rolling waves of sadness and emptiness as well as the ebb and flow of sorrow? Anyone who has lost a loved one discovers sooner or later that grief hits home. Like it or not, each stage of mourning does present itself in the face of loss, and one must navigate the accompanying emotions.

Give sorrow words; the grief that does not speak
knits up the o-er wrought heart and bids it break.
—William Shakespeare, *Macbeth*

Having experienced grief in the past when my mother died, I
naively thought I had a handle on the process. After all, I know
what the stages of grief are, and I understand one must experience
the full range before arriving at acceptance and peace. Silly me!
Knowing the four phases in no way precludes the inevitability of
suffering through them.

I'm sharing this experience with you so that when grief hits—and,
I say *when* because it definitely will at some time in your life—
you will be aware that it comes in waves. Like the movement
of the ocean, there's an ebb and flow to sorrow, and it bears an
indefinable, unpredictable shape. You can't see grief. Tears are
only a by-product. You will feel it in every cell in your body, but
it's impossible to describe. And its depth and breadth are ever
changing. Sometimes a shallow wave of melancholy sweeps over
you fleetingly. At other times it's more like a massive undulating
swell of a wave that threatens to suck you under its tow and
drown you.

One moment you're okay, and then quite unexpectedly, something
you see, hear, or remember will trigger an overpowering, gut-
wrenching sense of loss and sadness. It seizes you. You may know
exactly what triggered this response, or it might blindside you.
You're suddenly (as I was today) engulfed in this powerful, illusive
surge of grief that holds you in its grip. And you wonder why at
this moment it happened.

I know all the right words of comfort, all the rationale to be happy
for the loved ones who have passed. They had great lives. They
are no longer suffering. I know all the reasons to feel joy instead of

loss. My dad was with Mum. They were together in a magnificent place. Again, knowing these things doesn't prevent the flood of emotion. Grief is more powerful than knowledge.

Of course, on some level it does help to use comforting self-talk as described previously, but there's no denying that it doesn't remove the emptiness or pain of the loss. It's perfectly okay to be happy for the ones who have passed, to feel the joy that they're in a better place with loved ones who passed ahead of them, but it's also okay to allow yourself to *feel* that overwhelming sense of lamentation. So go ahead and mourn your loved ones, and acknowledge the space inside that *they* so vibrantly filled when they were alive.

Be kind to yourself. Permit yourself to feel the entire range of emotions, and ride the undulating wave of grief. Remember the ebb and flow. What wells up also subsides.

So as suddenly as I was gripped by grief this morning, this evening I'm engulfed in a wondrous sense of hope and joy! I recall Dad's words to me on the day he died. I sense his reassuring hand on mine and the love in his eyes as he urged me, "Anthea, I don't want you to be upset!" I rejoice in the sense of excitement he felt as he prepared to meet his maker and reunite with my mum, the love of his life.

And almost immediately, I am engulfed in love, the strongest of all emotions. The power of love knows no boundaries; it transcends all other emotions. Love never fails. It conquers all!

He heals the brokenhearted and binds up their wounds.
—Psalm 147:3 (NIV)

Fleeing the Fiery Furnace

For more than an hour, the flames had flickered intermittently inside the chimney of the fiery furnace in the garden. Suddenly and quite unexpectedly, the blaze surged upward in a vigorous manner. A fiery rush blasted through the opening of the incinerator accompanied by a powerful whooshing sound, originating deep within the bowels of the bricks where the inferno was hottest. This draft of heat, as it built to a crescendo, created a strong current of air that belched through the top of the kiln. The four of us stood speechless, rooted in place. We gazed in utter disbelief as the intensity of the thrust forcefully spewed something skyward.

What in the world was that?

I'll never forget that day—the day Dad was to be cremated. It happened a few days after my father's celebration of life, later than we had expected because the local crematoriums were struggling to keep up with the demand. The unusually high number of deaths because of influenza was causing delays in cremations. It was on my mind when I awoke that morning, but I quickly dismissed the thought of my dad's earthly body remains entering a fiery furnace to be incinerated and reduced to ashes. As a family we had decided not to attend the cremation itself, choosing instead to say our farewells to him after the remembrance service in the church sanctuary, but I must confess the moment I opened my eyes, I knew what day it was and the significance of what was to take place.

In his final years, whenever we visited him, Dad would impress upon each of us the importance of taking our time to sort through all his belongings after he had departed. We were told not to rush. We might inadvertently destroy something of value or great importance if we hurried. He was adamant we should be patient and diligent. My husband, our three children, and I were instructed to look through each page of every single book, of which he had many. He also owned an entire wall of formidable shelves in his study, where he kept dozens of large binders filled with folders that were in turn packed with papers and envelopes, some dating back decades. There were letters received, copies of letters he sent, bills, invoices, notes on painting techniques, and pottery secrets, many treasured WWII documents and manuscripts bulging with records detailing many years of searching for his biological parents.

It was an overwhelming and intimidating assignment life dealt us. But true to our natures, we would keep our word and honor Dad's wishes. So the day after his celebration of life, the five of us took some collective deep breaths, rolled up our sleeves, and began to tackle the massive undertaking, one tiny step at a time. We scoured everything we touched with the scrutiny of eagle eyes, looking in front, behind, inside, and out of each item. We sorted into containers what would keep and what needed further sorting. We tossed that which was disposable into giant black trash bags.

After three days of sorting from the early morning hours until late at night, we had gathered an excessive amount of papers for disposal. The small shredder I'd sent Dad was begging for mercy, and we remembered that he never trusted it anyway. His choice of safe, secure disposal was to fire up the brick furnace in the back garden. He'd engineered and built this kiln with his own hands to burn to ashes any and all unwanted debris. Since it was a chilly but sunny February day, we decided to honor his memory and dispose of all the trash in his very efficient brick incinerator. He would for sure be so proud of us all. Many times Dad demonstrated which bricks to remove to initiate the most efficient burn. He instructed us in how to arrange the kindling to get a strong start and how to feed just the right amount of unwanted papers through the opening in the top to produce a roaring blaze that would dispose of it all quickly with little to no smoke.

So here we were—my husband, our two sons, and me. We surrounded the furnace, each feeding a few pages into the fire, glancing again at what we were about to destroy to double-check that it was nothing of significance. The fire was hot and roaring, literally consuming everything we threw into the blaze almost instantly. It was surreal and symbolic in a way. Here we were facing the fiery furnace my dad had built, while his remains were about to meet a similar fate at the crematorium.

I was thinking those very thoughts when it happened!

The powerful surge of air forced the flames to leap higher as the chimney belched a gust of wind and spewed something high into the air from within the fiery furnace.

What in the world?

The flying projectile descended directly into the outstretched hand of my astonished husband while our two sons and I looked on, speechless. We'd been burning hundreds of papers for almost thirty minutes, and nothing like that had occurred. Not a single thing had blown or flown out of the top! What in the world was it, and how in heaven's name did it survive this flaming inferno?

To all outward appearances, it looked like a rectangular piece of paper. It resembled a legal-size envelope folded over at one end. It wasn't anything remarkable at all. Looking closer, we marveled at its appearance. There was no smoke damage and no burnt edges, and it wasn't the least bit singed. How very strange, and it was indeed a singular incident. I'm so grateful to have had reliable witnesses to this odd occurrence who could testify that I wasn't crazy or weird or that the event wasn't a figment of my imagination.

I can assure you that none of us would ever knowingly have tossed *this* item into the furnace. It somehow must have been hidden from our eyes amongst other papers of no value. This one sheet was far too valuable a scrap of paper. To our family, this and similar bits of paper are considered treasures to be cherished— remnants of my dad, his talent, and his life work.

The paper projectile was a pencil sketch of a farm that he had drawn at the scene years ago. I soon recognized the drawing as the subject of one of Dad's paintings. What a blessing indeed. Thank You, Lord! It was like my dad had sent a message loud and clear that he was there watching over us, saying, "No, not this one!"

I felt a surge of warmth and deep emotion. I know my family experienced it too. Of all my father's earthly belongings, his beautiful paintings, of which he had many, were the most treasured. It would be so like him to use such an item to assure us he was there in spirit and that he had made the transition to the next life.

God works in such mysterious ways. Little miracles occur every day, but if we allow busyness to rule our lives, we can easily misinterpret the source of these little wonders or even miss them altogether. God often speaks to His children in simple ways. In meaningful ways that we can understand, if we are spiritually open to Him and accepting of His love and grace.

I encourage you to be open and observant. Let God in. Look for Him amid the life and times of now. He is full of special surprises, and He loves to delight His children. You never know when, where, or how He may appear with a blessing or a little miracle.

God moves in a mysterious way, His wonders to perform.
He plants his footsteps in the sea,
and rides upon the storm.
—William Cowper

Solitude—Where Silence Speaks

Solitude is a gift to be savored and cherished. The soul longs for quiet moments alone away from the pressures and demands of daily life. We human beings crave inner peace, relief from the never-ending noise of the present times. When we lose ourselves to solitude, we are not lost at all. There in the aloneness, we find our true selves. We are better able to think, to dream, to plan, and to recuperate from the all-consuming busyness. It's where we gain a perspective on life and relationships, and alone with our thoughts, we become comfortable with who we are and whose we are. In the silence of solitude, words of truth appear to lift the spirit and quench the thirsty soul.

In solitude, we're more in tune with our spiritual sides. We are more aware of our surroundings, and we develop a greater appreciation for the beauty of life and the meaning of our existence. Deep in thought with no external distractions, we can interpret more accurately our innermost thoughts and feelings. We gain clarity and a greater understanding of our place in the universe. When we shut out all the worldly noise, we obtain the strength of resolve, and inspiration meets us there. It's in the peace that we discover our sense of purpose. When we're still, the mind rests and gives space for gratitude to surface. Where gratitude resides, happiness thrives. We are content in knowing we have enough, and we are enough. We feel joy, and we are at peace.

> One can be instructed in society, one
> is inspired only in solitude.
> —Johann Wolfgang von Goethe

In today's world silence and serenity are almost nonexistent. We've chosen to crowd them out of our day. We've pushed them to the bottom of our to-do list and relegated them to the back burner of our nonstop lives. As a race, we humans have unscheduled precious quiet moments to reflect. We've replaced the space on our calendars with a plethora of activities, permitting no room for anything but work, chores, and other continuous comings and goings that are a higher priority to us. We've filled the spaces where solitude once lived, with a never-ending cycle of busyness! People always surround us, and we get next to zero time alone.

Nowadays most people don't know what solitude is or where it went, yet it is so critical for our well-being, including our sanity. Spending time by oneself and apart from others is renewing and revitalizing. Taking intentional time by oneself away from the madding crowds of people, the demands of work and family, the cell phone interruptions, the emails and texts, the social networks, the computers, and the TVs helps us discover that *being* is more valuable to us than *having and doing*.

We discover our true worth in the silence of solitude. Alone on a mountaintop, adrift on a vast expanse of water, or lost in the serene beauty of the woods is where we connect with God in all His glory. When we're quiet, we hear Him call our name. I've found that God doesn't usually shout over the noise. He speaks through the silence. He whispers His messages to us, and when we listen, we better understand His ways. In solitude we feel His deep love. We are one with God. He is in us, and we are in Him.

In quiet wonder we discover while we are most alone that we are *not* alone at all.

The place of solitude is a state of being for each of us to rediscover, protect, and visit often. I encourage *you* to find those spaces of time in your life to shut out the roaring static that stimulates you, sends your mind reeling into oblivion, and dulls your senses. Seek time and space to be alone, and while you're there, breathe in the peaceful silence. Look up to the sky, and feel the stress and strain evaporate from your physical being.

Rejoice in the peace, tranquility, and gratitude of the moment. Marvel at the beauty of nature and the miracle of the clouds. Soak up the warmth of sunrays or feel the joyful pitter-patter of gentle rain from the heavens. Release the burdens of life weighing you down. Be thankful. Count your blessings, and as you contemplate the gift of life, set your spirit free to soar on wings like eagles.

Listen for the still, small voice of God. Hear Him whisper your name in the silence of solitude. As His peace encompasses you, feel His unfailing love. Rejoice in the moment, and your soul will sing.

> That my soul may sing praise to You and not be silent.
> O LORD my God, I will give thanks to You forever.
> —Psalm 30:12 (NASB)

Epilogue

My Soul Sings
to You, Lord

So very often, Lord, You softly call my name,
In the early morning light or gentle drops of rain.
I see You in the clouds. I feel You in the breeze.
You beckon me to meet You, near the old oak trees.

Many times I heard Your voice yet didn't heed the call.
Demands of work and daily life required I give my all.
So I hurried past You, Lord, and didn't stop to pray.
I'll visit You tomorrow. I'll make time another day.

I had such great intentions to carry out Your will.
But goals and plans took over, and I was never still.
It took trials and tribulations to knock me to my knees.
Humbled, I implored You to hear my prayers and pleas.

As I reflect upon my life, I must confess it's true
In choosing many things to do, I gave less time to You.
I thank You, Lord, for loving me, for always being there,
For choosing me, for blessing me and showing me You care.

You're calling me again, my Lord? I feel You in the breeze.
I race into Your arms with joy, beyond the old oak trees.
I praise You for unfailing love. I beg forgiveness too.
I set aside all worldly things. My soul will sing to You!

—Anthea

About the Author

Anthea Gillian Tripp gracefully weaves inspirational messages and impactful life lessons into true short stories. Authentic and unflinching in her passionate writing style, she awakens the soul with timely topics about life's defining moments. She runs Anthea's Anthology, a blog where she pours out her heart in words. Anthea is a devoted wife, mother, and grandmother, and she is an ardent advocate for healthy living. She and her husband, Chuck, cofounded *Get Super Healthy*.